and lover of Texas history.

Ducit Amore Patriae,

Jeffrey D. Murrah

NONE BUT TEXIANS

A HISTORY OF TERRY'S TEXAS RANGERS

Jeffrey D. Murrah

EAKIN PRESS 🔲 Austin, Texas

To Lois Helen Tate Murrah,

my grandmother,
who gave me love and a godly heritage
to pass on to my children.

Contents

CHAPTER 1

Prelude to War
(1860–1861)

"Has it so soon come to this?"
—Robert E. Lee

The story of Terry's Texas Rangers is a story of friends, acquaintances, and neighbors who in the call of liberty and preservation of a way of life came to the aid of their state and compatriots.

As events of 1843 suggested that the Republic of Texas would soon be annexed to the United States, people began moving there from the United States and other nations. Among the immigrants was a young, small, temperamental Baptist lawyer from Monroe County, Mississippi, named Thomas Harrison.[1] The young lawyer brought his wife and children with him to the new nation. He hoped he could make a life for himself with family members who had already moved to Texas. Harrison entered the law office of his brother-in-law, a Texas veteran and former secretary of state, William Houston Jack, and they set up their law office in Brazoria County.[2]

Brazoria County was a center of national activity at the time. Many of the Republic's notables resided in and around the county, among them the Terry and Johnston families. The two families were friends of each other.[3] Albert Sidney Johnston, former secretary of war of the new nation, had recently returned to Texas remarried with his new bride, Eliza Griffin. The Johnston family settled at China Grove in Brazoria County. Ben Fort Smith, a veteran of the Battle of New Orleans and the War for Texas Independence, had raised the sons of his sister, Sarah Terry, on his plantation, since their mother died in the 1830s. One of the sons was Benjamin Franklin Terry, It was here, in Brazoria County that Thomas Harrison, Benjamin Franklin Terry, and Albert Johnston began associations forever changing their lives.

When the possibility of war with Mexico arose in 1846, a call for volunteers went out. A young, outspoken, congressman from Mississippi who staunchly defended states' rights was organizing a state militia unit from his home state. This promising young congressman was Jefferson Davis. Although Thomas Harrison was now a "Texian," he returned to his native Mississippi to volunteer for service in the state militia unit known as the "Mississippi Rifles."[4] Like Harrison, Albert Sidney Johnston also left Texas to serve in the Mexican War. While in the volunteer regiment, Harrison discovered there were other Texians present. There among fellow volunteers, he met fellow Texan, W. P. Rogers.

The Mississippi Rifles fought bravely in several military engagements. The regiment distinguished itself in the Mexican War and brought recognition to its commander, Colonel Davis. When military officials offered Davis a Federal commission, he refused, citing that the Federal government did not have jurisdiction over state militia regiments.

After the Mexican War, Harrison returned to Texas. Initially, he practiced law in Houston. After a brief period in Houston, he moved to Marlin, then moved his office to Waco. His brother, James E. Harrison, moved from Mississippi to join him in Waco. There Tom Harrison settled down and proceeded to raise his family.

With the cessation of hostilities with Mexico, the period from 1850 to 1860 was productive. In many portions of Texas this period was one of growth and economic expansion. One family benefiting from the growth at this time was the Terry family. Although raised by their uncle, the young men established themselves as prominent citizens in the community. The Terry sons were Benjamin Franklin Terry and his brothers, Clinton, David, Nathaniel, and Aurulius.

By 1860, Benjamin Franklin Terry was thirty-nine years old and powerful, both physically and financially. Peers described him as frank, generous, courtly, kindhearted, and a man of brilliant mind.[5] Standing six feet tall, with broad shoulders, he towered above other men of the time. Terry was also a tireless rider and unerring shot.[6] His home was full of Christian hospitality and activity, serving as a social center of Fort Bend County.

Terry was born in Russelville, Logan County, Kentucky, on February 18, 1821. His family moved he and his three brothers to the territory of Texas in 1831. The family originally settled near Stafford Point. His father, Joseph Terry, remained in Kentucky, and later married Bethenia Phelps. His parents divorced after his father built a gambling hall, of which the mother disapproved.[7] His mother died in 1834, when he was thirteen.[8] Before her death, Mrs. Terry left her sons to be raised by her brother, Ben Fort Smith, and his wife, Obedience, who were staunch Baptists. Ben Fort Smith owned a large sugar plantation near Stafford Point in Brazoria County. He maintained a school at the plantation for his nephews and neighbors. Benjamin Franklin Terry resided in Texas when the nation came into existence. During the War for Texas Independence, he had left home with the intent of joining Gen. Sam Houston's army, but arrived too late.[9] He married Mary Bingham on October 12, 1841. Mary was the daughter of Major Bingham.[10] She was also an original resident and one of Stephen F. Austin's "Old Three Hundred."

As a sugar and cotton planter in Fort Bend County, Benjamin Franklin Terry, who often went by "Frank," prospered and increased his influence. He grew into one of the richest men in Texas. He jointly owned 133 slaves on the plantation, named Oakland, which he ran with a partner, William J. Kyle.[11] In an effort to improve Oakland, he joined in a venture to build the BBB&C (Buffalo Bayou, Brazos and Colorado) railroad west from Harrisburg to Richmond. [12] Terry hoped to build a spur right up to his sugar mill. Financing for the project was arranged through the help of Thomas S. Lubbock. The BBB&C was the first railroad built in Texas.[13] His partnership brought him into contact with Sidney Sherman, who was instrumental in improving Texas since Republic days. Sherman developed the Harrisburg end of the rail line.

Besides running his sugar plantation, Terry also involved himself in military matters by participating in what was called the "Cortina War." His involvement consisted of supporting a Mexican leader named Carijal. Carijal was the rival and sworn enemy of the Mexican bandit Juan Nepomuceno Cortina, who had been raiding towns in southern Texas in 1859.[14] The lands in Texas south of the Nueces River had been contested and fought over since the formation of the Republic. Juan Cortina intended to return the lands to Mexico.

Local citizens complained to the United States military authority, David E. Twiggs, when Cortina raided the city of Brownsville. In his raid, Cortina took over an abandoned army barracks (at Fort Brown) and controlled the area in and around Brownsville. Cortina monitored mail coming into and out of the city. He also conscripted locals into his private army and levied fees on citizens. When Cortina talked about pushing Anglo Americans back to the Nueces River, changes occurred in United States strategy. Specifically, they decided to forcibly remove Cortina. The plan was to use a combined force of Federal troops, Texas Rangers, and armed citizens.

After some initial confusion and delays, an expedition was finally authorized. The leader of the expedition would be the Federal cavalry commander, Robert E. Lee. Lee was given authority to pursue Cortina across international boundaries into Mexico. Once given the formal approval to carry out orders, Lee left with the expedition. The men hunted, fought with, and pushed Cortina back into Mexico in a series of gunfights. Although they contained Cortina in Mexico, they did not eliminate him.[15] It was on this expedition of the "Cortina War" that Frank Terry fought together with later Union cavalry commander George Stoneman, John A. Wharton, John S. "Rip" Ford, and Robert E. Lee.

John A. Wharton had befriended Frank Terry shortly after

moving to Fort Bend County. The two became lifelong friends.[16] Wharton was a Presbyterian[17] and law office partner of Clint Terry. He also served as Fort Bend County district attorney and operated a plantation, which he called "Eagle Island." [18] The plantation was between the Brazos River and Oyster Creek, twelve miles from the Gulf of Mexico. He had inherited the plantation from his parents. Eagle Island had long been considered a place of hospitality. John Wharton was thirty-one years old at this time and was described as "a man of strict temperance, the restraining influence of his moral character was felt wherever he went." [19]

Like Frank Terry, John Wharton had strong roots in the young state of Texas. His father was one of Stephen F. Austin's original settlers. His uncle fought for Texas independence at San Jacinto and was called "the keenest blade of San Jacinto." [20] John Wharton was born four miles from Nashville, Tennessee, on July 3, 1828. His parents later immigrated to Texas, when it was a territory of Mexico. He was initially raised at Eagle Island. At age eight he was sent to his uncle Leonard Groce's plantation, Bernardo. There he was instructed by Mr. Dean, a tutor from Boston. After the home education, he attended college at Galveston, until the age of fifteen.

Deciding he needed to further his education, he left Texas to study law in Columbia, South Carolina, under William C. Preston. As part of his training, he focused on rhetoric and elocution. He graduated at age twenty. While there he met and married Penelope Johnson, the only daughter of Governor David Johnson of South Carolina. Penelope and John married in 1848. Wharton's training in elocution and love of poetry later served to entertain many soldiers on the battlefields of America.[21] His family would achieve economic prominence by bringing the first cotton gin to Texas.[22]

On returning to Texas, sometime between 1848 and 1850, Wharton studied law under his cousin "Jack" Harris, John Woods, and E. M. Pease in Houston. Pease was elected governor in 1853 and again in 1855. Pease ran on the Democratic ticket. The Democratic platform "strictly adhered to principles of states' rights, that congress did not have the right to interfere in state affairs and condemned the attacks of the North on the integrity of the constitution and rights of the South." [23] This legal apprenticeship training brought Wharton a clear understanding of politics, adherence to states' rights issues and respect for the Constitution. After finishing his studies under the two prominent lawyers and obtaining his license, Wharton joined Clint Terry in the law firm of Wharton and Terry.[24] Wharton also served as a presidential elector for the 1860 election.

A legal associate of Wharton was the twenty-six-year-old Fort Bend County judge, Gustave Cooke. Cooke was born in Alabama and came to Texas alone in 1850, when he was fifteen. After educating himself, he established himself as a lawyer and judge.[25] He was well acquainted with the Terry brothers and John A. Wharton.

In addition to John Wharton, Benjamin Franklin Terry had a close friendship with Thomas Saltus Lubbock. Lubbock was forty-four years old, and although born in South Carolina, he actively participated in the struggle for Texas independence. He and his five brothers made significant contributions to Texas independence. Tom joined the New Orleans Greys in Louisiana to join in the fight for Texas. He participated in the Siege of Bexar but missed the Battle of San Jacinto.[26]

After the War for Independence, he joined the Santa Fe Expedition, serving as lieutenant. The expedition was to be a retaliatory military expedition against Mexico. Observers of the expedition noted that he exhibited leadership abilities. When Mexican forces captured and sent members of the expedition to Mexico City, Lubbock escaped confinement by jumping from a balcony. Back in Texas, he joined a second expedition, named the Somerville Expedition, to return in a punitive action against Mexico. Although this expedition also failed, the adventures provided Lubbock with military experience and helped him develop determination in character and a willingness to take risks.

Tom Lubbock made his living raising and selling financial stock in Harris County. His business connections included individuals who had initiated railroad and banking construction, going back to the days of the early republic. His brother, Francis R. Lubbock, had been lieutenant governor in 1857. Francis supported Jefferson Davis and secession at the Democratic convention in 1860. All of the Lubbock brothers supported Texas and the secession issue. Tom, an influential, wealthy and powerful personality, experienced in business and military matters, maintained membership in organizations devoted to the secessionist cause.

The election of November 1860 brought many changes to the sleepy county of Fort Bend. After a three-way race, a candidate won office even though his name was not on the ballot in Texas; nor had he won a clear majority of the popular vote. The candidate's political career had not been exceptionally noteworthy. He was the product of a political machine rather than being a shining star political hopeful. Citizens in Fort Bend County and the rest of Texas met the election outcome with concern. The candidate was Abraham Lincoln, and the office was president of the United States. These election results were answered by many, including Frank Terry, with talk of secession. John Wharton used his talent of rhetoric for speeches regarding the "oppression" of the Union, the importance of states' rights, and the need for secession. Before the month was out, many counties held mass meetings to consider their options.[27]

In Brazoria County, home of John Wharton, citizens held a mass meeting on November 17. They declared for secession, recommended holding a secession convention, and requested that the chief justice of the county appoint delegates to the convention. They then elected John A. Wharton to represent them at the convention.[28]

In Lavaca County a convention met on November 21, which favored secession. The convention went on to recommend that the governor "convene the legislature or provide for a state convention." [29]

Along with talk of secession, reports circulated through the state of African-American uprisings and wholesale poisonings of communities. These reports served to make citizens feel increasingly threatened, especially after the Cortina episode. The reports of uprisings and poisonings were unfounded, although they served to agitate the citizens. Incendiary fires occurred in many parts of the state, and many communities expelled any abolitionists they found.[30] Governor Sam Houston attempted to alleviate fears associated with the election. He admitted a distrust of Lincoln and the North, yet believed in the Constitution and the Union.[31]

With increasing talk of secession, counties across the state elected representatives to attend the secessionist convention.

Frank Terry, Tom Lubbock, and John A. Wharton were elected
as delegates to attend the secessionist convention in Austin.
Terry, representing Fort Bend County, was already a fiery secessionist. John Wharton, a staunch defender of states' rights who
represented Brazoria County, advocated immediate secession.
Frank Terry's friend Thomas S. Lubbock represented Harris
County along with lawyer W. P. Rogers and a physician. Rogers
had served with Thomas Harrison in the "Mississippi Rifles"
during the Mexican War.[32] Texas Supreme Court Justice O. M.
Roberts presided over the convention.

One hundred and seventy-seven delegates came to the convention from all over the state. Most of the delegates were
lawyers (40%) and planters and farmers (35.3%). The average
age of the delegates was forty-two, which made Terry and
Wharton some of the younger of the participants. Terry and
Wharton were also some of the wealthiest delegates present. At
this convention, and in subsequent actions taken by its young
delegates, associations began that lasted until long after the war
for some and until death for others.[33]

John A. Wharton, and Frank Terry joined the other delegates at the Texas secessionist convention on January 28.[34] Once
in Austin, Frank Terry renewed his acquaintance with John S.
Ford, the Texas Ranger whom he had previously worked with in
the Cortina affair, as well as Thomas Lubbock and W.P. Rogers
of Harris County. On the first day, the delegates were seated and
then formed various committees. An oath of office was administered that they would "faithfully discharge their duties" and
"pledge allegiance to the state."[35]

On the second day of the convention, Wharton was selected
to deliver the resolution for secession. He was chosen because of
his "great ability as an orator with great force of argument and
conviction." The resolution stated "that without determining
now the manner in which the result should be effected, it is the
deliberate sense of the convention that the state of Texas should
separately secede from the Federal Union."[36] The resolution was
adopted 152 to 6.

During the next few days, speakers from different states addressed the delegates. Resolutions from Tennessee and New
York were also discussed and reviewed. The legislature of New

York formally offered money and troops to President Lincoln, in order to coerce certain sovereign states of the South into obedience of the Federal government.[37] On February 1 the delegates invited the governor and judges of the supreme and district courts to attend when they voted on the articles of secession.[38]

At the convention, all five men (Terry, Wharton, Lubbock, Rogers and Ford) were solidly in the secessionist camp. Finally, on February 4, the closing day, the ordinance of succession passed on a vote of 166 to 8.[39] Upon passage of the ordinance, thunderous cheers broke out. Delegates replaced the U.S. flag over the speaker's platform with a handmade Lone Star flag. The people would then decide the secession question in a ballot. Tom Lubbock's brother, Francis, captured the attitude after the convention: "... Our people preferred to fight Massachusetts rather than Louisiana if fighting should become necessary."[40]

The reasons for secession were prefaced with this summation:

Whereas, the Federal Government has failed to accomplish the purposes of the compact of union between these states in giving protection either to the persons of our people upon an exposed frontier or to the property of our citizens; and whereas the action of Northern states of the Union, and the recent development in federal affairs, made it evident that the power of the federal government is sought to be made a weapon with which to strike down the interests and prosperity of the Southern people, instead of permitting it to be as it was intended, our shield against outrage and aggression:

Therefore, ...[41]

A synopsis of the reasons follows:

1. A hostile majority in the North adopted policies excluding southern states from "common territory." (For example, congressmen from northern states refused to allow southerners to settle in "common territory," although they had made up a majority of the Mexican War veterans.)

2. This same hostile majority permitted outlaws to war on the people of Kansas. (This refers to the mass murders at Pottawatamie, Kansas, by John Brown.)

3. The U.S. government failed in giving adequate frontier protection. (This refers to the Cortina affair, where Twiggs took little action, and to continued problems with Indians.)

4. Northern states violated the fugitive slave law. (This refers to the Supreme Court decision on Dred Scot, which northern states refused abiding by.)

5. Northern leaders promoted strange doctrines of "the equality of all men irrespective of race or color" and "a higher law than the constitution."

6. Seventeen Northern states elected a president hostile to southern interests.[42]

The convention also formed a fifteen-member subcommittee known as the "Committee of Public Safety." This committee was to organize the transitioning from being a state in the United States to a sovereignty. W. P. Rogers was one of those named to the committee.[43]

On concluding the convention, Tom Lubbock, John Wharton, and Frank Terry decided to share a stagecoach ride home, since they lived close to one another. On the way home, Lubbock, Wharton, and Terry discussed war as an impending event. As the stagecoach rumbled across the cold Texas plains, the three resolved to offer the new Confederate government a regiment of Texas cavalry.[44] This regiment of cavalry would later become "Terry's Texas Rangers." While Terry, Lubbock, and Wharton journeyed homeward, the Committee of Public Safety they helped form was already taking action. This committee formulated plans culminating in the demand for peaceful surrender of all Federal facilities in Texas.

Four days later, on February 8, 1861, the Committee of Public Safety directed Col. Ben McCulloch, hero of the Mexican War and Indian fighter, "to collect men to secure and protect public property in San Antonio, the headquarters of Federal forces in Texas." The committee also demanded that Federal property be turned over to Texas. They then began a series of correspondences with the military commander (U.S. Gen. David Twiggs) regarding the surrender. The committee was not all talk. Within two weeks, they sent McCulloch to make good on their correspondences.

Gen. David Twiggs had been anxious about the political situation in Texas since December.[45] He had been in correspondence with Governor Sam Houston as well as Federal authorities in Washington about his concerns. He did not want to be the first to shed blood as secession swept the state.[46]

Early on Saturday morning, February 18, Ben McCulloch's troops amounting to about 650 men surrounded General Twiggs and his 160 men in San Antonio.[47] After capturing him at gunpoint, McCulloch's men told Twiggs he was a prisoner of war. They then brought him to McCulloch. After exchanging greetings, Twiggs said, "Ben McCulloch, you have treated me shamefully, ruining my reputation as a military commander and I am too old to reestablish it." [48] McCulloch replied, "I am serving my State, the State of Texas, sir." David E. Twiggs then formally surrendered U.S. forces at San Antonio to McCulloch and his group of armed Texans.[49]

Among this group was a future member of Terry's Texas Rangers, James Knox Polk Blackburn. Blackburn reported that after surrendering, Twiggs wept. As part of the surrender, the American flag was lowered. About 2:00 that afternoon, two Federal officers arrived in San Antonio via an ambulance and were amazed at the absence of the American flag. One of those officers was Robert E. Lee.[50] Upon exiting the ambulance, he was told what happened earlier that day. Lee then asked, "Has it so soon come to this?"

Twiggs' command included many talented young officers. Among those surrendered were Edmund Kirby Smith, Fitzhugh Lee, Henry Hopkins Sibley, and John Bell Hood. These officers later resigned their commissions to join the Confederacy, where they became generals.[51] After surrendering the Federal forces and facilities, Twiggs left Texas. The U.S. Army then dismissed Twiggs from the army for "treachery to the flag." [52] After his dismissal from the Federal army, he too joined the Confederacy.

On February 18 the irascible lawyer from Mississippi, Thomas Harrison, along with H. B. Granbury,[53] joined in a state militia unit commanded by William C. Dalrymple in bringing about the surrender of U.S. troops at Camp Cooper.[54] Capt. S. D. Carpenter commanded the U.S. forces at Camp Cooper.[55] After the capture of this camp, Harrison organized a militia unit in

Waco, which later became a company in Benjamin Franklin Terry's cavalry unit. All across Texas, Federal forces surrendered facilities to local troops. Many remaining Federal troops were heading toward the coast. They set up a temporary camp at Green Lake, Texas. From there, they hoped to evacuate through the port of Indianola.

John A. Wharton and Frank Terry joined an expedition raised by John S. (Rip) Ford sailing toward Brazos Santiago.[56] Ford was sent by the Committee of Public Safety after reports were received of shots celebrating Lincoln's upcoming inauguration coming from the fort.[57] Terry held the rank of colonel; however, when the main force reached the nearby island of Brazos Santiago, command arrangements were readjusted. Because Hugh McLeod liberated Brazos Santiago prior to the arrival of the main force under Ford's command, Terry yielded his colonelcy to McLeod and became major of the force.[58]

With Brazos Santiago out of the way, John Ford directed his efforts at securing Fort Brown, which was commanded by Capt. Bennet H. Hill and George Stoneman. The Union commanders refused to leave the fort unless they had a proper order to do so.[59] Negotiations were soon under way concerning the fort and its guns. During that time, Frank Terry served as a liaison between the two forces. After a series of negotiations, the Union forces surrendered the fort. Confederate forces under John S. (Rip) Ford[60, 61] finally secured the fort, and defenders lowered the U.S. flag without firing a shot. Ford commanded about 1,500 men at that time. With its location on the Rio Grande, just north of Matamoros, Mexico, and with many artillery pieces, Fort Brown[62] and Brazos Santiago island posed potential threats to international trade. When the Federal forces finally relinquished control of the fort, the Confederates marched into the front of the fort, where they gave a thirty-two-gun salute to the Stars and Stripes as it was lowered. After surrendering, Bennett Hill and his Federal troops withdrew from Texas soil on board the *Daniel Webster*. George Stoneman and his 114 men withdrew on the steamship *Mustang*.[63]

The seizure of all Federal installations in Texas occurred without major incidents and with minimal loss of life. These seizures were completed before hostilities at Fort Sumter. After securing Fort Brown, Terry and Wharton hurried back to Fort Bend County.

While Frank Terry and John Wharton busied themselves in the Brazos Santiago Expedition, Tom Lubbock had other plans. He hurriedly left Texas for Montgomery, Alabama, and there, at the Confederate capitol, he sought permission to raise a cavalry regiment. Lubbock competed with many other adventurers seeking commissions and offices in the new nation. He finally succeeded obtaining an audience with the War Department.[64] The initial response from the secretary of war, Leroy P. Walker, was negative. The reason given was that the war would be over before Texas could ready its troops. Even after several weeks of continual efforts and appeals, the War Department response was unchanged.[65] Thomas Lubbock then returned to Texas, still determined to pursue his goal.

As events leading to war showed its inevitable occurrence, people in California considered what they should do. Two friends, miles away from hostilities in Texas, considered the actions they would take. The two men were Albert Sidney Johnston and Judge David Terry. They met and discussed matters with each other. Johnston resigned his military position as commander of the Department of the Pacific, and David Terry left his judicial position. Both men left California for Texas via the difficult overland route across the desert.[66]

Shortly after the events of Fort Sumter on April 12, Benjamin Franklin Terry rejoined his friends Tom Lubbock and Thomas J. Goree. Given that Lubbock's effort at obtaining permission to raise a cavalry regiment failed, they decided to travel to Virginia to pursue other options. The three men then took the overland route to Virginia. Once in Virginia, Goree obtained an appointment to James Longstreet's service.[67]

During the time that his friends were on their way to Virginia, John Wharton was eagerly obtaining arms for Confederate troops gathering around Col. Earl Van Dorn at Galveston.[68] While sailing a schooner on an armament run from New Orleans, Federal blockade vessels near Galveston captured Wharton. He threw the arms overboard before being boarded. The Federals considered Wharton a prisoner of war, and gave him the choice of taking the Federal oath of allegiance,[69] which

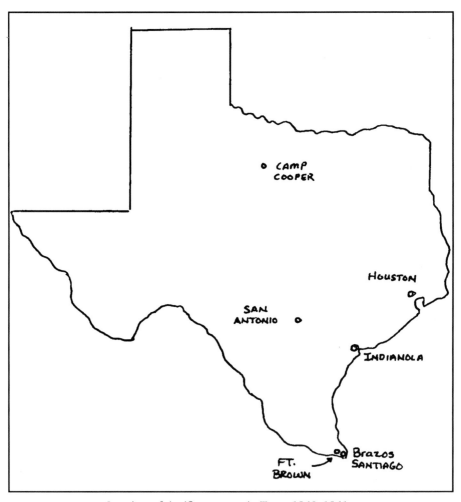

Locations of significant events in Texas, 1860–1861.

would allow him to return home or be sent to Key West, Florida, for imprisonment. Wharton's response was "to Key West forever." Upon seeing the futility of their efforts, and Wharton's resolve, the Federals released him two weeks later.[70]

Eventually, Terry, Goree, and Lubbock arrived in Virginia and served as volunteer aides and scouts on the staff of Gen. James Longstreet at the Battle of Manassas (July 21). Longstreet wrote in his report:

> About an hour after my position was taken it was discovered by a reconnaissance made by Colonels Terry and Lubbock that the enemy was moving in heavy columns towards our left, the position that the general [Beauregard] had always supposed he would take. This information was at once sent to headquarters, and I soon received orders to fall back upon my original position of the enemy's batteries. They made a very gallant and complete one, and a hasty sketch of his entire left.

After the battle, Longstreet presented Gen. Pierre G. T. Beauregard with captured Union colors taken in the battle. One of the flags had been shot down from the Fairfax County Courthouse by Terry. Terry, who was a crack shot, severed the lanyard holding the Union flag and thereafter replaced it with the Confederate colors.[71] One account claims Terry was on horseback when his shot broke the lanyard.[72]

Benjamin Franklin Terry, John A. Wharton, Thomas Lubbock, and Thomas Goree, then in good favor, secured authorization from the War Department to recruit a cavalry regiment in Texas for the Confederate army in Virginia, on specified conditions. These conditions included that the men furnish their own arms and equipment, including Colt's repeating pistols.[73] The unit would serve in Virginia. This authorization was what the men had originally come for. The dream discussed on a stagecoach ride from Austin was becoming a reality.

CHAPTER 2

Recruitment and Deployment (1861)

"For the war! For the war!"
—Cry of the new recruits

Once in Texas, Terry, Lubbock, and Wharton selected a muster center and ten recruiting captains. Some of these men selected as officers were former Texas Rangers,[1] though Terry himself had not been one. Terry selected Houston as the muster center. On August 12, 1861, he commissioned ten men as captains. He then sent out the recruiting captains with their instructions.[2] Fortunately, many of the local colleges were near graduation time. In Ranger lore, it is claimed that Terry and his captains recruited at the college campuses.[3]

Some of the recruiting captains and counties assigned were as follows: John Austin Wharton (Company B-Brazoria/Matagorda counties); Wharton's brother-in-law, Louis N. Strobel (Company K-Fayette, Lavaca, and Colorado counties); James G. Walker (Harris/Montgomery counties); Mark L. Evans (Company C-

Gonzales County); Stephen C. Ferrell (Company D-Bastrop, Hays, Travis, and Burleson counties); Leander M. Rayburn (Company E-Gonzales County, a.k.a. "The Gonzales Rebels"); Isham G. Jones (Company I-Gonzales County, a.k.a. "The Gonzales Rifles"). (See page 18 for full list.) Initially, each company was known by its captain. Numeric designations were later made when the unit reached Kentucky.[4]

Instructions given to each recruiting officer included raising a company of 100 horsemen. Each of these volunteer horsemen was to furnish his own weapon, a pair of six-shooters, bridle, saddle, spurs, lariat, and mount. After receiving these instructions, the officers went into the counties of Central and Gulf Coast Texas, including Bastrop, Hays, Travis, Burleson, Matagorda, Brazoria, Harris, Montgomery, Fayette, Colorado, Lavaca, McLennan, Gonzales, Bexar, Goliad, and Fort Bend.[5] The recruiting captains were to sign up the men, then assemble in Houston, Texas.

Some of the Texas State Troop units had already mustered for service. In those situations, the recruiting captain's duty consisted of agreeing to meet in Houston. Although many militia units had formed, authorization was needed from the Confederate War Department to make their formation official. Units had already organized in Gonzales, Brazoria, McLennan, Harris, and Fort Bend counties. Recruiting in those counties was rather simple. Some had been operational since May 1861 under the authority of the Militia Act of 1858.[6]

The State of Texas set up drill and instruction camps, where volunteers received instructions on how to fight.[7] In these camps, drill masters introduced the men to drills, military tactics, and formations. It was often at these camps where volunteers were mustered into service.

Some of the counties (Gonzales, Harris, Bexar, and Goliad) previously experienced military engagements during the War for Texas Independence. Additional military experience was gained in the war with Mexico in 1846, the Cortina War, and ongoing dealing with Indian hostilities. Since Texas was a relatively new country, patriotism ran high. Men experienced with firearms and previous war training in Texas' military activities provided inspiration for many of the young recruits.[8] In March

Commanding Officer	County of Origin	Company Designation	Nickname or Local Designation
Thomas Harrison/ Rufus Y. King	McLennan and adjacent counties	A	Prairie Rovers
John A. Wharton	Brazoria and Matagorda	B	Mounted Rangers
Mark L. Evans	Gonzales	C	Wauls Confederates (?)
Stephen C. Ferrell	Bastrop, Hays, Travis and Burleson	D	Bastrop Rangers
Leander M. Rayburn	Gonzales and adjacent counties	E	The Gonzales Rebels
John T. Holt	Fort Bend	H	The Terry Guards
Isham G. Jones	Gonzales	I	Gonzales Rifles[9]
Louis Strobel	Fayette, Lavaca, and Colorado	F	Lone Star Rangers[10]
W.Y. Houston	Bexar, Goliad	G	Javalinas
John G. Walker	Harris, Montgomery	K	Tom Lubbock Guards
	Wharton	L	Wharton Guards

a Gonzales military unit formed with the invasion of Mexico as its goal. The invasion never occurred, although military preparedness in Gonzales and other cities remained high.

The majority of men volunteering for service were young, usually in their late teens or early twenties.[11] Their vocations included cowboys, farmers, and shopkeepers, and many were college-educated men, either recently graduated or still in college.[12] Many were experienced horsemen, proficient in using a lariat and pistols. John A. Wharton, Gustave Cooke, Thomas Lubbock, John Rector, D. F. Lily, Samuel Marion Dennis,[13] Thomas McKinney Jack, James Love, and Thomas Harrison were all lawyers who left their professions to join the unit. The lawyers understood the legal ramifications of secession and the choices they were making. Later in the war, one observer of the unit commented that he was surprised to find in the regiment many men of intelligence, polished manners, and good fortunes.[14] These volunteers knew what the issues were and what it may cost them. They were men willing to stand for what they believed in.[15]

Before leaving for the final formation and mustering of his unit, and the war, Benjamin Franklin Terry dressed himself in a new Confederate uniform. After dressing, he attached his uncle Ben Fort Smith's sword. The sword that hung at his waist was previously carried into battle at New Orleans and San Jacinto.[16] He left the home with his oldest son, David, and then visited the older slaves at his plantation. He paid his respects to them and exchanged personal farewells, and instructed them to take care of "Miss Mary" and the children. As he was about to leave, an older black woman brought out his youngest son, five-year-old Kyle, who had been crying at his father's departure.[17] After comforting Kyle, Frank rode off with David Terry and a servant. At Houston, David would rejoin his companions in John Holt's company.

In Bastrop County, Stephen Ferrell designated Bastrop as the organization center for the company. The night before muster day, potential recruits entered town, drinking and celebrating. On the morning of muster day, citizens gathered to watch the departure ceremonies. Women, old men, and children mingled with the recruits. They prayed, cried, and asked for blessings on the recruits for their patriotism and heroism. After securing blessings and wiping away the tears, the company rode out of town.[18] Such emotional departures were common at ceremonies in nearby counties as men left in defense of their country.[19] Ferrell's company arrived at Houston on Saturday, September 7, and was joined by five other companies.

Less than twenty days after the call for volunteers went out, the unit officially formed at Houston on Monday, September 9, 1861. The muster center consisted of a warehouse serving as makeshift headquarters on the outskirts of the city. At the appointed time, the men lined up on three sides of an open square. When Lt. John Sparks stepped forward, the assembly of men quieted themselves. Lieutenant Sparks then addressed the men and led them in the oath of service. The oath made them official soldiers of the Confederate States.[20] Sparks himself had recently resigned from the U.S. Army.[21] The enrolling officer

Confederate banner under which Companies E, I, and C of Terry's Texas Rangers formed in Gonzales County. Company A of the Fourth Texas (part of the Texas Brigade) also formed under this banner.

— Courtesy of Gonzlaes County Historical Museum

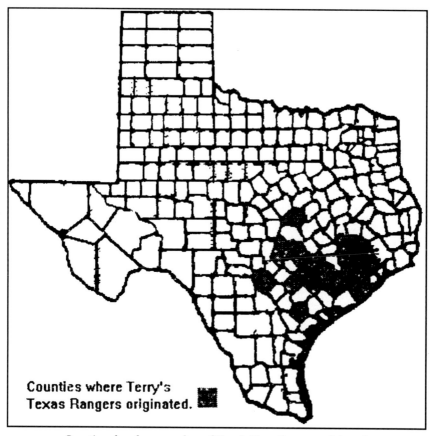

Counties where Terry's Texas Rangers originated. ■

Counties where large numbers of Terry's Texas Rangers originated.

then stood and asked them, "Do you wish to be sworn into service for twelve months or for three years or for the duration of the war?" In a loud, unanimous shout, the men proclaimed: "For the war! For the war!"

After being sworn into service, the men celebrated with demonstrations of horsemanship along Congress Avenue. They practiced such skills as dismounting and remounting at a full gallop, and picking up objects on the run. Thomas Harrison met with his nephew, Thomas McKinney Jack, who had joined John Wharton's company.[22]

The regiment consisted of ten companies of 100 men each. The total manpower strength of the regiment was 1,170, which was larger than many other regiments formed in Texas.[23] Terry and Lubbock shared command.[24] Terry refused the title of colonel, until his men elected him to that office.[25]

The regiment split into separate groups for travel. Terry led the first group, accompanied by Francis R. Lubbock, the newly elected governor of Texas. This group departed Houston on September 10.[26] Francis Lubbock's brother, Tom, served as the officer in charge of the second group. While waiting to move out, some of the men remaining in Houston occupied their time by showing off their skills and horsemanship to citizens. The men formed into small groups and practiced cavalry charges down city streets. They also broke wild horses on streets where the public could view them in amazement. These activities led to write-ups in the local papers regarding their excellent skills. Morale was high, and the men wanted to fight.

Being that the Union blockade was under way, transportation to New Orleans would be overland. The first group rode to Beaumont on rail. From Beaumont, a riverboat then took them to the Sabine River. It was there that the horses were sent back home.[27] At Niblett's Bluff, on the Sabine River, S.W. Allen and Governor Lubbock obtained some wooden carts.[28] The men were then loaded six to eight to a cart. The carts had no seats or springs and were powered by two pair of oxen. The rough-riding carts carried them into Louisiana. Several miles into Louisiana, the unit headed toward New Orleans by rail. Since the railroad did not go all the way through to New Orleans, the men got off at New Iberia and marched about 100 miles to Brashear City (present-day Morgan City, Louisiana). Some of the men chose not to walk, instead finding some wild horses which they broke and rode for the distance. At Brashear City, the men once more boarded a train headed to New Orleans.

Along the way to New Orleans, some members of the unit referred to themselves as "Texas Rangers." On reaching New Orleans a week later they were surprised to find that many citizens considered them the Texas Rangers of law enforcement fame.[29, 30] While in the city, the men lodged in a cotton compress building. The Rangers attempted procuring some tents and mess gear from the local commander, who previously commanded the Federal forces in Texas, Maj. Gen. David E. Twiggs,

CSA. His reply was that "Rangers" didn't need to be bothered with such unnecessary things.[31] In New Orleans, the men waited while further transportation arrangements were being made.

While in New Orleans, Terry received orders that he was to go to Kentucky and serve under Gen. Albert Sidney Johnston.[32] Some accounts report Johnston went to New Orleans and met with Terry concerning the unit and his need for men, which is unlikely. Johnston did, however, visit Texas in the weeks prior to the unit's departure.

Albert Sidney Johnston already figured prominently in Texas and the minds of its citizens. He was the former commander in chief of the Army of Texas, secretary of war during nationhood, and leader of a Texas volunteer unit in the Mexican War. Johnston and Terry also knew each other well and were well aware of the reputation each man had earned.[33] Johnston claimed to have intervened with the War Department and reassigned Terry's unit to his command. Along with the intervention from Richmond, Johnston promised Terry that his unit would remain an independent command and never be brigaded. It is likely that Terry was also promised that the finest horses which could be furnished by Kentucky would serve as their mounts.[34] Although originally assigned for the Army of Northern Virginia, the unit found itself on the way to Kentucky.

The Rangers in the first group met to review the news about the assignment and take a vote regarding moving to Kentucky and serving under fellow Texan Albert Sidney Johnston. The news about going to Kentucky rather than Virginia disappointed them.[35] Their disappointment was compounded since their fellow Texans in the First, Fourth, and Fifth Texas Infantry preceded them to New Orleans by a few days and then went on to Virginia. The main advantage of the Kentucky move was serving under a Texan commander and his promises made to Terry. The Rangers conducted their vote and agreed to serve in Kentucky. The second group left Houston around September 30.

From New Orleans, the men boarded on the Mississippi Central Railroad and traveled to Grand Junction, Tennessee. The unit waited there for further commands from Colonel Terry. At the time Terry was in Chattanooga with Francis R. Lubbock. The message came that the unit was to proceed to

Nashville. Francis Lubbock left his friend, Frank Terry, for the last time and continued on to Richmond to meet with President Jefferson Davis.

In Nashville the men camped at the old fairground in West Nashville for ten days. While there, a measles epidemic broke out. Large numbers of Rangers contracted the illness, with many becoming severely ill. Many of the Rangers had never left Texas before, and the change of climate affected their health. Local citizens from the churches came to their assistance with nursing aid and housing. This assistance led the Rangers to develop a high regard for the women of Nashville. The local population continued helping the men in recuperating from the illnesses even after the main body left. Help often included allowing them to stay in private residences. Besides helping the Rangers, the "people of this vicinity [Nashville] nearly all maintain pretensions towards religion, principally Baptists." [36]

Those men in good health often displayed their horsemanship skills to the citizens of Nashville. The fairgrounds were filled with activity such as breaking wild horses and picking up handkerchiefs, gloves, and fifty-cent pieces from the ground while at a full gallop as they did in Houston. This was the closest thing to a Wild West show the citizens of Nashville had ever seen. After a while, the spectators began putting coins of lesser denominations on the ground since the Texans effectively accomplished the task of picking up the coins. [37]

The Wild West show atmosphere was further enhanced by the Rangers' dress. The men initially had their civilian clothing tailored into the style of a military uniform. They wore red shirts trimmed with dark collars, cuffs, epaulets, and pocket flaps. The collars and cuffs maintained the red themes. Even their trousers sported red stripes, which was a practice reserved for officers. Their headgear varied widely. Some wore sombreros, some bandana handkerchiefs, and others low-crowned, broad-brimmed hats. Texas stars were affixed to hats, holsters, and belt buckles. [38] Later in the war, they were issued more standardized uniforms, although they kept the Texian idiosyncracies.

Terry assigned guards over the camp at night. The guards were to keep the men from going into town. Frequently, some of the men managed sneaking past the guards and made their way

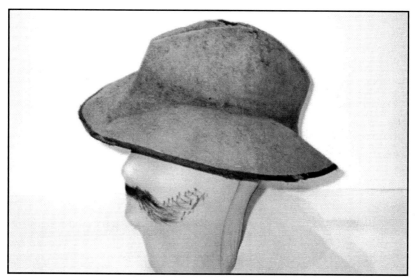

Hat worn by Col. Gustave Cooke. The use of broad-brimmed hats was common among members of Terry's Texas Rangers.

— Courtesy of The Museum of Southern History

into town. Limits were placed on the number of men officially allowed to go into town and the duration of their visit. Once in town, many began drinking and eventually were locked up in the local jail.

One evening, several Rangers went into town and began their usual drinking. Then they attended a performance of a play about Pocahontas. During the performance, one of the men discharged his pistol so as to protect the leading female character, after stating that "his mother taught him to always protect a lady when in danger." The police quickly arrived, and a fierce brawl ensued. The fight resulted in two policemen being killed and one wounded. News of the Pocahontas episode quickly arrived at Johnston's headquarters, and he ordered Terry to immediately report to him on the first train to Bowling Green.[39]

Terry proceeded to Johnston's headquarters and received the regiment's assignment. In that meeting, Johnston ordered Terry to assemble his men in Oakland, Kentucky, about fifteen miles northeast of Bowling Green. At 1:00 A.M. the unit marched out of camp to board the next available train ("take the cars") to their new camp.[40] The next train left at 2:00 P.M.

Once in Kentucky, the men set up camp and the regiment proceeded with the business of organizing and electing officers. The men chose Terry as their leader with the rank of colonel.[41] They then elected the other officers, all the way down to corporal. Numeric designations were given to the companies, and the unit was designated the "8th Texas Cavalry." A roster was made of those present, then forwarded to Richmond. The men avoided the numerical designation when referring to the regiment, instead preferring to call themselves "Texas Rangers."[42] Terry and Johnston renewed their friendship as neighbors and fellow Texans. Another fellow Texan, George Whythe Baylor[43] of Fayette County, was part of Johnston's staff.

The Rangers were assigned to Johnston's command in Kentucky, and many of them were without horses.[44] Since Johnston needed the cavalry for reconnaissance work, obtaining horses was a priority for Terry. The first 500 men were assigned horses by drawing for them.[45] A detail was later assembled and sent to Nashville to bring up more horses.[46] The last of the Rangers arrived on October 21. Besides obtaining horses, Terry sought further improvements for the regiment by purchasing more weapons for the regiment and himself. A letter written by a member of the regiment indicates that sixty African Americans were with the regiment at this time.[47]

Many members of the unit continued struggling with illness, and now they were to set up camp at Oakland. The wet, cold winter weather came early, and snow was already on the ground. The men were not used to such conditions. The detrimental effects of inclement weather were amplified by this area of central Kentucky, which was damp and unhealthy due to all the dripping springs, caves, and sinkholes. One Ranger described the area as "awful mean country. Nothing enticing that I have seen in it. Nothing but rocky hills covered with black jack hickory and post oak and occasionally a walnut."[48]

The men who were well enough to report for duty then performed work and picket duty in the snow. The duty proved very strenuous since they had to do double duty with so many ill compatriots.[49] These hardships strained the stamina of many of the Rangers. Even in the midst of such problems, some gambling and drinking occurred, despite a ban on these activities. Not all the Rangers engaged in such vices, as church services were held regularly and some Rangers attended. Another activity included listening to a regimental band from Mississippi perform nightly in the camp.

Arming a regiment posed a major concern. At the time of muster, a list of the men in the unit was completed along with a list of armaments. The armaments list included pistols and rifles.

One stipulation placed on members of the regiment required furnishing their own firearms. Each volunteer horseman furnished his own weapon and a pair of six-shooters. Later, shotguns would often be used in combat, along with muskets and rifles. Double-barrel shotguns were desired over muskets and rifles. Pistols were a favorite weapon of the Rangers, with some members having as many as four.[50] Frank Terry bought a revolver for himself, adding to the four pistols he already carried. Later, as men died or were wounded, fellow Rangers often kept their pistols. Gen. Albert Sidney Johnston noted that although the Rangers were armed better than most units, they were equipped with weapons consisting of a wide variety of calibers.[51] The varying caliber weapons made equipping the men with proper ammunition (rounds) problematic. An early list of the unit's arms showed the following:

597 Double-Barrel Shotguns
91 Common Rifles (.54 Cal)
29 Mississippi Rifles (.54 Cal)
14 Sharps Rifles
13 Sharps Six-Shooting Rifles
5 Minnie Muskets
5 Harpers Ferry Rifles
5 Carbines
3 Colt's Six Shooting Rifles
3 Morse Rifles
3 Double Rifles
3 Musketoons
2 Muskets
579 Navy Colt Revolvers (.36 Cal)
92 Army Colt Revolvers (.44 Cal)
65 Colt Five-Shooters

21 Holster Pistols
11 Starr Revolvers (.42 Cal)[52]

The Rangers were better armed than many other Confederate units. The abundance of rifles over muskets contrasts with units where muskets predominated arms equipage. Shotguns would necessitate closer quarter engagements than afforded by rifles.

The six-shooter allowed for a faster rate of fire than did the rifle. When .36- or .44-caliber percussion pistols were used, the impact from the bullet would knock down an opponent, even when only grazing him. This type of impact strength, combined with rapidity of fire, reduced the need for pinpoint accuracy in aiming.[53] Thus, speed provided through technological advances allowed the Rangers an edge in close-quarter conflicts during the early years of the war.

The shorter barreled .36-caliber Navy Colt (or "Navy Six" as they called it[54]) was preferred over the .44-caliber Army Colt due to easier handling. In combat the men often carried two or more pistols to allow for increased rapidity of fire. Since self-contained ammunition was not in existence at the time, the time necessary to reload the weapons was a problem, especially when riding. Carrying multiple loaded weapons allowed a Ranger to deliver more firepower without stopping to reload.[55]

The first major duty was assigned on November 5, 1861. The unit patrolled and picketed all the section of the front from Bowling Green, Kentucky, north to Woodsonville[56] on Green River. The large number of turnpikes crisscrossing in the vicinity made the area difficult to secure. While the Rangers were in Kentucky, the story originated that "Terry had 500 Indians and 500 white men with him, and he had raised the black flag."[57] Stories such as the black flag helped create the Ranger mystique.

One of the cities patrolled in the area was Jamestown, Kentucky. Jamestown lay four miles east of Bowling Green.[58] The Rangers referred to Jamestown as "Jimtown." On Sunday, November 15, when patrolling, two companies provided cavalry escort for some companies of infantry. Thomas Harrison led the cavalry companies. The Confederate infantry forces they were escorting were commanded by Col. Patrick Cleburne. When the

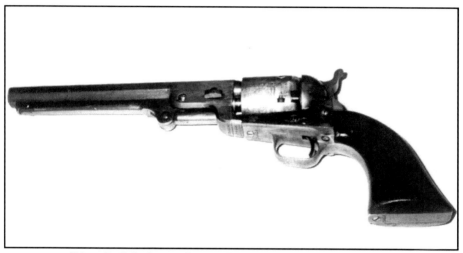

"Navy Six," the favorite firearm of members of Terry's Texas Rangers.
— Courtesy of The Museum of Southern History, Sugarland, Texas

Confederate force and its cavalry escort were attacked by Federal forces, Harrison discovered the Federals possessed a larger force than he and Cleburne combined. While under Federal fire, Harrison ordered the two companies of Rangers to withdraw and seek reinforcements. When the requested reinforcements arrived, they attacked and dispersed the Federal force. Despite the victory, this action earned Harrison the title of "Jimtown Major" and displeasure with the men due to his withdrawal.[59]

On Tuesday, December 17, the Confederate commander, Gen. Thomas C. Hindman, advanced toward Woodsonville. The Union forces had steadily pressured an advance in the Green River area since December 10. The Union commander, Gen. Alexander McCook, hoped to capture or build a bridge over Green River, since the Confederates had destroyed the railroad bridge in reaction to his advance. General Hindman decided that the Union advance needed to be countered. The Union troops had recently built a pontoon bridge near Woodsonville and established outposts near the railroad to guard their achievement. At Green River, the Yankees had already established outposts on the north bank.

Hindman then sent in skirmishers, who drew fire from the enemy and revealed their positions. At that point Hindman was called away, and he delegated command of all the forces in the area to Colonel Terry. Hindman left instructions to decoy the enemy up the hill, where Confederate infantry and artillery could fire on them more effectively, and the Union infantry would be out of range of their own artillery.[60] Terry began following the plan. A small force was sent to attract the notice of the Federals. After gaining their attention, the Confederates withdrew across the bridge. The Union troops advanced across the bridge and up the hill, chasing the decoy force. Immediately, Terry divided the Rangers into two forces. He commanded one group and sent Captain Terrill to the road by the rail line, with the intent of catching the Union forces in a pincer move.

Terry's command was with Major Phifer's cavalry on the heights overlooking Green River[61] when Federal troops suddenly fired on Terry's position. Terry and about 75 Rangers found themselves under fire from about 300 men from the 32nd Indiana Infantry.[62] The 32nd Indiana was commanded by Col. August Willich,[63] a veteran officer of the Prussian army.[64] The Germans of the 32nd Indiana poured fire from a blackjack thicket east of the Rangers' location.[65] Things looked bleak as the novice Texans faced a larger veteran Prussian force. Terry immediately ordered a charge, which he emphasized with an oath.[66]

Terry then led his regiment in charging Federal positions. Each of the Rangers carried loaded shotguns and pistols, which they knew how to use effectively. They headed straight toward the infantry occupying the thicket. The Federals were lying ready with bayonets in a "kneel and parry" formation.[67] The Rangers charged within fifteen to twenty yards of the Federals and then opened fire with pistols and rifles.[68] The charge and firepower from the weapons decimated the Federal line. With this charge, in which mounted cavalry went up against standing infantry, the enemy was routed and driven back. Terry's men pressed the Federals from their position back across Green River. The Federals' retreat carried them across the rocky ground, partway through a cornfield, and back across the bridge.[69]

While leading the charge, Terry was hit by a bullet in the head, which instantly killed him. On witnessing Terry's death, Mort Royston rode back under enemy fire to deliver the tragic news.[70] When word of his death reached the wagons, Terry's

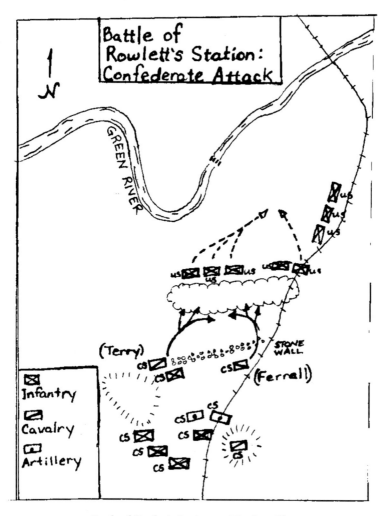

Battle of Rowlett's Station, or Woodsonville.

slave became belligerent. He demanded revenge for Terry's death. Several Rangers dismounted and restrained the slave, who attempted arming himself and riding out to avenge his master's death.[71]

The other body of Rangers, under Captain Ferrell and located on the right side of the turnpike, were also attacked. In this attack the Federals fired from their positions, hidden behind haystacks and a fence near the railroad. The Rangers also charged and repulsed the attack at this location. Ferrell charged the Federals three times and was halted each time. The Federals finally withdrew when the Confederate infantry, who had been supporting the cavalry, arrived where the fighting occurred. At the conclusion of the action, lasting several minutes, Colonel Terry and three other Rangers had been killed and eight wounded. Union losses were 163 killed and 218 wounded.[72] One Ranger reported that "there was a large reward offered for Terry's body, dead or alive. When he was killed there were about fifteen men killed or wounded over his body."[73] From the Battle of Woodsonville[74] episode, the Rangers learned the importance of always sending out men to protect the flanks prior to attacking.[75]

Afterward, superiors and followers of Terry mourned. One Ranger said, "The death of one hundred sixty three men, not even American citizens would not cover the death of that one [Terry] that day."[76] Another of the men in the regiment, after the war, said that in the loss of Terry the South had lost "another Forrest and veritable Napoleon of cavalry."[77]

General Hardee's orders said of Colonel Terry: "His regiment deplores the loss of a brave and beloved commander; the army one of its ablest officers."[78] Tom Downey of Victoria collected Terry's body from the field, and from there it went to Cave City, Kentucky, and then to Nashville Tennessee. In Nashville, the state legislature adjourned for two days to pay respects. Respects were also paid in New Orleans, Louisiana, before the body returned to Texas.[79] News of Terry's death reached Austin, Texas, on December 26. The Texas Senate chamber was draped in black, and state senators resolved to wear mourning badges for the next thirty days. Terry's body arrived in Houston by train and was then carried in a procession occupying twelve blocks until reaching the Tap and Harrisburg Railway depot. Ironically, the railroad he helped found now carried his body home. From the depot, his body was sent by train to Sugar Land.[80] There he was buried at the family graveyard on his plantation.[81]

Shortly after Terry's death, the regiment experienced disorganization. With their commander dead and leading officers ill, morale sunk. In keeping with traditions of self-reliance, the men then held another election of a commanding officer. Thomas S. Lubbock, although ill, was chosen as their commander, passing Thomas Harrison, who was also ill. The men still disapproved of Harrison based on their opinion of his ordering a withdrawal from the earlier engagement near Jamestown, Kentucky. During this time, Thomas McKinney Jack (Thomas Harrison's nephew) transferred to Albert Sidney Johnston's staff and served as an aide-de-camp.[82]

One of the few encouraging moments came a few days after the Woodsonville battle, when a Federal officer was captured. The officer had participated in the fight with the Rangers. Among the papers found on him was a letter to his sweetheart. The letter said, "The Rangers are as quick as lightning. They ride like Arabs, shoot like archers at the mark, and fight like devils. They rode upon our bayonets as if they were charging a commissary department, are wholley without fear themselves, and no respector of a wish to surrender." [83]

Illness in the form of measles, camp fever and respiratory infections plagued the unit.[84] By December 30, Gen. A. S. Johnston reported the unit at half its original numbers due to death and sickness. Some of the ill were transported to Nashville, where they were split between hospitals and private residences. It was there that Thomas Lubbock died of typhoid fever a month later. The date given for his death was January 9, 1862.[85]

CHAPTER 3

The Battle of Shiloh
(1862)

"To fight with the Rangers was to be in advancement in this world or the next."
—Ranger L. B. Giles

The Rangers rested the first two weeks of January 1862 in the Green River area.[1] During that time, they reorganized the able-bodied men in the regiment after all the losses. They also obtained more horses. Their time at camp was filled with frequent drills and inspections. The men in the regiment developed friendships with men in Kentuckian John Hunt Morgan's cavalry regiment, whom they shared camp with.[2]

Thomas Lubbock's body was sent to Texas and buried with military honors in Houston. The regiment now needed a new commander. The Rangers looked among their ranks for an officer whom they would willingly follow.

The Rangers and General Johnston disagreed on the best way to select officers. Johnston insisted on regular promotions, while the Rangers believed it important that they vote on the matter. The general finally relented after a delegation of the regimental captains met with him. In the subsequent election of officers, the men chose John A. Wharton colonel. Wharton's promotion violated the traditional promotional system. Although still ill from measles, Wharton assumed his new responsibilities.

After their brief rest, the Rangers rode out of camp and relieved "Adams Cavalry" of Mississippi in the forward positions of the army. While at this assignment, their responsibilities included picket duty near Bell Tavern, Kentucky.[3]

In one of the first engagements of 1862, Confederate Gen. Felix Zollicoffer attacked Union forces under George Thomas at Mill Springs, Kentucky. General Zollicoffer hoped the fog would aid his efforts; however, Federals halted Zollicoffer's attack and defeated the Confederate offensive. Among the casualties was General Zollicoffer. This defeat at Mill Springs (also referred to as Fishing Creek) and the loss of General Zollicoffer started the year with discouragement regarding the Confederacy's new independence.

On January 31 a detachment of Rangers joined the party sent to recover General Zollicoffer's body from Union lines.[4] While on this assignment, the forty Rangers dressed as Indians and Mexicans, adorning themselves with buffalo robes and sombreros.[5] While retrieving the body, the Union and Confederate soldiers exchanged verbal barbs. One Ranger commented to Union troops that "he hoped to return the favor" to them.[6]

In a brief break from the monotony of camp life, Thomas Harrison and sixty Rangers left camp on February 7 to visit Mammoth Cave. While there, the Rangers relieved the cave's pro-Union owner of some supplies. Since there were not many known caves in Texas at that time, they decided to explore the cave. They traveled the cave on foot by candlelight. On their journey, they saw the register chamber, lover's leap, fat man's misery, star chamber, and the giant's coffin. After their exploration, they returned to camp.

Two days later, on February 9, the Rangers withdrew from the Green River area of Kentucky and moved to Bowling Green. Muddy roads from an earlier snowfall slowed progress of the withdrawal. Along the way, further bad news arrived for Gen. Albert S. Johnston: the Confederates had lost Fort Henry. The other main defensive position at Fort Donelson was under siege.

These positions were important in maintaining the Confederate defensive line through Tennessee. On realizing that the defensive line holding Tennessee was untenable, General Johnston decided to withdraw his army from Kentucky in the midst of winter.

Beginning February 11, the Rangers and other Confederate troops began evacuating the state in snow and freezing rain. As the day wore on, the snow worsened. The weather continued deteriorating, with blizzard conditions on the 13th. Despite the inclement weather, the survival of the army depended on the safe withdrawal of its men.

On February 15 the Rangers, as the last unit to leave Bowling Green, were assigned the destruction of the rail depot and public stores, thereby preventing capture by invading Federal troops. Federal guns had begun shelling the city the day before. The Rangers continued the job of destroying the Confederate supplies amidst the explosions from the cannonade and inclement effects of a snowstorm. They successfully completed the task before leaving the city. The Rangers then assumed the responsibility of rear guard for the retiring Confederate forces.[7]

The other troops in Johnston's army leaving Kentucky moved through Nashville to Murfreesboro, Tennessee. The Rangers traveled through Nashville for the last time as the army was abandoning the city and burning or transferring the large amounts of supplies stockpiled there. They entered the deserted streets of Nashville at 2:00 A.M. on Thursday, February 17, just hours before the scheduled destruction of the bridges leading to the city at 4:00 A.M.[8]

From there, the Rangers were ordered to retrace their route to Charlotte, Tennessee.[9] On leaving Nashville, women from the city braved the winter conditions and poured out onto the city streets. In the early morning hours, the women cheered them on, and were joined in their cheers by Confederate troops moving through the city.

In Charlotte the Rangers joined fellow southerners in Nathan Bedford Forrest's command assisting troops escaping the surrender of Fort Donelson.[10] Forrest and his men had been at Fort Donelson prior to its surrender, but Forrest refused allowing surrender. His men escaped the surrender along with many infantrymen by leaving the fort before the official surrender occurred. Assisting the troops meant adding a passenger to one's horse. The added passengers combined with cold, windy, inclement weather made the journey difficult. A difficult part of the task was crossing the rivers and streams, encrusted with ice, with two in a saddle. Yet the Rangers successfully brought the survivors back to the Confederate lines. (For cavalry units, Confederate lines meant Murfreesboro, Tennessee.)

The assignment taxed the regiment's constitution, including that of its commander, Colonel Wharton. He was left to recover in Franklin, Tennessee, and Maj. Tom Harrison then led the unit on its withdrawal through Tennessee.[11]

Along the way, Major Harrison disciplined two straggling and insubordinate soldiers by having them "mark time" under guard while on the Shelbyville Pike.[12] The humiliation of cavalrymen receiving discipline was heightened by passing infantry observing them. The men in the unit disliked the action and expressed their displeasure by threateningly moving toward Harrison. Capt. S. "Pat" Christian quickly intervened to keep the men from attacking Harrison. Christian assisted Harrison in quieting down the troops and restoring order.[13] This episode led to Harrison being called the "Mark Time Major." He had previously lost favor with the men in Kentucky, and this incident added to the dislike the men had for him.

In March the cavalry forces of Johnston's army broke camp and moved farther south to Corinth, Mississippi. The route went through Shelbyville, Tennessee, to Huntsville, Alabama. From Huntsville they went through Decatur and Tuscaloosa, Alabama, and Iuka, Mississippi.[14] From Iuka they went on to Corinth, Mississippi. While marching to Corinth, the Rangers served as the rear guard.[15]

In Corinth the strength of the unit, along with morale, increased. This surge of strength occurred when survivors of illness returned to camp and new recruits arrived from Texas. Colonel Wharton also rejoined the regiment. Among the recruits coming from Texas were Clinton and David Terry. Clinton was Benjamin Franklin Terry's younger brother and Wharton's law partner. David was Frank Terry's other brother, a former judge in California.

The men in the regiment were confident of their military abilities, and often bragged about their fighting prowess. A letter written by the chaplain, R. F. Bunting, stated:

> Colonel Wharton has authorized me to say that he will not admit amateur fighters into the Regiment and further, . . . This opens the way for joining a cavalry regiment that has seen more perilous service and which already enjoys more reputation than any other in the army. We want none but Texians.[16]

On the evening prior to leaving Corinth, General Johnston paid the regiment a visit. The men cheered as he arrived in the camp. In response to the cheers, he commented, "With a little more drill, you are the equals of the 'Old Guard' of Napoleon." [17]

Now in high spirits, the Rangers moved from Cornith to a position north of the Union forces bivouacked on the banks of the Tennessee River. The Rangers camped next to Owl Creek, a tributary of the Tennessee River. Dense, secondary-growth trees and thickets covered the area at the Rangers' campsite. At that time of the year, the woods and brush around the area were filled with wildflowers and peach blossoms from the numerous orchards nearby.[18] One Federal commander described the area: "The ground was undulating, heavily timbered, with scattered clearings the woods giving some protection to the troops on both sides." [19] The thickets were so much of an obstacle that the Union commanders did not send out pickets.

Saturday, April 5, was the original planned day of a Confederate attack.[20] Gen. A.S. Johnston was desperate for a victory after withdrawing from Kentucky, and losing Forts Henry and Donelson, Fishing Creek, and Nashville. A council of war was called in Johnston's tent. Attending were Generals Braxton Bragg, P.G.T. Beauregard, Leonidas Polk, William Hardee, and John C. Breckinridge along with members of their staffs.[21] In his desperation, Johnston considered many plans. Everyone was hopeful concerning the upcoming battle. Beauregard added, "In the struggle tomorrow, we shall be fighting men of our own blood, Western men, who understand the use of firearms. The struggle will be a desperate one, and if we drive them back to the

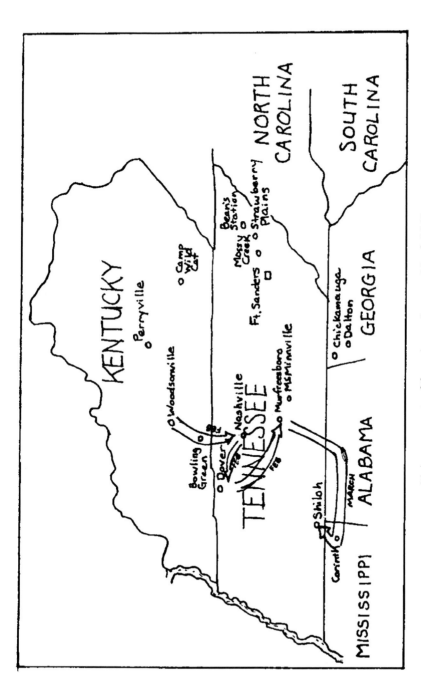

Major movements of the regiment, January–March 1862.

brink of the river and they make a determined stand there, our troops will be repulsed and our victory turned to defeat."[22]

The original plan of attack, prepared by General Beauregard, was modeled after Napoleon's order of battle for Waterloo. Beauregard's plan called for having men brought into action in three successive parallel lines. General Hardee and his line would attack first, followed by General Bragg. General Polk[23] would support the left and Breckinridge[24] the right flanks.[25] It was believed the successive waves of Confederates would present a force the enemy could not break through.[26] The use of such a plan presumed the geography to be a plain rather than the timbered and wrinkled landscape where the army was located.

Unfortunately, heavy rains turned the roads into mud, delaying the planned attack until the next morning.[27] The heavy rains soaked the equipment and weapons of the Rangers. Several of them approached Colonel Wharton seeking permission to discharge their weapons, to make sure they would fire. Wharton approved the request and allowed them to go outside of camp and fire the weapons. The massive amount of shooting sounded as if a skirmish was under way. On hearing gunfire, General Polk sent a brigade of infantry to find the source.[28] Wharton was arrested later that day for the episode.[29] His commanders were concerned that the discharging weapons may have given away Confederate positions. As Johnston considered consequences for the incident, Wharton earnestly appealed the decision, saying he "would rather be shot than not allowed to go into the fight."[30] He received a severe reprimand from commanding officers.

After the reprimand, Wharton spoke to his men, informing them they needed to redeem themselves. He asked them to wipe out the stain by showing gallant behavior in the coming battle. Indeed, they would ride further into the enemy's ranks than any other regiment.[31]

On the evening of April 5, prior to the initial attack, Beauregard visited the Ranger camp and met with Wharton in Wharton's tent. At one point, members of the regiment formed a wall around the tent where Wharton and Beauregard visited. Beauregard then made a speech to the regiment, which was received with a hearty reception.

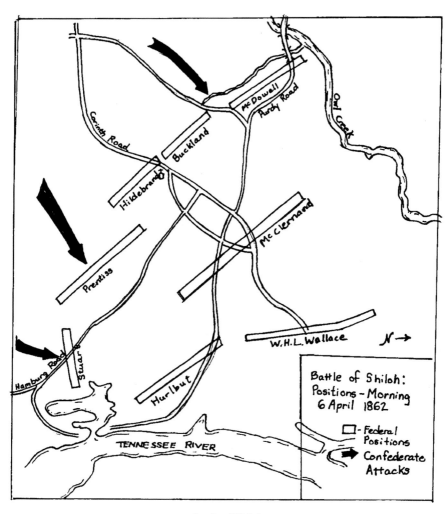

Battle of Shiloh.

Each general was to have his men ready to advance by 6:00 A.M. Readiness included equipping each man with three days' rations and 100 rounds of ammunition.[32] Albert Sidney Johnston gave orders to the soldiers that they would not be allowed "to strip or rob the dead," and that anyone running away would be "shot on the spot."[33]

On Sunday morning, April 6, the Confederate attack began. Initially, the Rangers were in the rear of the left wing in columns. The initial Confederate assault was released, and the Rangers had to wait. The wait seemed like hours to the restless Texans, who heard the fire of cannon and rifle and eagerly desired to join the fight. As the hours passed, the men stayed apprised of the situation through couriers dispatched from the front. Finally, Maj. Thomas McKinney Jack, a former Ranger who had recently been promoted to General Johnston's staff, galloped up. With his face smiling, he relayed the order to move. The Rangers shouted joyfully, then burst out in columns of four.[34] Their first action was described by Beauregard:

> Learning about 1 P.M., that the Federal right (Sherman and McClernand) seemed about to give way, I ordered General Hardee to deploy his cavalry (the Rangers) to turn the flank and cut off their retreat to the river, an operation not affected, because a proper or sufficient detour to the left was not made, and the gallant Texans under heavy fire became involved in ground deemed impractical for cavalry and had to fall back.[35]

The "impractical ground" was a boggy ravine the Rangers tried to cross single-file. The creek was littered with the tell-tale signs of fighting, including canned goods and empty bottles of whiskey and champagne.[36] While crossing through the mud of the ravine, they came under fire from Federal troops hidden in the underbrush, behind a rail fence. Wharton decided not to risk his men any further and ordered the regiment to attack the Yankee positions. The Rangers surged forward, tearing down and leaping over the fence. Once they cleared the fence, pushing the Federals back, they were attacked with cannon. The grape and canister shot forced the regiment to pull back.[37] During the enemy fire, Clint Terry was mortally wounded. He had been riding by the side of Wharton. Wharton then drew the men off and had them support Company A, Alabama State Artillery, which then came under fire from Union skirmishers.

The Union battery was causing considerable trouble for the Rangers. Gen. William Hardee ordered Wirt Adams' regiment to take the battery, which they refused to do. The call then went out for volunteers among the Rangers. The Rangers answered the call, and promptly charged the battery. The Federals, surprised at the sudden charge upon them, surrendered the battery. The volunteers took the Union battery without firing a shot.[38]

Wharton finally ended up dismounting half the regiment. Once afoot, the Rangers drove forward until the Federal skirmishers left the field.[39] The Federal commander of that area later reported that every attempt made to turn that part of the Federal right was repulsed, although to prevent the success of the Confederates the men took positions to the rear.[40] After their participation in the initial attack, the Rangers were put into reserve status and later returned to supporting the Confederate artillery battery.

Later that afternoon, they and other units held in reserve were told to prepare themselves for a final rush to drive the Federals into the Tennessee River. However, the push was called off about 4:00 P.M. The cancellation of the attack disappointed many of the men, who questioned this halt of movement at such a crucial time.

The first day's casualties included John Wharton, who was wounded in the leg. General Johnston and Clint Terry both died of wounds on the battlefield. Johnston was shot about 2:30 P.M. and later died from the loss of blood. He was in the arms of Thomas McKinney Jack when he died.[41] Command of the army then went to P.G.T. Beauregard. The remaining Terry brother, David, stayed in a command role, serving as a staff officer for the regiment.

Heavy torrents of rain and artillery bombardment from the Federal gunboats *Tyler* and *Lexington* filled the night with discomfort. These conditions allowed little sleep for the Confederates. Some of the Rangers raided the abandoned Union sutlers' stores, helping themselves to needed supplies for themselves and their horses.[42] Medical supplies were a favorite object of the raids. The Rangers were specifically blamed as the body of Confederates raiding Federal Gen. Benjamin M. Prentiss' camp, which had been overrun that morning.

On the morning of the second day, Monday, the Federals received fresh reinforcements and counterattacked. The Rangers fought a mounted rear-guard action covering the Confederates' retreat from positions gained on the first day. About 10:00 A.M., Beauregard ordered the Rangers to ride

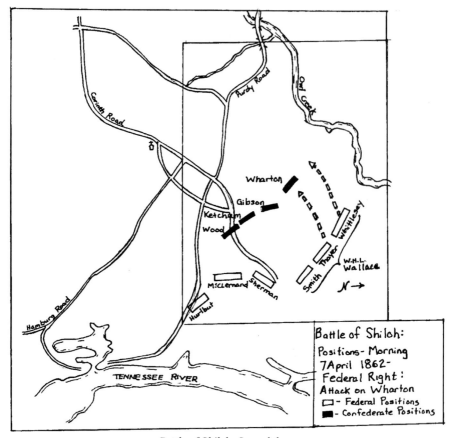

Battle of Shiloh: Second day.

around the Union right.[43] After circling, they met with Thayer's brigade[44] advancing on the right. Thayer's men belonged to Lew Wallace's division and were fresh reinforcements. Thayer's infantry fired several volleys into the Rangers. One volley killed Wharton's horse. Wharton then ordered the men to withdraw and dismount.

As the Rangers skirmished, Wharton sent word to Beauregard about the Union reserves coming in force. In one of the Confederate counterattacks, the regiment fought dismounted and joined with a brigade of Louisiana infantry.[45] This action occurred beginning in Sowell field and ended in the crescent field to the north. After covering the retreat to Shiloh church on the Confederate left, Wharton was ordered to the right side of the line.

Tuesday, in order to recover from his severe wound, John Wharton turned regimental command over to Maj. Tom Harrison.[46] "Old Tom," as some called him, was a small man. He seemed out of place on the large bay horse he rode. He wore a red bandana on his head, replacing the hat he had lost in the fighting on Monday night.[47]

At about 4:00 that afternoon, Col. Nathan Bedford Forrest, John Hunt Morgan, and Wirt Adams with the 3rd Tennessee (Forrest's original unit) were assembling a force to attack Federal infantry under William T. Sherman, then pressing on the right of the Confederate rear on the road to Corinth, Mississippi.[48] In the midst of a rain shower, the cavalry assembled at the edge of an expanse filled with felled timber. Forrest came up with forty men, then lined them on the right of the Rangers. Forrest, being the senior officer, waived the command to Harrison with his 300 men.[49] Forrest then prepared to charge the enemy. Harrison rode up and down the line, telling the Rangers to prepare for the charge and that "Breckinridge's men are broken down and must have time to clear a marsh they were trudging through." Then he told them to reserve fire and aim low.[50] Harrison concluded, "Boys, go in twenty steps of the Yankees before you turn your shotguns loose on them." He added, "Now, by God, follow your Jimtown Mark-Time Major!"[51]

Harrison ordered the men forward. Before giving them the orders concerning the speed they were to go, the Rangers charged. The Yankee skirmishers fired a volley and fell back. About the time the skirmishers of the 77th Ohio returned to battle line formation, the Rangers reached their twenty steps in front of the main line. Since the Federals had already fired at the charging Confederates, they didn't have time to reload. The Federals then assembled in two lines with bayonets fixed. Those in front kneeled with bayonets fixed at right angles while those in the rear had bayonets fixed at a horizontal level, positioned between the heads of men in the front line. Within a brief moment, the barrels of each shotgun discharged toward the Federal line. The Ohio regiment's commander yelled "Stand to me my brave Ohioans! You've never deserted me yet!" before he fell.

After his death, the Ohioans broke and ran. The effect of this was devastating to the Federal line.[52] Many men left their guns and retreated.

The Rangers and their companions hung their shotguns on their saddles and opened fire on the retreating Ohioans with revolvers. The Confederate force continued the action, riding over the front line, and engaging the 4th Illinois Cavalry. The pursuit continued until the retreating Federals reached their reserve forces. At that time, the Rangers and other Confederate cavalrymen left.[53]

Col. Jesse Hildebrand of the 77th Ohio, who experienced the charge, said, "So sudden was the charge, shooting our men with carbines and revolvers, they had not time to reload or fix bayonets." [54]

Major Harrison of the U.S. forces reported, "We were forced to fall back under cover of our cavalry. The rebel cavalry literally rode down the infantry."[55]

This action was called the "Battle of Fallen Timbers." Fallen Timbers serves as the closing act of the battle now known as Shiloh.[56] At the conclusion of Shiloh, the Rangers lost nine killed and sixty wounded.[57] One of those killed was Clinton Terry.[58] Another soldier who was almost killed in the action was William Tecumseh Sherman, who had ridden up with the 77th Ohio. As a result of the Battle of Fallen Timbers, the Rangers ended their dissatisfaction with Thomas Harrison and never referred to him as "Jimtown Major" or "Mark Time Major" again.

CHAPTER 4

After Shiloh
(1862)

"I would rather be a private in that regiment than a
Brigadier General in the Union army."
—Gen. Augustus von Willich, USA,
regarding Terry's Texas Rangers

After the Battle of Fallen Timbers, the Rangers bivouacked on the ground and proceeded at a leisurely pace the next day.[1] They covered the army's unmolested withdrawal back to Corinth, Mississippi.[2] Colonel Wharton left the unit for a pass in order to recover from wounds, and the regiment stayed in Corinth the next two weeks. From Corinth they went to Reinzi, Mississippi,[3] and stayed there for two weeks. From Reinzi they went through Florence, Alabama, and then into middle Tennessee.

Sometime in early May, after Wharton returned, Beauregard brigaded the regiment with the 1st Kentucky Cavalry commanded by Col. John Adams. Since Adams was the senior officer, he commanded the brigade despite Wharton's contesting of Adam's seniority. Wharton believed Adams was reluctant in engaging the enemy.

Wharton was hesitant in resuming command of the regiment and its assignment under such undesirable conditions. Together the two regiments went on a raid into middle Tennessee.[4] The target of the raid was the town of Bethel on the Elk River.[5] While on this raid, the Rangers fought a skirmish with Union forces under Union Gen. J. S. Negley's command. The Federal forces guarded a railroad bridge over the Elk River, near Bethel, in Giles County, Tennessee (one of the Federal units was an Ohio regiment).[6] Initially, the Rangers planned surprising their opponents at the Union encampment and cutting off their retreat. As they prepared for the attack, several Federal troops left the camp using a railroad hand car. The squadron on the railroad led by Lt. Fergus Kyle realized they must be intercepted.[7] The Rangers chased them down and finally caught them. The firing in this episode alerted the main force at camp, resulting in an intense gun battle. When it was over, seventeen Union troops were killed and forty-nine taken prisoner.

While on the raid, some Rangers and Kentucky cavalrymen obtained alcohol and drank to intoxication.[8] The drunken men then took an unauthorized trip into Winchester, Tennessee. They later returned safely to the main body of troops in Giles County, Tennessee. The men incurred the wrath of Wharton for their irresponsible behavior.

The regiment found themselves in a cat-and-mouse situation with the Federal cavalry. The Yankees tried cutting them off while behind enemy lines. The Rangers and Kentuckians evaded their pursuers for eighteen days, until they reached Chattanooga, Tennessee.[9] Wharton was so dissatisfied with the course of events in the raid and so unwilling to have his command sacrificed that he insisted on withdrawing his regiment from Adams' brigade.[10] Colonel Wharton expressed his exasperation at General Adams' conduct the entire trip and told him to take his Kentucky regiment and go to Halifax with it, if he wanted to. Wharton intended remaining in middle Tennessee and doing what he could to carry out the original order of General Beauregard.[11]

After this episode, Wharton unsuccessfully attempted transferring the regiment to either the Department of the Trans Mississippi or Texas by sending an agent to the government in Richmond, Virginia.[12]

The Rangers then camped at the foot of Lookout Mountain for a rest. While there, Col. John Hunt Morgan visited with Colonel Wharton. The Rangers occupied their time by writing letters, sightseeing, caring for their horses, and performing other routines of camp life. Occasionally, they went out on scouting missions. While on these missions, the Rangers purchased necessary foodstuffs.

One of the scouting missions involved responding to a gunboat threat. General Mitchell of the Federal army had built a gunboat and planned to capture Chattanooga. When the gunboat was to move up the river, a party of twenty Rangers went to investigate. Armed with shotguns, the party positioned themselves on a high bank of the river. The reports of a behemoth of destruction proved false. The gunboat was only a small riverboat lined with cotton bales. The Federal troops were leisurely lying about the deck; some troops were even playing cards. As the boat reached the high bank the Rangers opened fire, and the blasts sent cards flying and men scurrying. The Rangers forced the craft into Battle Creek, where it remained and was used as a bridge for troops.[13]

While commanding the Army of Tennessee, Gen. P.G.T. Beauregard on June 9 put the Ranger regiment along with the cavalry units in north Alabama and middle Tennessee under the command of Nathan Bedford Forrest.[14] This was one of Beauregard's last official acts as commander of this army. Forrest had already earned a reputation as a fighter, having risen through the ranks as a non-professional soldier.

Forrest stood six-foot-two and had a stern demeanor. There were two liberties no one ever attempted: disobeying his orders and abandoning the field in the presence of the enemy. He was stern and his language rough. The Rangers had fought with him before at the Battle of Fallen Timbers and in the withdrawal from Fort Donelson.

Regiments included in Forrest's brigade included the 1st Kentucky Cavalry commanded by Adams and 1st Louisiana Cavalry commanded by Col. John S. Scott. Forrest already exhibited noteworthy leadership in commanding his cavalry units with the 3rd Tennessee. Both the Kentuckians and Louisianans raised objections to Forrest's background as a slave trader. The

Rangers instead evaluated Forrest on his leadership. As a result of these objections, the new brigade composition of Forrest's command included the Rangers, the 1st and 2nd Georgia Cavalry (also known as Lawton's Georgians, led by Col. William J. Lawton), Major Smith's Tennessee Battalion, and Captain Taylor's Kentucky Battalion.[15] The 1st Louisiana Cavalry was then sent to Kingston, Tennessee. After assuming command, Forrest proceeded to organize and gather information about Yankee troops in Tennessee.

Forrest led the newly formed brigade on a raid into middle Tennessee, leaving from Chattanooga on July 8. After a march in the rain, the brigade reached McMinnville, Tennessee, on July 11.[16] While in McMinnville, the force was joined by Morgan's Georgians and two companies of cavalry from Kentucky (Maj. Baxtor Smith's command). Forrest then met with the regimental commanders in planning an attack on Murfreesboro. Murfreesboro lay more than forty miles away, with a guard of 2,000 occupying Federals under command of Gen. Thomas Crittenden.

Crittenden had been increasing his harsh rule on the citizens of Murfreesboro. At the start of the week prior to Forrest's departure, twelve citizens were held under an armed guard of 200 troops. The arrests continued, and by week's end at Friday, the number swelled to 400 citizens.[17] The prisoners were held under martial law, and Crittenden was turning up the heat, even to the point of destroying farm utensils and fences.[18] He ordered all residents into the town square, and from his podium announced scheduled executions for several citizens on July 12.[19] He told the citizens that previously they had "had a good time," but he would initiate an "iron rule" and that "they would not raise any crops that year." Those scheduled for execution were held in the jail portion of the courthouse.

While Crittenden was basking in his occupational power, Forrest had other plans. He called his commanders for a council of war. In the meeting they jointly planned the upcoming raid. Forrest led the brigade on an all-night ride, stopping only to feed and water the horses. When the brigade passed through Woodbury, the townspeople came out during the late night with food for men and horses,[20] including meals they had prepared for Sunday dinner.[20] The Confederate raiders reached the outskirts of Murfreesboro just before daylight. Forrest then sent a company of Rangers to silently capture the pickets. The Rangers accomplished the task as ordered.[21]

About five miles from town, the unit halted and readjusted their saddles and girts.[22] Forrest then learned from the returning company of Rangers that Crittenden had split his forces and gave their location.[23] In the midst of early morning darkness, Forrest split the Rangers into two groups. Wharton commanded the group attacking a military camp on the north side of town and Forrest led the remainder into the town itself.

Wharton prepared his 120 Rangers for the attack on the Union camp north of Murfreesboro containing the 7th Pennsylvania and 9th Michigan Infantry (located on the Murfreesboro-Woodbury road). After positioning themselves quietly, the order came to charge. The Rangers charged the 7th Pennsylvania encampment with a yell. The sudden attack surprised their sleepy opponent. Abruptly awoken Federal troops emptied out of their tents in their night clothes,[24] then fled before the attacking Confederate cavalry.[25] The cavalrymen pursued the retreating troops into the camp of the 9th Michigan. The infantry attempted forming a square against the cavalry attack, and the square slowed down the momentum. Wharton soon found his force outnumbered and lacking the support troops needed. Placed in a desperate situation, he developed a plan of persisting in repeated attacks until he overcame the Federals.[26] In the three-hour battle, Wharton received wounds severe enough that he shifted regimental command to Tom Harrison.[27]

Those Rangers in the force attacking the city found encouragement from local women, who, when they heard gunfire, came out into the streets in their robes telling the men "God bless you."[28] The ladies began begging the Confederate liberators to attack the courthouse. Colonel Morrison of the 2nd Georgia led his men in attacking the courthouse.[29] Federals guarding the courthouse jail (a company from the 9th Michigan), housing 150 political and citizen prisoners, began shooting into the cells containing citizens. The prisoners' situation worsened when one of the guards, as he fled, lit a bundle of paper and stuck it under some loose wooden flooring, then took the keys with him. The prisoners survived the Federal shootings and fire by clinging close to the walls.[30] The Georgians attacking the courthouse forced the Yankees to leave and quickly put out the fire. After extinguishing the fire, they searched for a way to open the large iron door. They found an iron bar, which they used to pry the door open enough for someone to crawl through, then escaped by crawling under the door. The prisoners expressed their gratitude to the Confederates as their saviors.

Forrest gathered six companies of cavalrymen and attacked the camp of the 3rd Minnesota. He then personally led the first charge of about 350 cavalry against 1,200 Federal infantry. The infantrymen repulsed the initial charge, and Forrest pulled back and exclaimed in anguish, "Great God, have the Rangers deserted me and disgraced themselves and their state forever?" He then sent for the six companies of Rangers under Wharton. About that time Wharton and his companies of Rangers rode into town just as Forrest demanded surrender of the remaining members of the 9th Michigan Infantry, telling them, "If you refuse, I will charge you with the Texas Rangers under the black flag."[31] The Federal troops promptly surrendered.

The Confederate troops in town secured the jail, railroad depot, telegraph office, and courthouse. They also searched homes and taverns looking for Federal officers, including General Crittenden.[32] Once the officers were collected, they were lined up in front of the jail's former inhabitants, who were told by a Confederate officer, "They tell me these men treated you inhumanely while in jail. Point them out to me."[33]

Forrest sent a similar demand to the remaining members of the 3rd Minnesota, commanded by Colonel Lester. Lester and his men had been fighting in hand-to-hand combat with the other Confederate cavalrymen led by Col. Baxter Smith. Lester requested time to allow for a conference with Colonel Duffield, and Forrest agreed to the request. Lester was shown the strength of Confederate forces on the way to meet with Duffield. Unknown to Duffield, Forrest kept moving his men so as to appear a larger force. After conferring, Union commanders Lester and Duffield both surrendered.

General Crittenden initially refused a parole from Forrest. He claimed that Forrest was a guerrilla, with whom he could not deal. Forrest reportedly turned him over to the Rangers. The Rangers serving guard duty were of such villainous demeanor and appearance that Crittenden suspected plans on his life. Within a couple of hours in such company, he accepted the parole.[34]

At the conclusion of the Murfreesboro raid, fifteen companies of infantry (six of the 9th Michigan, nine of the 3rd Minnesota), seven companies of cavalry (four of the 4th Kentucky and three of the 7th Pennsylvania), and two sections of Hewett's battery (containing new Parrot twelve-pounders) were captured.[35] This amounted to about 2,000 troops captured by 1,300 Confederates. What supplies and arms the Confederates couldn't appropriate were burned. The enlisted men were paroled by General Forrest. He even gave the band back their musical instruments. They returned the favor by playing favorites like "Dixie," "Bonnie Blue Flag," "The Girl I Left Behind Me," and other southern songs.[36]

The Rangers escorted captured Federal officers to McMinnville, Tennessee. Orders were given, "If any man makes a break from the column, shoot him down without halting him." Since the Rangers rode continuously over the previous forty hours, many of those guarding prisoners fell asleep on their horses while transporting them. Nevertheless, the prisoners arrived without incident in McMinnville.[37] The capture of Murfreesboro netted the entire Federal force, with General Crittenden, in addition to stores valued at almost one million dollars.[38]

After three to four days' rest in McMinnville, the Rangers went to Lebanon, Tennessee, in order to capture the occupational Federal garrison there.[39] The Yankee cavalry departed before the Rangers arrived. Residents greeted the Rangers with "unbounded hospitality" and fed them poultry, pork roast, ham, cakes, and pies.[40]

After losing Murfreesboro, the Federal commander of the region, Gen. Don Carlos Buell, reacted angrily. He ordered Gen. William Nelson to retake McMinnville and Murfreesboro. Nelson promptly set out on his mission. The Rangers under Forrest managed circling around and positioned themselves at Nelson's rear. The Confederates then destroyed two railroad bridges located between Nashville and Nelson's pursuing force.[41]

This cut Nelson off from the men he was to capture, and embarrassed the commander.

The Confederate force then visited the Hermitage, home of Andrew Jackson. While there, they inspected Andrew Jackson's home and joined some of the local young ladies visiting from Nashville. Together they picnicked at the Hermitage, commemorating the anniversary of the Battle of Manassas.[42]

On the return trip to Confederate lines, the cavalrymen proceeded to destroy some of the railroad bridges. Often the bridges were guarded by wooden stockades manned by occupational forces. At one of the bridges, Forrest ordered the Rangers to charge a stockade.[43] Federals occupying the stockade met the charge with heavy fire. The Rangers were driven back from their unsuccessful charge with 180 killed or wounded.[44] After realizing the futility of this attempt, Forrest withdrew. The Rangers ended up participating in the destruction or burning of half a dozen railroad bridges before reaching Sparta, Tennessee.

The men finally rested on July 26 in Chattanooga, Tennessee. With the raid's conclusion, the men engaged in rest and leisure. During this period they created a Masonic Lodge for their members. The "Terry's Military Lodge" began on August 9, 1862. Camp routine still consisted of skirmish drill in the morning and a review every afternoon. Discipline was kept strict when not on patrol and was often administered by Thomas Harrison.[45] Sometime during that summer the Rangers received their second flag.

In the fall, Gen. Braxton Bragg of Georgia, now commanding the Army of Tennessee, commenced his Kentucky campaign. The Rangers were included in this new offensive. Bragg disliked Forrest and sent him back to Murfreesboro after the army reached Bardstown, Kentucky. Bragg transferred command of the combined cavalry brigade to fellow Georgian Joseph Wheeler. John Austin Wharton continued commanding the Terry's Texas Ranger regiment. While under Wheeler, the Rangers formed part of the right wing of Bragg's two-pronged parallel columns headed for Kentucky. At the Tennessee–Kentucky line, the unit skirmished some with Union General McCook's corps on August 30 at Altmount, Tennessee.

Once in Kentucky, the unit quickly found itself in combat situations. At Munfordsville, Kentucky, the Rangers blocked off the escape of Federal troops under Col. John Wilder. This maneuver had them near where B. F. Terry was killed the year before. After some skirmishing and the taking of a fortification, the advance was completed which then had Colonel Wilder caught in a pincer move between the Confederate forces of Polk and Hardee.[46] On September 17, Bragg formally demanded that Colonel Wilder surrender his force. Wilder, who before the war was an Indiana industrialist, lacked military experience. Under a flag of truce he went to Confederate Gen. Simon Buckner's headquarters to ask advice. He had heard that Buckner was a soldier and a gentleman. Buckner already knew what surrender was like, after being part of the force surrendered at Fort Donelson. Buckner declined giving Wilder advice, claiming "that is not the way wars were fought." Buckner told him to defend his position as long as it helped his commander and the Confederates surrounded his forces. Wilder then asked to see the Confederate forces, which Buckner allowed. After reviewing the forces, Wilder said, "I believe I'll surrender." Colonel Wilder finally surrendered his force on September 20, 1862, to General Buckner. (Munfordville occurred on the same day as Sharpsburg.)[47]

While on the Louisville Pike near Mt. Washington, Kentucky, the Ranger regiment stopped for lunch. As they ate, they were attacked by Union forces commanded by General Buell. They quickly mounted, formed skirmish lines, and attempted to hold back the sudden attack. In the engagement, Ronald Chatham received a wound in the center of his forehead. Despite the wound, he remained on his horse and with the regiment until the fighting stopped. He then went to the rear. On passing some women in Mt. Washington, he showed them his gun, and they remarked, "Just look at that poor Texas Ranger; shot through the head and still wants to fight." [48]

On October 4, near Bardstown, a brigade of Union cavalry positioned themselves between the Rangers and Confederate lines.[49] The Rangers were on the Louisville Pike, about four miles west of Bardstown.[50] Wharton assumed that Joseph Wheeler was covering his flank, yet discovered he wasn't there. The Federals continued increasing their numbers and kept advancing in a slow, steady manner. The combined advance of heavy forces and Wheeler's lack of coverage placed the unit in a precarious situation.

That afternoon, at about 3:00, Bob Elgin of Chappell Hill rode up the pike from Bardstown and told Wharton about approaching Union troops. Wharton, quickly realizing the seriousness of the situation, consulted with Maj. Tom Harrison on what to do next. Major Harrison implemented a strategy, and shouted "fill up the lane boys, fill the lane up." The Federal cavalry drew up in force and prepared to charge. The unit, then a force 250 strong, formed in a line. Wharton then ordered the bugler to sound charge when the enemy approached within forty yards.[51] At the sound, the men charged with Rebel yells at a full gallop. Colonel Wharton and Major Harrison led the brigade riding side by side. The men rode four abreast down the Louisville Pike. The Confederates broke the attack and continued forward, heading straight toward the main body of Federal troops. Enemy forces consisting of four regiments (1st Kentucky, 4th Kentucky, 3rd Ohio, and 2nd Indiana cavalry regiments), an artillery battery and infantry fired but could not stop them. The Yankees held until the Confederates were about fifty yards from the line. At that point, the main Union line broke. The Federals ran away, with the Rangers pressing them. In the first two minutes, the Rangers captured several men and weapons. Three minutes into the battle, Federal infantry began arriving and artillery shells began falling. The Rangers then quickly departed the battle, heading toward Confederate lines. When the Rangers returned safely to Confederate lines, they brought 200 prisoners with no losses to the Rangers. As a result of the action, John Wharton and Thomas Harrison were both promoted.[52]

In the post-battle responsibilities after Bardstown, Lieutenant Dechard of the Rangers met with Captain Cupp, a Union cavalry officer, during a brief truce to exchange wounded men. The two would meet again the next year, although under more dire circumstances. Gen. Leonidas Polk praised Wharton and Harrison after the Bardstown battle. He said they were "worthy of applause and emulation of their comrades of all arms in the army." [53]

At Perryville on October 8, the unit was stationed on the right flank of the Confederate line with a small detachment on the left side. On the battlefield, Union forces positioned themselves on the west side of Doctor's Creek and Confederates on the east side. The area between the armies consisted of a deep creek within a valley surrounded by hills on either side. The hills contained no breastworks but had timber in places. Both sides positioned their artillery on the hills. Doctor's Creek served as the main water supply for the area. Since the Confederates arrived in the area first, they controlled the creek. The Confederates waited until early afternoon for the Union forces to attack. While waiting, the artillery of both sides dueled across the valley, causing the earth to tremble.

About 2:00 P.M. the artillery duel faded, and the Rangers were summoned to service.[54] When finally called into action, they charged across the bridge spanning the creek in columns of four. Once across, they formed five lines, one behind the other. With a loud Rebel yell they then charged up the hill. Benjamin F. Cheatham's infantry followed up the charge. The Rangers brushed the defending Yankees from the hill and its woods.[55] When "recall" was sounded by the bugler, the unit returned. In the charge, the acting regimental commander, Mark L. Evans, was killed at the head of the regiment. Thus three regimental commanders had been lost in less than twelve months.

By day's end, the battle was over. The Confederates retained the battlefield, the Federals were driven back and two Union generals had been killed (James S. Jackson and William R. Terrill). General Bragg believed he could not remain in Kentucky and maintain such a large force. Despite the victorious situation, Bragg took his army back to Tennessee. This decision demoralized many of the men.

After the Battle of Perryville, the unit returned to Tennessee via the Cumberland Gap to Knoxville. General Buell, whom the Rangers previously embarrassed in Tennessee, pursued the Confederate army as far as London, Kentucky. The regiment finally passed through the Cumberland Gap on October 22. Wharton's brigade and B.F. Cheatham's brigade served as the rear guards throughout the withdrawal. As rear guards they were frequently skirmishing to cover the withdrawal.[56] Skirmishes were so frequent that the Rangers rarely were able to unsaddle their horses. The march was further complicated by an early cold spell with snowstorms and short rations.[57] Troops suffered from hunger, cold, lack of sleep, and lack of forage for the horses. Through their associations, Wharton and Cheatham developed a warm, personal friendship. Their two brigades participated in almost constant skirmishing and building obstacles to slow their pursuers, both day and night.

Overall, the Kentucky campaign lasted thirty-eight days and covered more territory than any other of the war.[58] Members of the regiment reported that the Rangers were under fire forty-two times with fighting or skirmishing daily and some days more than once. One member reported thirty-four battles or skirmishes in thirty days. The last seventeen days contained daily skirmishing.[59] Because the supply wagons were with the main army, whose retreat they covered, the Rangers had no shelter and little food. One Ranger wrote, "We had to form line and skirmish several times a day. The service was very trying. For more than a week, there was no order given to unsaddle." [60]

Another Ranger recalled, "from the day we entered Kentucky until the day we passed out of the state, thirty-eight days, our regiment in part or as a whole had been under the fire of the enemy's guns forty-two times, including Perryville Battle as one of the times." [61]

In the closing part of the Kentucky campaign, on October 13, command of all cavalry regiments in the Army of Tennessee, except the Rangers, went to Joseph Wheeler. The Rangers were then attached to Gen. Leonidas Polk's corps. General Bragg had been ordered to Richmond, Virginia. Bragg was to give account of the activities of the campaign, but he was known for his censure and blaming of others when events were less than ideal.[62] Although associated with Polk's command, the Rangers functioned as an unattached, independent command.[63]

During October the Rangers received new tents and uniforms. The Rangers also received a written commendation and promotions for their fight at Bardstown, Kentucky. Colonel Wharton was promoted to general and Thomas Harrison to colonel. With the promotion, Harrison became regimental commander. Wharton's new position was at the brigade level of command.[64]

Polk then took the army to Chattanooga and from there to

Murfreesboro. Once at camp in Murfreesboro, the soldiers brought increased social life to the small Tennessee town. The town had suffered during another occupation by Federal troops, and its residents were grateful to see the Confederates return. After the brief stay at Murfreesboro, the Rangers moved their camp to Nolensville, Tennessee, about fifteen miles south of Nashville. Their duty consisted of watching the Federal army assembled at Nashville. While in Nolensville, there were periodic skirmishes with Union cavalry and reconnaissance missions. Skirmishing with enemy troops often involved stopping enemy foraging parties.

Several ladies from Nashville visited the unit at camp that December. The women successfully traveled through Union lines carrying assorted supplies under their skirts. During the middle of the month, President Jefferson Davis visited the Army of Tennessee, which included a review of the troops. The day after his review, cavalryman Gen. John Hunt Morgan married in nearby Murfreesboro. Wives and sweethearts alike turned out for Morgan's marriage. Along with the wedding, there were parties, receptions, horse races, and a grand banquet held for the president and Confederate leaders. One Ranger claimed that this month was one "among warm-hearted and hospitable Tennesseans. Warm firesides, square meals and the smiles of pretty girls made an Eden on Earth for the war-worn soldiers."[65]

Not everyone enjoyed the hospitality. General Bragg, who returned from Richmond, issued an order on the subject.

"The country for miles around our military stations is full of officers and soldiers, visiting, loitering and marauding. Many of them quarter themselves on the people of the country, claiming as a right they should be entertained. Such parties are not only not authorized, they are denounced as highly pernicious to the discipline and efficiency of the army, and the general calls on commanding officers and citizens to aid in suppression of the evil." [66]

Christmas Day in Murfreesboro featured horse racing, card playing, and other festivities.[67] While the Army of Tennessee enjoyed themselves in Murfreesboro, the Rangers were largely thinking of home and loved ones while in Nolensville. Holiday festivities came to an early close, with Federal Gen. William S. Rosecrans leaving Nashville on December 25 and marching out

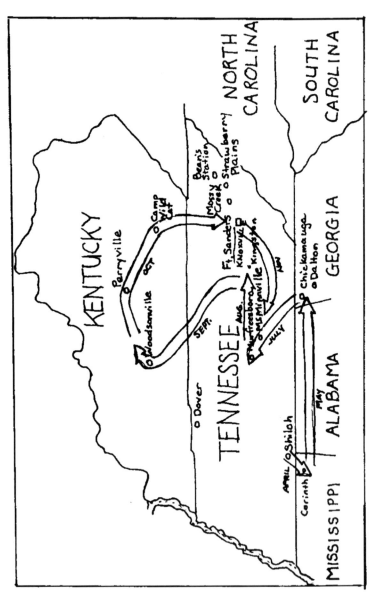

Major movements of the regiment, April–December 1862.

to meet General Bragg and the Army of Tennessee. Rosecrans took advantage of Bragg's cavalry brigades under Forrest and Wagner not being with the main body of troops.[68]

Around noon, as some of the Rangers enjoyed their holiday egg nog, Federal troops surprised them, driving in the pickets.[69] The main body of the regiment hastily mounted their horses and advanced in two columns. Colonel Harrison ordered the men: "Form your company on this rise and hold the position while I form the regiment behind you in supporting distance."[70] Federal infantry and artillery were soon firing on the main body of the regiment. The Union artillery quickly gauged their range and poured in shells on top of them. One Ranger reported a shell hit near him, covering him in blood and horseflesh. After an attempted stand, the unit fell back. Wharton reported the attack by the Union troops to General Bragg, who initially ordered Wharton to delay them until he was certain that they were advancing.

The Rangers went out to assess the situation. On reaching the rise, they discovered a solid line of Union infantry lying down. The regiment quickly retreated, with the infantry pursuing.[71] Thus began a day of skirmishing and stalling.

On December 26, as Union forces continued advancing, the Rangers charged and engaged the advance troops most of the day. News of the fighting was relayed through General Wheeler to General Bragg. With Union troops continuing their advancing, Bragg eventually issued orders for Wharton to "let the enemy come on."[72]

On the 27th, in a cold misty rain, the Rangers again engaged advance Union troops at daylight. Wharton positioned himself on some hills north of the Triune Road. The Rangers held their position most of the day. By holding this position, Wharton kept Gen. William Hardee's troops from being flanked. Wharton managed maintaining the position through most of the rainy day, until the fog lifted in the afternoon. With the lifting of the fog, artillery fire drove them out of their position. By night, Wharton fell back to Eagleville.

The two opposing armies finally met outside of Murfreesboro, on the Stones River. The terrain was open country with rough, uneven ground. Outcroppings of limestone ledges broken by deep crevices and boulders strewn about created numerous obstacles on the battlefield. There were densely wooded tracts or brakes of Tennessee red cedar and thinner ones of oak.[73]

At Murfreesboro, the Rangers were stationed on the extreme left of the Confederate line. On the 29th, Wharton received orders from Bragg to move forward, "engage the enemy and bring on the attack," which he successfully did.[74] On the 30th, Hardee ordered Wharton to "make a detour of the enemies right and fall upon their flank and rear."[75] The day was also filled with artillery duels.[76] From this position, at daylight, Wharton led the regiment and other units in his brigade around the Union right to within 600 yards of Rosecrans' headquarters, where they attacked a wagon train and the Nashville Pike. In the action, four cannon were captured, along with prisoners from the 75th Illinois Infantry regiment. Also captured were papers indicating the number of Federal troops there to be between 60,000 and 70,000.[77] The Rangers could not hold the ground they gained, and withdrew from their position.

In his report of the action, General Hardee said, "Captain S.P. Christian of the Texas Rangers with four companies, charged and took a complete battery of the enemy with all its guns, caissons, horses and artillerists."[78] The next day, December 30, the Rangers moved farther down the Pike in the direction of Nashville, and again encountered the same supply train. They then attacked before daylight and finished the job they had begun, managing to capture several pieces of artillery, over 2,000 prisoners, and numbers of supply wagons. This attack earned Wharton the title of "Invincible" from General Bragg.[79]

Fighting continued throughout the day. The Confederate troops began attacking about 6:00 A.M. in a cold, drizzling rain. The regiment was dismounted and assigned to form a skirmish line ten feet apart. The line was on one side of a field grown up with long weeds.[80] Once in position, they waited for the Yankees to attack. Finally, Col. Tom Harrison surveyed with field glasses and observed Federal cavalry (15th Pennsylvania regiment) preparing to charge with sabers. He said, "Now boys, we will have some fun. There is a regiment out there preparing to charge us armed with sabers. Let them come nearly close enough to strike and then feed them with buckshot." The

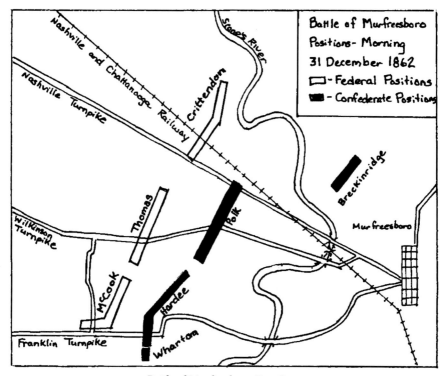

Battle of Murfreesboro: Day One.

Yankee cavalry then charged them. The Texans stood their ground, which caused the Pennsylvanians to run within a few steps and stop. At that moment, the Rangers released their deadly volley. The effect scattered the attackers.[81] Many Federals surrendered and the Rangers chided them, "Why did you stop? . . . Are your sabers long range weapons? . . . How can you kill a man with these things [referring to the sabers]?"[82, 83]

In another episode that day, subsequent to Federals being driven through a cedar brake by a rapid Confederate charge, Blackburn records the Rangers captured a Union officer who spoke with a Prussian accent. They asked him his name and rank, and he said, "General Willich."

"The same who commanded the 32nd Indiana as a colonel?" he was asked.

"Yes the same, and who are you?" demanded the general.

"Terry's Texas Rangers" was the reply.

"*Mein Gott*," said General Willich, "I would rather be a private in that regiment than be a Brigadier General in the Federal army." [84]

On January 2, Confederate General Breckinridge led his division in an attack ordered by General Bragg on Union positions. Breckinridge was to drive the enemy back, crown the hill, entrench his artillery, and hold the position. [85] Although Bragg claimed to have ordered the cavalry to aid with the attack, the messengers said they could not find Generals Wharton and Pegram to deliver the orders. Breckinridge followed orders and launched the attack in the midst of a hard rain. The Confederate attack was halted from making progress against Union lines. After the attack was blunted, the Federals pounded Breckinridge's division with fifty-two pieces of artillery. [86] Although by now the rain had turned to sleet, the bombardment incessantly continued. The attack and bombardment decimated the "orphan brigade," which required assistance in order to disengage from the fighting. Confederate forces were sent to assist the brave brigade. The Rangers dismounted and joined the Confederate forces sent to cover the retreat of Breckinridge's forces. [87]

Bragg ordered the army to retire at will. The Army of Tennessee ended up retiring only twelve to fifteen miles from the battlefield. [88] By the time the Battle of Murfreesboro ended, the Rangers had captured over 2,000 prisoners, as well as guns, wagons, and equipment. Although he wore sheaths of iron, the regimental commander, Col. Tom Harrison, received a flesh wound. The wounded Colonel Harrison refused going to the rear. Because he was wearing the iron sheaths, others began referring to him as "Ironsides."

After the battle, ambulances, chaplains, and burial parties surveyed the results of the battle. The Rev. Dr. Joseph Cross of the Army of Tennessee described the scene after several days fighting:

Here they lie, friend and foe, in every possible position, a vast promiscuous ruin. . . . After a pretty thorough inspection of the ground in the rear of our lines, from Stone River on the extreme left, I rode to the front, where the dead lie thick among the cedars, in proportion of five Yankees to one Southron. Here are sights to sicken the bravest hearts—and lessons for human passion and oppression. Here is a foot, shot off at the ankle—a fine model for a sculptor. Here is an officer's hand, severed from the wrist, the glove still upon it, and the sword in its grasp. Here is an entire brain, perfectly isolated, showing no sign of violence, as if carefully taken from the skull that enclosed it by the hands of a skillful surgeon. Here is a corpse, sitting upon the ground, with its back against a tree, the most natural position of life, holding before its face the photograph likeness of a good-looking old lady, probable the dead-man's mother. Here is a poor fellow, who has crawled into the corner of a fence to read his sister's letter, and expired in the act of its perusal, the precious document still open before him full of affectionate counsel. Here is a handsome young man, with a placid countenance, lying on his back, his Bible upon his bosom, and his hand folded over it, as if he had gone to sleep saying his evening prayer. Many others present the melancholy contrast of scattered cards, obscene pictures and filthy ballad books—"miserable comforters" for a dying hour. One lies upon his face literally biting the ground, his rigid fingers fastened firmly into the gory sod; and another with upturned face, open eyes, knit brow, compressed lips, and clenched fists, displays all the desperation of vengeance imprinted on his clay. Dissevered heads, arms, legs everywhere; and the coagulated pools of blood gleam ghastly in the morning sun. It is a fearful sight. . . .[89]

CHAPTER 5

Advance
and Retreat
(1863)

*"I would rather fight for Tennesseans
than anyone else except Texans."*
—John A. Wharton

The rain never seemed to let up that January. Cold, wet days of clambering through mud welcomed the Rangers as they provided cover for the retreating Army of Tennessee. The retreat took them away from the familiar town of Murfreesboro. After protecting the rear of the army, they were assigned constant winter picket duty on the Shelbyville-Murfreesboro pike in Tennessee.[1] Occasionally the monotony of cold, wet days was broken up by skirmishing with Federal troops. Some days, they fought up to half a dozen skirmishes. In one rare break from the routine, orders came for the Rangers to locate the daughter of a Confederate colonel (Colonel Tillard). The mission took several days.

After leaving Confederate lines, the Rangers witnessed Yankee troops setting fire to homes belonging to men in the

Confederate army. It seemed as though the invading Federals were not just fighting against them but punishing Confederates for defending their homes.

Finally, on January 25, the Rangers were ordered on a longer mission. The new mission was a raid, and as part of Wharton's brigade they would join up with regiments in Forrest's brigade. Joseph Wheeler, the newly appointed cavalry commander for the Army of Tennessee, would lead the raid into western Tennessee. Wheeler at that time was twenty-six years old. The young, small commander in his restless 120-pound Episcopalian frame did not readily inspire the men.

A small stature combined with a receding hairline and beard barely masked the youth of this newly appointed general from Georgia. Wheeler graduated from West Point in the class of 1859. While there, classmates dubbed him "the point," since he lacked length, breadth, or thickness. Bragg's new cavalry commander sported a crimson sash, a large black plumed hat, and loved consuming wild honey. His small stature soon earned him the nickname of "Little Joe" among the Rangers.[2]

The men outfitted for the raid with food and ammunition. Although the commander was arrayed in a dapper fashion, the regiments quickly discovered the amount of ammunition provided was inadequate for the mission before them. The low ammunition concerned the men and angered Generals Forrest and Wharton.[3]

January weather in Tennessee is extremely cold. For the Rangers, the frigid temperatures made any raid an arduous undertaking. Nevertheless, the regiments departed camp for a location in western Tennessee. When crossing streams, ice formed on the horses' legs and tails. Their path took them through snow three feet deep in places. Six men froze to death while crossing the Cumberland Mountains.[4] Some of the only encouragement received came from women who brought them meals along the way.

After a week of traveling under frigid conditions, they reached their destination, Fort Donelson. It was only a year before that the Rangers were in this part of Tennessee, rescuing Confederate troops escaped from the fort. They arrived about 10:00 in the evening. A deep snow fell earlier that day and the previous evening, and the light of a full moon on untrampled snow revealed that no pickets were on duty.

The men rested briefly before beginning their assault. Before daylight the next morning, on February 3, Wheeler ordered an attack against Forrest's advice.[5] The selected target was Dover, a fortified post of Fort Donelson. Dover, under the command of Union Colonel Harding, was positioned on the Cumberland River, a roaring, muddy torrent swollen with extra water from recent rains.[6]

Wheeler initially sent the Union commander a demand for surrender signed by all three generals participating in the raid (Wheeler, Wharton, and Forrest). After the Union commander refused the demand, the attack on Dover commenced. In the opening attack, Forrest and his brigade approached from the north and east. Wharton attacked from the Fort Donelson side.[7] A total of eight mounted regiments attacked. Forrest's brigade captured the outer works and Wharton's command captured a cannon. Since ammunition ran low, both commanders withdrew their forces after three hours of fighting with great loss of life. Wharton held the Rangers in reserve that day, so they did not participate in the attack.

That night, in the darkness, the Federals sent four gunboats and troop transports up the swollen Cumberland River. Their mission was to shell the Confederate forces, land troops, and attack. One Ranger described the destruction produced by the firing gunboats. The shells were "cutting from the trees along the banks limbs as large as a man's body."[8] Under the cover of darkness, Ranger Sam Maverick[9] jumped into the cold river with matches in his hair. He swam hand over hand to one of the gunboats, which he set ablaze.[10] He then swam back through the frigid waters to safety on the shore. There he obtained a promotion and a pint of liquor. After he returned to camp, the cavalry forces fell back further since troop transports accompanying the gunboats had begun unloading additional Federal forces.

Both brigade commanders (Forrest and Wharton) objected to the unsuccessful attack on Dover before its occurrence, which caused them to lose more respect for Wheeler. They already had little respect for him based on the poor outfitting done prior to the raid. The day's losses increased the resentment toward his leadership. That evening, after the attack, the commanders

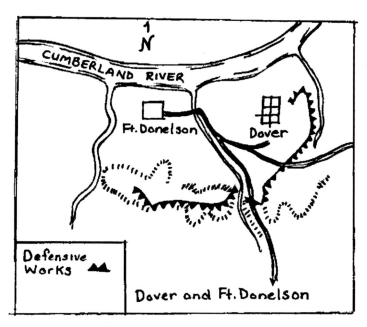

Map of Dover, Fort Donelson, and fortifications.

gathered in a farmhouse. Wheeler sat beside the fire dictating his report. Wharton sat opposite Wheeler, and Forrest lay on the floor warming his feet by the fire. As Wheeler dictated the report, he was interrupted by Wharton and Forrest's disapproval of what he said and did regarding the raid.[11] Forrest was especially upset since he had two horses shot from under him that day. Forrest was so resentful, he offered Wheeler his resignation over the matter.[12] Wheeler declined acceptance of the resignation. Forrest went on to state he would be in a coffin before he would serve under Wheeler again.[13]

Now demoralized, the force retreated to Duck River, where they discovered another obstacle. The ferry needed to transport the troops was on the opposite side of the frigid river. Two Rangers volunteered to swim the river and return with the ferry.[14] The volunteers bravely plunged into the river and completed the difficult task.

The frigid conditions remained such that hands stuck to the metal gun barrels and the horses' bits. The men were concerned that those same bits were being placed in the horses' mouths.[15] Despite the problems with the cold, during one of the few relaxed moments the troopers engaged in a snowball fight and purposely involved Col. Thomas Harrison.[16]

Federal troops continued pursuing and engaging the Rangers constantly until they returned to Confederate lines. As a result of the hardships associated with the travel and attacks involved on the raid, whenever a Ranger wanted to describe suffering, they referred to "the Donelson trip." [17] In an effort to improve morale, after the Rangers returned from the Donelson trip, Wharton hosted a military ball for his men.

The Rangers camped near Louisberg, Tennessee, for a while in February. Periodically, they went into town for entertainment for the evenings. Entertainment often consisted of singing songs and playing piano at the homes of citizens. Louisberg also served as a jumping-off point for several days of foraging patrols. It was a welcome break after the hardships of Donelson.

In March the Rangers moved their camp near Wartrace, Tennessee. Frequent drill and inspections filled the month with activity. Duties for the regiment included picketing on the pike, as well as scouting and spy missions around Murfreesboro. The pickets periodically skirmished with Yankee troops.

Sometimes special raids and missions took place. Typically, a call for volunteers went out since these raids were often more hazardous than those associated with campaigns. One such raid was organized by Ranger Stephen Ferrell. That April, John Hunt Morgan and Maj. Dick McCann's Tennessee cavalry reported to Ferrell for special service which included raiding the railroad lines in Tennessee. The main targets were the Louisville and Nashville Line (L&N) and the run between Nashville and Chattanooga. During the raiding mission, the Confederate cavalry frequently skirmished with Federal forces. One of the skirmishes occurred on April 10, about five and a half miles from LaVerne, Tennessee, when Confederates ambushed a train. After removing some track, Confederate cavalry hid in the nearby bushes. As the train slowed, the Confederates opened fire on the troops guarding the train. The train ran off the tracks during the skirmishing. In the midst of fighting and confusion of a train derailment, the guards were soon overpowered.[18] In the skirmish, the combined Confederate cavalry force fought against members of the 10th Michigan Infantry.

When the fighting ended, the Confederates had success-fully captured the train. The Rangers escorted female passen-gers from the train to the nearest house, and then returned to the train to open the mail bags. An iron safe was found, and the Rangers attempted opening the safe with rocks. Finally, they managed breaking it open. As part of the booty, the Rangers ob-tained Old Rosy's (Union General Rosecrans') pistol and $30,000 in Federal cash.[19] The volunteers returned safely to Confederate lines near Tullahoma, Tennessee, and turned over the cash and booty to Wharton. He later used the cash in buying more horses for the unit.

When April finally came, spring fever also arrived. The reg-iment decided a horse race was needed. The "Grand Horse Race" would be between their commanders, Tom Harrison (a.k.a. Old Ironsides or Old Tom) and John A. Wharton. With the go-ahead signal, both leaders spurred their horses from the starting line. In the race, Wharton's horse hit a tree, knocking him off the horse, leaving Harrison to win. Wharton ended up on crutches for a while after the fall during the race.

In May, Wharton sent the Rangers to Sparta, Tennessee. They were ordered to hold the town of Liberty until a force under General Morgan arrived to relieve them. Besides holding Liberty, they carried dispatches between commanders and headquarters.

With the arrival of June, Gen. Braxton Bragg suspected a new Union offensive. In anticipation of this he ordered some commands into fortifications. The Rangers were sent to Hoover's Gap, Tennessee, in order to defend the area from in-vading Yankees. The Rangers camped and patrolled the area for several days. Bragg was right; the Yankees finally invaded through Hoover's Gap on the Murfreesboro-Shelbyville Pike. The anticipated invasion occurred on June 24. Union forces at-tacked in full force. The Rangers held their position, yet other units faltered. Despite their resistance, the Rangers fell back be-fore superior Union numbers and the threat of being flanked.[20]

The Union offensive continued to rapidly push into south-ern Tennessee. Several days later, on a rainy June 30, Bragg evacuated Tullahoma. The Rangers, the 11th Texas Cavalry, and a newly consolidated Texas infantry brigade under Churchill[21] guarded the rear of the Army of Tennessee's retreat.[22] Although the distance was only eight miles, much of the road had mud knee-deep. As part of the retreat, the Texans cut down trees and threw up obstacles, slowing the advancing Union forces.[23] The Confederate troops in the Army of Tennessee departed so hurriedly, they discarded anything that would slow them down.[24] In covering the Confederate army, the Texas units skirmished and fought daily with Union pursuers, alternating with the 11th Texas Cavalry.

Heavy fighting occurred July 4 as Union forces (1st, 5th, and 9th Kentucky regiments) conducted a three-pronged attack against the Texas troops. The Federals initially cut off one company and pushed a second back. The Rangers engaged the Federal troops at University Place, Tennessee (now the University of the South) in the Cumberland Mountains.[25] The Confederates eventually drove the Federals back with well-delivered volleys. After halting the enemy advance, the Rangers pursued their attackers back to their reserve units. The efforts of the Rangers and the 4th Tennessee Cavalry (Starnes-McLemore's Regiment) succeeded in slowing the Union advance. In the action, Union forces lost nine killed and almost thirty wounded. Finally on July 5, the Army of Tennessee safely reached Chattanooga. Although the Rangers' engagement met with success, the morale of the Army of Tennessee shrank as General Bragg continued his retreat through the state.[26] Regimental Chaplain R. F. Bunting expressed his disappointment in a letter, stating, "Doubtless the Grand Army of Tennessee has fulfilled its mission—for it can out-retreat anything in the Confederacy."

Several days after arriving in Chattanooga, Wharton arranged for another ball for his men to bolster their morale. Within a few days, the regiment was ordered to Rome, Georgia.

That summer, the Rangers camped at Rome in order to procure more horses. They arrived on July 15. While there, the Rangers participated in dress parades and inspections. Dr. Bunting began a series of religious camp meetings at a Primitive Baptist Church there, which resulted in men being saved and pledging themselves to "the better life." [27] The meetings occurred twice a day and lasted five weeks. Similar religious revival services occurred within the main body of the Army of Tennessee while at Tullahoma.[28] During the religious revival, over half of the nearly 400 troops comprising the regiment converted to Christianity. The men formed a "Christian Association" and chose Col. Gustave Cooke as president.

The Rangers also took up a collection to buy a horse for John A. Wharton, who now held the rank of general. With the collection, the regiment presented Wharton a thoroughbred horse (a bay charger). The horse was presented along with a $1,000 silver saddle on August 5.[29]

The presentation occurred during a grand review and barbecue. The "Bloody Sixth" Arkansas band provided music for the event. In his acceptance speech, Wharton said he would rather fight for Tennesseans than anyone else except Texans. This comment angered the Georgians present.[30] After Wharton's speech, Tom Harrison made a few remarks, and then Reverend Kaufman led the men in prayer. The barbecue was followed by a ball in Rome, which some of the Rangers did not attend due to religious objections regarding dancing.[31]

Later that summer, since the Confederacy experienced defeats at Gettysburg and Vicksburg, a special day was called for by President Jefferson Davis. President Davis set aside Friday, August 21, as a national day of "fasting, humiliation and prayer" for the Confederate cause. In his official proclamation, Davis stated:

> . . . It is meet that when trials and reverses befall us, we should seek to take home to our hearts and consciences the lessons which they teach, and profit by the self-examination for which they prepare us. . . . Let us rather receive in humble thankfulness the lesson which He has taught us in our recent reverses, devotedly acknowledging that to Him, and not to our feeble arms, are due the honor and glory of victory; that from Him, in his paternal providence, comes the anguish of defeat, and that, whether in victory of defeat, our humble supplications are due at His footstool . . .[32]

On that day, while many locals were assembled in their houses of worship, Union artillery began firing on the city of Chattanooga, thus signaling the beginning of a new Union military offensive. Shelling continued on a daily basis. By September 9, Union forces occupied the city.

In the early part of September the Rangers patrolled the mountain passes around Lookout Mountain. By mid-month, on September 19, the Rangers moved into position in the Confederate lines at Glass Mill, Georgia. While moving into place, they met Gen. James Longstreet's corps arriving from Virginia, which included Hood's brigade. Hood's brigade consisted largely of Texan soldiers. Being fellow Texans, Hood's brigade considered the Rangers the only command as good as themselves.[33] The Rangers also met with Granbury's brigade while positioning. The all-Texan Granbury's brigade would later gain notoriety in the Atlanta campaign.

Later that day, along Chickamauga Creek, the regiment covered the southern flank of the Confederate line, holding the Union right in check. At one point, Federal cavalry (George Crook's division: 1st, 2nd, 3rd, and 4th Ohio Cavalry) attempted attacking the Confederate rear. Wharton's brigade and the Rangers received the attack at Glass Mill, stopped the advance, and repulsed the Union attack.

After resting during the night the regiment followed up on their previous success. The next day, Wheeler launched an attack on Crook's division.[34] While the other regiments made a frontal assault, the Rangers fell upon the enemy flank charging through a lane, straight into the camp of the 1st, 2nd, 3rd, and 4th Ohio Cavalry regiments. After heavy fighting, they defeated the 4th Ohio Cavalry, captured two regimental colors, and mortally wounded their colonel.[35] In the last great charge of the battle, the regiment pursued the cavalry of McCook and the once-before captured General Crittenden. The Union cavalry retreated back to Chattanooga, with Confederates on their heels through the cedar brakes and blackjack thickets of the area.[36]

After the charge ended, couriers brought a message to Lt. George M. Dechard of the Rangers. The message came from the wounded Lieutenant Colonel Cupp of the 1st Ohio. After reading the message, Dechard hurriedly returned to the portion of the battlefield where Cupp lay mortally wounded and met with him. The two men met had previously after battles in the Kentucky campaign, with one of those times at Bardstown,

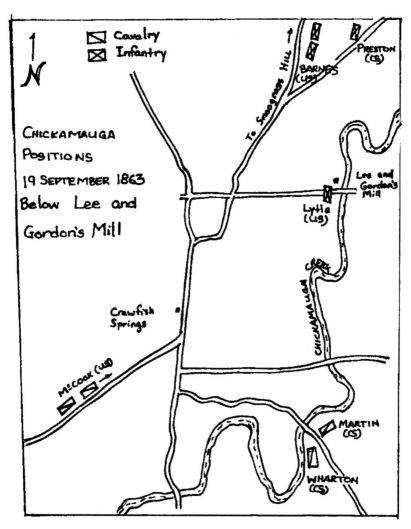

Positions of the regiment at the Battle of Chickamauga.

Kentucky. On reaching the part of the battlefield where the officer lay, Dechard dismounted, and said, "Why, it's my old friend Major Cupp. I am sorry to see you thus."

"Lieutenant Colonel Cupp," replied the other, "but I've had my last promotion. You people have got me this time."

In the Chickamauga meeting, Cupp requested Dechard take his watch and other items and send them to relatives in

Ohio. Dechard honored his request, and these items were sent via a truce a few days later to his family in Ohio.[37]

The following day, September 21, the Rangers crossed Chickamauga Creek at Lee and Gordon's Mills and pushed toward Lookout Mountain. They were to take the Chattanooga Road and hold it until released. Along the way, they skirmished a couple of times with Federal cavalry. A portion of the regiment left the main body and intercepted fifty Union supply wagons coming from McLemore's Cove to support Union troops along Chickamauga Creek. The wagons never reached their intended destination. The Rangers helped themselves to the wagons' contents and returned to camp loaded with supplies. The next day, they were sent to clear Lookout Mountain of any remaining Yankee troops.

In the days immediately after the Battle of Chickamauga, the Rangers performed picket duty along the south side of the Tennessee River. On the opposite bank was the 1st Ohio Cavalry, whom they had recently fought at Chickamauga. At one point, the two units arranged a truce. During the truce, the men swam, swapped stories, exchanged supplies, traded newspapers, and enjoyed each other's company. Blackburn recorded the following exchange as an example of their activity: A Yank said to Johnnie Reb, "Where is Old Ironsides (Col. Tom Harrison) today?" "At camp," says Johnnie Reb. "Where is Colonel Cupp?" (calling by name the colonel of the 1st Ohio). "Oh the devil, you know where we left him over at Chickamauga," was the answer.

Such truces commonly occurred in the absence of commissioned officers.[38] Col. John McIntyre, a fellow Texan with the 4th Ohio, was once asked by a Ranger which Confederate unit was the toughest. His quick reply was "The Texas Rangers. They have killed over seven hundred men for me; I have had to go back to Ohio and recruit four times." [39]

In the aftermath of Chickamauga, General Bragg met with Gen. James Longstreet. After the meeting with Longstreet, Joseph Wheeler was summoned. In the meeting, the leaders discussed sending a cavalry expedition north of the Tennessee River. The objective was to break Rosecrans' communications behind the Union lines. Wheeler told Bragg that few of the horses would be able to withstand the strain of such a mission.

Bragg insisted, so a few days later, Wheeler assembled the best collection of mounts he could find. As often occurred with General Bragg, the original orders were countermanded on the day of departure. The new orders were to first clear Lookout Mountain, then proceed on the raid.[40] The Rangers, along with other cavalry units, cleared the Union pickets from Lookout Mountain, then began the mission in earnest.

On September 30 the regiment, along with the 4th Alabama Cavalry (commanded by Col. A. A. Russell), the 4th Tennessee Cavalry (Starnes-McLemore's regiment), elements of the 11th Texas, 3rd Arkansas (from Randolph County, Arkansas) and the 51st Mounted Alabama Infantry, assembled.[41] The combined regiments would begin their mission under the overall command of Joseph Wheeler. The scope of Wheeler's authority now included the regiments previously under Forrest's command. Wheeler thus assumed the command of Forrest's regiments. Forrest disliked being under Wheeler's command (due in part to the Dover episode) so much that he sought and received an independent command from President Davis.

As the force under Wheeler journeyed along the Tennessee River, the men of the 4th Ohio Cavalry mimicked the movements of the Confederate forces from the opposite side of the river. This action irritated and embarrassed Wheeler, who commanded the raid.[42] Finally, the Confederates began crossing the Tennessee near Cottonport, Tennessee. They were opposed by companies of the 4th Ohio Cavalry, on the opposite bank of the river.[43] The opposition slowed Wheeler's forces. Wheeler disliked being slowed down, and ordered the artillery brought up. The Union cavalry then dispersed as Wheeler brought up the artillery pieces to the riverbank. The artillery quickly cleared the remaining Federals from the opposite side of the river. The men then proceeded crossing the river. Since it was dry season, the river was only two to three feet deep.

Once on the other side of the river, Wheeler split his forces into two parts. One, led by Wheeler, was to attack a large supply train (800+ wagons) in the Sequatchie Valley.[44] The other, led by Wharton, was to take McMinnville. From there, the force led by Wheeler made their way across Walden's Ridge and into the Sequatchie Valley at Anderson's Cross Roads on October 2.[45]

The Rangers were in the group led by General Wharton with 2,500 men that headed to McMinnville. Units from the 4th Tennessee reached the village first. A charge led by Colonel Hodge captured Federal rifle pits that provided the outermost Federal defensive perimeter. When the main Confederate force arrived, the forward forces dismounted and deployed. An advance battalion drove in the Union pickets. Wharton then met with the regimental commanders and considered his options. He decided on approaching the garrison under a truce and demanding their surrender as done in the 1862 raid on McMinnville. Wharton's idea was used, and Colonel Hodge was ordered to deliver the request.[46] To everyone's surprise, the Federals were interested in accepting Wharton's offer.[47] The Federal commander, Maj. Michael Patterson, would only surrender if it could be proven to his satisfaction that he was outnumbered. Wharton refused the request to view the numbers of Confederate troops, whereupon Patterson surrendered.[48] The Confederates then helped themselves to quartermaster supplies and pro-Union merchants as they saw fit. After equipping themselves, they destroyed the remaining quartermaster and commissary stores.

On October 5 the combined force left McMinnville and headed for Murfreesboro. Outside the city, the force captured a stockade on the Stones River. After the stockade's capture, the raiding force began cutting the telegraph, chopping down trestles, and tearing up railroad tracks.[49] The subsequent day, the force destroyed a locomotive, railroad stock, and the trestle bridges between Murfreesboro and Wartrace, Tennessee.[50]

On October 6 the Rangers reached Shelbyville, Tennessee. They proceeded to the shops of Yankee store owners and appropriated more supplies. As other units arrived, order disappeared and anarchy developed. In the anarchy, citizens were robbed at gunpoint. Among the supplies acquired were dress coats and paper collars. The cavalrymen, who had not washed clothes in weeks, adorned themselves in the formal finery, placing them over their dirty uniforms. Those witnessing the event and the dirty cavalrymen's parade down the streets in formal finery found the sight. They also obtained a black "Prince Albert" coat, which was later presented to the chaplain, R. F. Bunting.[51]

Union cavalry forces had been aware of the raid since October 1. Brig. Gen. George Crook, commander of the Second Cavalry Division (which included the 1st Ohio Cavalry, 72nd Mounted Infantry of the Mounted Lightning Brigade, and 2nd Kentucky Cavalry) was ordered to seek out and destroy Wheeler in battle. Brig. Gen. Robert Mitchell, commanding the first division of Federal cavalry, was also enlisted to participate in pursuing Wheeler's force.

The Rangers left Shelbyville on October 7, passed through Farmington, and went north. After they were several miles past, a messenger galloped up to the commander and delivered an urgent message. The order wanted them to "come to Farmington double-quick." As usual, the commander (Col. Gustave Cooke) took charge, turned the column around, and led them back to Farmington. Since the weather was overcast and cloudy that day, the sight of the smoke-covered town did not alert them to the potential danger. Upon reaching a smoke-covered Farmington that afternoon, they were ambushed by Union General Crook's forces. Crook and his men positioned themselves in a cedar thicket armed with Spencer rifles. The initial volleys shattered the head of the column and injured many of the horses.

A drizzle began falling during the battle, which, combined with artillery smoke, limited visibility to very low levels.[52] In these conditions, soldiers could not see what they were shooting at. The Federals lined up on one side of the pike, firing at the sound of galloping horses, and pressed the attack, moving men forward. The advancing Federals shot at the retreating Confederates and sabered their horses.[53] The Federal cavalry present fought dismounted, since the topography hampered use of horses. The situation was chaotic at best for the regiment.

With much of the leadership wounded, Maj. Pat Christian salvaged the command, organized some of the Rangers, and gathered the wounded, including Colonel Cooke, by moving them to a defensible position.[54] General Wheeler managed to get orders to Tom Harrison to "form fours" and charge the Union position. The charge succeeded in temporarily driving the Federals back. The environment severely limited the use of horses and charges. Soon Federal reinforcements arrived and drove the Confederates from the field. Darkness fell before

Crook could launch an all-out attack, and in the darkness, a rear guard was formed to hold against advancing Federals. The main body then galloped at full speed for the Tennessee River.[55]

Wharton, Wheeler, and Harrison met to review events at Farmington. Wharton felt the regiment did the best they could, given the circumstances. Wheeler agreed with him, but Thomas Harrison expressed his frustration and disappointment: "It was not a fight at all! I'm ashamed of them! If they can do no better than that I'll disown them!" A staff officer said, "I always thought that regiment overrated anyhow." This angered Tom Harrison, who got up, shook his finger in the fellow's face and broke out furiously: "Who the ——— are you? There is not a man in that regiment who can not kick you all over this yard, sir!" As he strode off to his horse, he was heard to say: "By God, I'll curse them all I want to; but I'll be ——— if anybody else will do it in my presence."[56]

The disaster at Farmington demoralized the Rangers and raised further questions among the soldiers regarding Wheeler's leadership.[57] Wharton knew the situation needed prompt action. Immediately after crossing the Tennessee River to Confederate lines at Muscle Shoals, Alabama, Wharton left the unit. He proceeded to Richmond, Virginia, with his concerns. While there, he actively pursued transferring the Rangers and himself into another army across the Mississippi River. Although his efforts at obtaining a transfer met with failure, he received a promotion to major general. Such actions by the leadership in Richmond sent a confusing message to General Wharton regarding his concerns.

Although the Rangers experienced discouragement regarding the raid into Tennessee, some in Confederate leadership viewed the results differently. The captured supply wagons successfully made it to Confederate lines intact, and losses were light. The raid resulted in capturing more than 2,000 prisoners, and destroying miles of railroad and several major rail bridges. General Bragg gave General Wheeler and all the regiments a written commendation for the raid.

At headquarters for the Army of Tennessee, frequent disagreements occurred between Generals Bragg and James Longstreet. These disagreements continued one after another, and the need for a third party to resolve their issues was apparent. President Davis finally stepped in with a possible solution to

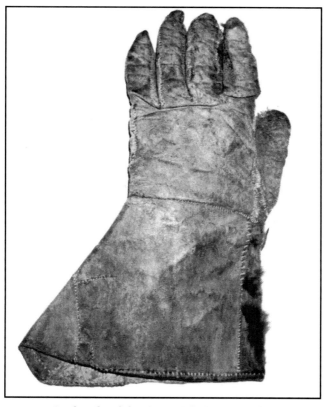

Leather glove belonging to Col. Gustave Cooke.
— Courtesy of The Museum of Southern History,
Sugarland, Texas

the differences between the generals. The solution called for Gen. James Longstreet to advance into eastern Tennessee with two divisions. Thus, a new campaign was initiated. On November 4, General Bragg sent General Longstreet's corps, along with Wheeler's cavalry, to reinforce forces near Knoxville. The plan was to force pressure on Union Gen. Ambrose Burnside's army still located in Knoxville, Tennessee. If Knoxville was recaptured, the rail line between Chattanooga and Virginia could be restored.

In preparation for the Knoxville campaign, the composition of the brigade changed. The new brigade contained the 8th Texas Cavalry, 11th Texas Cavalry, 3rd Arkansas Cavalry, and 4th

Fur haversack belonging to Col. Gustave Cooke.
— Courtesy of The Museum of Southern History,
Sugarland, Texas

Tennessee Cavalry. The regiments had often worked together in the past and coined names for each other. The 8th and 11th had previously brigaded together, and since both were from Texas, they were known as "Chums." The 3rd Arkansas (under Col. J. T. Morgan) were the "Joshes," and the 4th Tennessee Cavalry were "Paul's People." The name "Paul's People" came from one of their commanders, Lt. Col. Paul Anderson ("Old Paul"), who referred to the men as "my people."[58] The new brigade was commanded by Brig. Gen. Frank Armstrong.

In the Knoxville campaign, the Rangers were joined by the Texas Brigade from the Army of North Virginia. Some of the regiment in the Knoxville campaign included the 1st Texas (under A. T. Rainey), the 4th Texas (under J.C.G. Key), and the 5th Texas (under Col. R.M. Powell). These regiments were from the famous "Texas Brigade" (a.k.a. Hood's Brigade).

Longstreet provided Wheeler with instructions regarding the terrain and strategy for the campaign into eastern Tennessee. Shortly after the campaign began, Federal military papers were captured.[59] The papers showed the organization of Burnside's cavalry and some of the infantry. Armed with this information, the Confederate cavalry forces crossed the Tennessee River at Motley's Ford with high hopes of victory.

On the way to Maryville, Tennessee, at Little River, Wheeler's forces ran into the 11th Kentucky Cavalry (U.S.). As the units skirmished, the Confederate commanders devised a course of action. Plans were made to flank the Union troops and attempt positioning themselves behind them. The Confederate cavalry then positioned themselves into a line of battle necessary for the flanking maneuver. In the midst of the battle, before the flanking move could be made, a severe thunderstorm broke. The heavy rain hampered the Confederates' original plans for the attack. Instead of flanking the Union force, the Confederates only dispersed them. After first dispersing the 11th Kentucky Cavalry, Colonel Wolford reinforced the Federal force and attacked. The Union attack attempted flanking the Confederate forces. As the Confederates were threatened by a flanking move, more Confederate cavalry rushed forward. The Federal attack was met by the Rangers, 11th Texas Cavalry, and 3rd Arkansas, who successfully halted then drove back the Federal cavalry.[60]

The next day, the Rangers were ordered to press a Federal battery and dismounted cavalry about seven miles from Knoxville. The Rangers led a charge, combined with the 11th Texas Cavalry. Despite cannon fire from Union forces, they continued making forward progress until stalled by increasing numbers of Federal infantry. The Rangers fought until their ammunition was exhausted. They withdrew in an orderly fashion and were relieved by other Confederate forces. Although the Rangers withdrew, the effect of their charge was far reaching.[61] The mass of fleeing Federal troops that experienced the charge

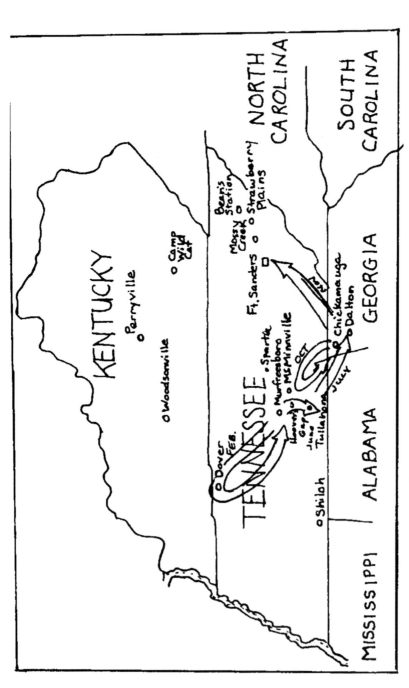

Major movements of the regiment, January–December 1863.

didn't stop until they were in the city of Knoxville, where they created a panicked disorder.

Since the main Confederate force was deep in the pro-Union countryside of eastern Tennessee, and Federal forces fortified themselves at Knoxville, Longstreet had to choose a course of action. In the campaign, he felt that the only safety for his forces was to attack the Federal positions.

As part of the preparations for the attack, the Rangers were given a special task. On November 22 it was reported that Unionist sympathizers floated supplies down the Holston River to Knoxville, where they were snagged by a boom on a pontoon bridge and brought into the Federal fort located there. In response to this, a young staff officer who was given temporary command of the regiment decided to construct a large raft cut from local trees at Boyd's Ferry.[62] The plan was to float the raft down the river in an attempt to damage the pontoon bridge and boom being used by the besieged Union forces.[63] The order was given at night to the Rangers, a regiment with no experience felling trees. Besides demoralizing the men, the action proved futile. During the late night and early morning, in cold winter darkness, the logs were cut and assembled into a raft. The green oak log raft sank when placed in the river.[64] Demoralization worsened as the men were not allowed to make fires for fear of being discovered.

On Sunday, November 29, Longstreet attacked Fort Sanders, which guarded Knoxville. The Federals had felled logs around the fort and placed wire entanglements to hamper approaching Confederates. Longstreet's attack plan opened with the Texas brigade advancing with fixed bayonets. After the advance reached the fort and planted the colors, they were repelled back. Broken terrain and felled timber hampered other portions of the attack. Longstreet's main goal of taking a Federal fort in Knoxville failed.[65] After pulling back, the supplies accumulated at Loudon were distributed. Unused supplies were burned.

After failing in his efforts to take Knoxville, Longstreet then directed the cavalry to march around the north of the city. From this position, the cavalry could keep reinforcements from reaching the city. Eventually this plan was abandoned and Longstreet pulled his force to a location near Morristown, Tennessee. He

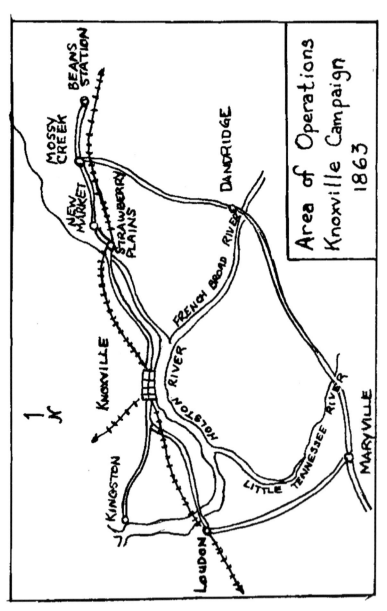

Area of Operations: Knoxville Campaign, 1863.

later moved his troops to winter camp positioned on the East Tennessee and Virginia railroad at Greenville, Tennessee.[66]

At Wheeler's headquarters the simmering conflict between Generals Wheeler and Wharton came to a head. Wheeler had believed that Wharton, being the politician he was, was plotting with an unnamed Texas congressman in Richmond. The plan involved securing the command of the cavalry for himself. The conflict erupted over a forged order purported to have been written by Wharton. Wheeler denounced Wharton as a "frontier political trickster." After this episode, political pressure was exerted at Dalton, Georgia, Richmond, Virginia, and Houston, Texas, to have Wharton transferred.[67]

While in winter camp, the Rangers often guarded the troops at night. Hostilities continued through winter with large engagements along the railroad lines at the Battles of Mossy Creek and Strawberry Plains. During this time the men subsisted on one pint of oatmeal a day, along with blue beef every other day. Any bread they desired had to be found through foraging.

On December 29, at Mossy Creek, the 2,000-strong Confederate cavalry was attacked by 4,000 Federal cavalry. Fighting raged on both sides of the railroad leading from the town of Mossy Creek to Morristown. The Rangers were part of General Armstrong's forces on the right side of the railroad. The Rangers were the only mounted regiment of the Confederates fighting in the engagement. After heavy fighting throughout the day, where ground changed ownership repeatedly, the Confederate commander withdrew when he felt he could not carry the position.[68]

On January 17, 1864, the Rangers joined the 11th Texas and some Confederate infantry in a clash with a Union cavalry brigade near Dandridge, Tennessee. Oscar H. La Grande commanded the Union brigade. In the fighting, the Texans pressed the enemy and almost succeeded in running off some of their horses. Federal reinforcements prevented the loss of the horses. By day's end, the Confederates drove the Federals from the field.[69]

CHAPTER 6

The Fight in Georgia
(1864)

"Only the fortune of war, only the fortune of war."
–Brig. Gen. Thomas Harrison

The previous year's fight at Farmington produced many casualties. Some of the casualties occurred when men were left behind the front lines due to being separated from the unit or being wounded. Eight of the Rangers who found themselves caught behind enemy lines soon met with Yankee troops on March 11. The Rangers had been caring for a wounded companion at a private residence. While at the residence, troops of the 5th Tennessee Cavalry (U.S.) surrounded the home.[1] The spokesman for the Tennessee troops demanded that the Rangers surrender, promising they would be treated as prisoners of war. The Rangers surrendered and turned over their arms. Afterward, the Yankees changed their minds and opened fire, killing all but one Ranger. The survivor overpowered the soldier guarding him and escaped back to Confederate lines. Once again with his compatriots, he reported the atrocity.[2]

During the Rangers' assignment in the Knoxville campaign, command of the Army of Tennessee changed from Braxton Bragg to Gen. Joseph E. Johnston. This change in command led to improved morale in the Army of Tennessee.[3]

On February 1, Tom Harrison traveled to Dalton, Georgia, where he tried to obtain a transfer of his brigade away from Longstreet's command and back to the Army of Tennessee. His efforts met with success, but the regiment didn't leave Tennessee until March 29.[4] The main body of the Rangers traveled from Tennessee east into North Carolina. Their route took them through Asheville, North Carolina. From North Carolina they travelled through South Carolina and then on to Georgia. In Georgia, they went through Athens and finally arrived at Resaca, where they rejoined the Army of Tennessee. By the time the Rangers reached Georgia, the Army of Tennessee was commanded by General Johnston. Returning to the main body of the army, the Rangers quickly found themselves in military action again.

Their first combat, in what would be part of a long campaign, occurred at Dug Gap, Georgia. Dug Gap was a stop located on the Western and Atlanta railroad between Chattanooga and Atlanta. The action brought the two Texan commanders, Tom Harrison and Hiram B. Granbury,[5] together. This was the first battle in which they shared commander roles since the two of them had fought together at the surrender of Camp Cooper in Texas. Both residents of Waco, Texas, were now commanding Texan units with reputations for fighting.

In the fighting at Dug Gap (May 8), the Rangers joined with Granbury's Texas Brigade, two regiments of dismounted Arkansas Rifles, and a brigade of Kentucky Cavalry (9th Kentucky).[6] In the action, Union Gen. James B. McPherson's army corps advanced into the mountain gap and met with 4,000 veteran Confederate soldiers. The Confederates stopped his advance. The Federals regrouped and launched attack after attack, but the Confederates met and repulsed each attack. By day's end, the Federals made five unsuccessful assaults on the Rebel positions. Federal forces then fell back to Snake Creek Gap.[7] In one of the Confederate counterattacks, the Rangers charged into Union lines, taking more than sixty prisoners. General McPherson later wrote to Sherman how Confederates met him with "considerable force." In spite of McPherson's reports, Sherman was puzzled by the failure of numerically superior Union forces to break the Confederate line at Dug Gap.[8]

The Rangers thus began participating in a series of battles involving the armies of Federal Gen. William T. Sherman and Confederate Gen. Joe Johnston. These battles included scouting and fighting, both mounted and unmounted. Fighting occurred throughout the hills of northeastern Georgia, roughly along the main railroad line through the area. Battles were fought at river crossings and gaps in the mountains. General Sherman, with superior numbers, attempted flanking the Confederate forces by maneuvers throughout the rough terrain. Battles occurred at Dalton, Varnell's Station, Adairsville, Cassville, Cartersville, New Hope Church, Big Shanty, and Kennesaw Mountain.

The next day at Dalton, Georgia, the Rangers succeeded in what observers described as "a brilliant charge" on May 9.[10] The charge managed to break the Union lines, with more than 100 Yankees captured. Among the captured was a Union colonel of the 2nd Indiana Cavalry. The colonel was informed that he had been captured by Terry's Texas Rangers. Col. Oscar LaGrange then said, "You have a prize indeed. I am Colonel La Grange. I did not know that you boys had got down here from east Tennessee. I knew you as soon as I saw you coming."[10] La Grange was then taken to Thomas Harrison. At that meeting, La Grange said, "I was in command of the brigade, and was anxious for the commission of brigadier general. I had some influential friends who were helping me. My division commander told me to go out, run in the rebel pickets, skirmish a little and send in a report which he would forward with strong recommendation for my promotion. I came out, ran into the Texas Rangers, and am a prisoner." Harrison responded, "Only the fortune of war, only the fortune of war."[11]

Meanwhile, Wharton finally secured a transfer for himself. In preparing for his transfer, he obtained letters of recommendation from his peers. Generals John Bell Hood, Patrick Cleburne, William Hardee, Howell Cobb, B. F. Cheatham, and

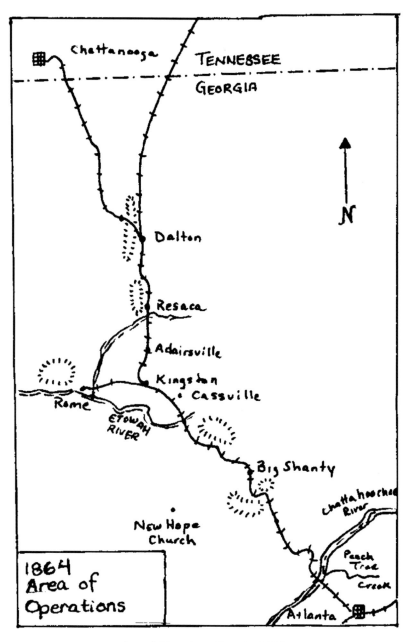

Area of Operations: Georgia, 1864.

Alexander Stewart recommended him to Generals Kirby Smith and John Magruder. All the letters contained praise for Wharton. Maj. Gen. Alexander Stewart, who commanded the regiment while in eastern Tennessee, stated, "His removal from here is a great loss to this army and a decided gain to yours." Gen. John Bell Hood wrote, "He (Wharton) will make himself known to you by his acts." Gen. Howell Cobb said that Wharton was a man of "sound judgement." Gen. B. F. Cheatham wrote, ". . . and feel confident that he will add fresh Laurels to the wreath he has earned in the Department of Service." The Confederate secretary of state, James A. Seddon, also wrote a letter on Wharton's behalf. His and Stewart's letters were both hand-delivered by Wharton to Kirby Smith and John Magruder.[12]

On May 17 portions of Union Gen. Oliver Howard's corps attempted advancing on Adairsville, Georgia, and the state arsenal there. The Rangers formed part of the Confederate resistance that fought from 4:00 to 9:00 P.M.[13] On May 24 at Cassville, the Rangers fought as mounted cavalry. Here they joined Confederate soldiers protecting the crossings of the Etowah River from Union advances.[14] The regiment finally withdrew before Union troops flanked them.[15]

In a rare break from fighting, the Rangers rested off their horses near Cassville, Georgia. Suddenly, some Confederate troops flew toward them in a confused state. The Rangers responded quickly by mounting up, forming, and moving out to meet the pursuers. The Rangers met the Federals, and fighting ensued. The fighting intensified, becoming hand to hand. Suddenly, the Federal commander, a Kentuckian, realized who they were fighting and said, "H—l men, we are fighting Texans, every man cover his own rear, and d— quick at that, or its h—l or Andersonville."[16]

At Varnell's Station, a Confederate brigade was bringing captured supply wagons back to southern lines. Yankee cavalry attacked the brigade containing the Rangers. The 8th Texas and the 2nd Tennessee Cavalry mounted a counterattack. Under regimental command of Col. Gustave Cooke, the Rangers charged the enemy ranks. In the charge, they captured more than 100 prisoners, including a brigade commander and other

Prayer book carried by Col. Gustave Cooke during the war. Penciled notations around Psalm 1 refer to his faith during the Battle at Averysboro, Georgia.

— Courtesy of The Museum of Southern History,
Sugarland, Texas

officers.[17] Despite heavy losses, the Union army, under Sherman's command, continued using its superior numbers to push a slow and steady advance. Battle by battle, Sherman was pushing closer and closer to Atlanta.

On May 27, under the leadership of Thomas Harrison, the Rangers fought dismounted at New Hope Church.[18] They were positioned on the right side of the Confederate line (attached to Hood's corps). In the battle, Confederate Gen. John Bell Hood sought to "develop the enemy" by sending an advance force toward Union lines.[19] Gen. Joseph Hooker reacted to Hood's ploy, and pushed his main Federal force (the Fourth Corps) up a road toward New Hope Church during a thunderstorm. At New Hope Church, Hooker charged through rain into Hood's main body of troops. The Confederates had quickly learned the value of defensive works, opening fire from behind the log barricades. Confederate troops fought in the mud, sheltered behind their log barricades, while the well-placed artillery provided cover fire for them. In the midst of the battle, the thunderstorm continued with a blinding downpour of rain as Union forces repeatedly assaulted Rebel lines. Union troops tried turning the extreme right of the Confederate lines, near where the dismounted Texans held the line.[20] The fellow Texans in Granbury's brigade caught the brunt of the Union efforts, throwing back seven assaults and making a final charge at 10:00 at night.[21] Hooker's men were eventually pulled back. The fierceness of the battle, use of sixteen guns firing canister shot and inclement weather would lead Hooker's men to later refer to this battlefield as "Hell Hole."[22]

On June 3 the Rangers fought at Big Shanty. After that battle, Gen. Joe Johnston slowed Sherman's advance at Kennesaw Mountain and Pine Mountain for several weeks. Eventually, after giving up more ground than Confederate leadership could tolerate, command changed. The Confederate leadership changed commanding general for the Army of Tennessee again in less than a year. Gen. Joseph E. Johnston was replaced with Gen. John Bell Hood on July 17, per President Jefferson Davis.

The new commander placed the Rangers as part of Wheeler's command. They were positioned on the Confederate right at the Battle of Peachtree Creek and were to support General Hardee's attack.[23] They formed part of a Confederate cavalry action to occupy McPherson's forces while Confederate infantry attacked George H. Thomas' forces. On July 17–18 they fought from behind breastworks to slow Union Gen. George H. Thomas' advance.

On July 23 General Hood approached Thomas Harrison with a special request. A Federal artillery battery had been giving him trouble, and he wanted a small group to see what they could do about it. Harrison selected the Ranger Alexander May Shannon for the mission. Shannon then handpicked some men, forming a unit known as "Shannon's Scouts." [24] The men donned Federal trousers and slipped through the Yankee lines. Once across the lines, the Rangers silenced the battery and began heading back to Confederate lines. Before returning, they each took a horse from the Yankee supplies.

The success of the mission impressed General Hood. On the unit's return, he ordered Shannon to organize a special detachment for intelligence gathering. Hood also assigned members of the Rangers other secret duties. Three Rangers (George Claiborne, Emmet Lynch, and George Archer) were sent into Tennessee for intelligence work that July, which included spying in the cities of Franklin and Nashville. Their mission included finding out troop strengths, location of forts and other military information. Hood provided them with gold and couriers. The spies mixed business with pleasure and visited local belles while in Nashville and Franklin. One of the spies claimed to have attended a dance given by a Union brigadier general in Nashville.[25]

On July 27, Harrison's brigade, including the Rangers, moved out to halt Federal cavalry that had crossed the Chattahooche River at Campbellton.[26] The Rangers and other cavalry regiments succeeded in halting the Federal advance at Latimer, Georgia.[27]

Two large Federal cavalry forces were sent out to free Union prisoners of war at Andersonville, Georgia. The POW camp population had swollen since Federal authorities halted prisoner exchanges. The first Federal cavalry force sent against Andersonville was commanded by E. M. McCook and the other by George Stoneman. On July 30 the Rangers, as part of Wheeler's 1,400-strong cavalry force, intercepted one of the Federal forces. After an intense battle, under the hot summer sun, Wheeler's force defeated the 3,600 Federal cavalrymen under Gen. E. M. McCook. The Confederates captured 2,000 men, several ambulances, a battery of artillery, and released 500 Confederate prisoners in an action known as the "Battle of Brown's Mill." [28] This battle occurred near Newnan, Georgia. McCook escaped by leaving behind captured Confederate troops and heading toward the Tallapoosa River.[29]

The other Federal cavalry force sent to liberate prisoners at

Andersonville was led by George Stoneman. Confederate cavalry stopped this force at Macon, Georgia.[30] After the Battle of Brown's Mill, Gen. John Bell Hood received vindication. Hood had always believed that Confederate cavalry was superior to Federal cavalry, and the battle proved him right because the Confederate cavalry defeated a force twice its size.[31] Hood, now filled with enthusiasm at being validated, decided to send Wheeler and the cavalry on a raid of Union railroads.[32]

Wheeler issued a call for volunteers, and many of the remaining Rangers and 3rd Arkansas Cavalry answered the call. Wheeler's force totaled about 4,000. This mission, or raid, has been called "the Great Wheeler raid into middle Tennessee." The cavalry departed on August 11 from Covington, Georgia. The mission was to burn and destroy the railroads in the rear of Sherman's forces. The force captured Dalton, Georgia, destroying track and raiding military stores.[33] Federal troops received reinforcement, causing Wheeler to leave. He then threatened a move toward Chattanooga. The cavalry force destroyed the rail lines between Cleveland, Tennessee, to Charleston and from Athens to Loudon. The Confederate raiders then crossed the Holston River above Knoxville and headed toward Knoxville. After some skirmishing action, the force crossed the Cumberland Mountains near McMinnville, then headed for Murfreesboro. While in Tennessee, members who were lost and separated from October's raid rejoined the regiment. They also discovered that some of the members of the regiment, after being taken prisoners by Federal troops, were shot.[34]

Outside of Murfreesboro, the force destroyed fifty miles of the railroad leading to Chattanooga. Railroad destruction was accomplished when men piled fenceposts on the track and set them ablaze. The rails then expanded and bent in the heat, thus making them useless until straightened out.[35] The Confederate force destroyed more than fifty miles of railroad. The system of blockhouses, repair facilities, and troops stationed at regular intervals on the Nashville-to-Atlanta line minimized the effects by quickly repairing any damage inflicted. After destroying the railroad, the Confederate force headed for Muscle Shoals, Alabama.

Finally, on September 6, they crossed the Tennessee River.

Fording the swift, treacherous river proved difficult. The river was over a mile and a quarter wide, with a swift current. The waters dominated some of the cavalrymen, pinning some against debris flowing downstream, while others clung to the tails of their horses.

After some brief skirmishing, they moved through Florence, Alabama, and back into Confederate lines. The regiment then rested at Tuscumbia, Alabama. On September 14 two women from Nashville made it through the fighting lines and presented the Texas cavalry regiment with their third flag. This third regimental flag was made for them by Mary McIver and Robbie Woodruff of Nashville. John McIver presented the flag to them. The Rangers admired its beauty and vowed to defend it. The second flag was folded up and sent back to the state.

On September 2 Sherman finally captured Atlanta, which lowered Confederate morale. With the loss of Atlanta, the leadership of the Army of Tennessee now considered its next course of action. The Army of Tennessee remained a formidable fighting force despite the loss of Atlanta. During this time, General Hood began moving the Army of Tennessee through northern Georgia and on its way to Tennessee. He also ordered General Wheeler to join him as soon as possible.[36] Hood's "Tennessee plan" moved forward on the condition that Wheeler's cavalry must stay south of the Tennessee River. Although the main bodies of the Rangers were under Wheeler, and therefore required to stay south of the Tennessee River, Shannon's Scouts continued answering directly to Hood.[37] Shannon did not go to Tennessee but rather continued operating in Georgia with orders to interfere with Sherman's activities as much as possible.

The Rangers then went to Rome, Georgia. which contained a foundry and important mill. At Rome the Rangers, as part of Harrison's brigade, joined Ashby's brigade and a battery of four guns. On October 13, as the guns were limbered, Federal infantry and cavalry attacked. The Rangers were dismounted at that time. As the Federal cavalry poured in, shouting "Clear the road for the Fourth Regulars," the Rangers ran for their horses.[38] After several rallies, the Federals ended up pushing the Confederates back five miles. In this action, known as the "Rome Races," the Rangers lost their third flag when the oilcloth casing enclosing it

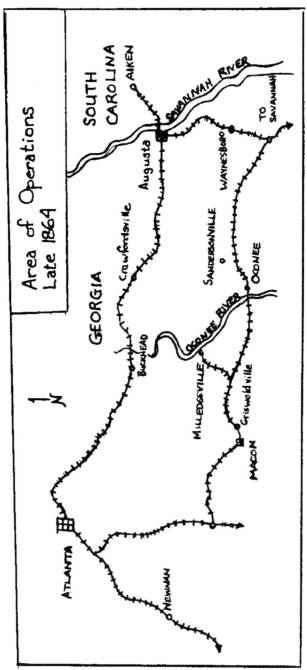

Area of Operations: Georgia and South Carolina, late 1864.

caught on some bushes during the escape.[39] J. J. Weiler of the 17th Indiana regiment found the "lost flag."

After occupying Atlanta for over two months, General Sherman began another invasion. On November 14, Federal troops set fire to Atlanta amidst bands playing "John Brown's Soul Goes Marching On." In the midst of the drama of fire and music, the Federal troops marched forward, thus beginning the "March to the Sea."[40] Sherman's army moved in four columns with Gen. Judson Kilpatrick covering the left wing of his march with Federal cavalry. The Rangers, along with the 11th Texas Cavalry, rode ahead of the Federals, ever harassing the wings of Sherman's march to the sea.[41]

The Eighth Texas Cavalry experienced its first taste of the "March to the Sea" about midnight November 20. That night, they met with Maj. Gen. Peter Osterhaus' corps near Clinton, Georgia. Several charges and countercharges were made without decisive results.[42]

Next, the cavalry went to Milledgeville, Georgia. Once there, they dismounted and assisted infantry who were already engaged. The Yankees finally pulled back after their attacks were blunted.[43]

After the fight at Milledgeville, the next fight was at Griswoldville.[44] Once again there were charges and counter-charges until the Union troops drove the Confederates from town.[45]

After the defeat at Griswoldville, Wheeler sent the cavalry to Saundersonville. There they met some Federal infantry. The Rangers found themselves hard-pressed and responded with a desperate charge led by Clem Bassett. After the charge, General Wheeler took off his hat and shouted, "Three cheers for Bassett," which was echoed by his staff. Wheeler offered Bassett a position on his staff, which he declined.[46]

General Sherman began sending out foraging parties known as "bummers." The mission of bummers was originally to forage for food in the countryside and bring it back to their original units. Eventually their mission turned into one designed "to consume and destroy": They were to consume everything edible by man or beast.[47] There were few, if any, restraints placed on these "bummers," who went marauding across the countryside.

No communications were maintained with these parties, and destruction of property was wanton. This led to their notorious reputation, even amongst Union troops and commanders.[7] Those bummers who fell victims to the Confederate cavalry were regarded by fellow Union soldiers as getting what they deserved.[49] Shannon's Scouts actively campaigned against bummers and their atrocities. In this campaign, they captured or killed bummers engaging in their depredations.

When the bodies of killed or captured bummers were searched, Shannon's Scouts recovered gold teeth, eating utensils, silverware, feather beds, quilts, jellies, hams, and potatoes. After "relieving" the Yankees, they distributed the goods to needy families they met.[50]

After Sherman left Atlanta, he sent his cavalry commander, Gen. Judson Kilpatrick, to Augusta, Georgia, with approximately 5,000 men. Augusta contained an arsenal and cotton factories. To oppose this force, the Confederates had General Joseph Wheeler, who commanded a cavalry force of 2,500 men, including the Rangers.

One evening, Kilpatrick and his accompanying cavalry camped at Rock Springs, Georgia. During the night, Shannon's Scouts captured all the pickets without firing a shot. The next morning, Wheeler's force rode into the camp, finding Kilpatrick and his men sleeping. The Confederates began firing their weapons. In less than fifteen minutes the Federals stampeded, with Confederate cavalry in pursuit, pressing their victory. The Confederates continued pursuit throughout the day. Kilpatrick left in such a hurry that he abandoned his gold-handled sword, a pair of ivory-handled six-shooters, and his saddle.[51]

Finally, at about 4:00 P.M., Kilpatrick and his men reached Buck Head Creek. After crossing the creek, the Union cavalrymen burned the bridge and entrenched themselves behind hastily constructed breastworks. The Confederates attacked the entrenched Federals. The attack failed to dislodge the Union troops. After failing to take the position, Wheeler had the cavalry retreat in order to regroup. In a final attack at sunset, the Confederates made it over the breastworks. They then pursued the Yankees through the brush until dark.[52] Darkness settled in before another charge could occur, so action was called off.

On November 26 the Rangers and other Confederate cavalry forces attacked Gen. Judson Kilpatrick's camp at Waynesboro, Georgia. In the attack, the Confederate horsemen scattered pickets and galloped over the wooden barricades. The subsequent effects produced fright in the awakened Federals. Kilpatrick, who had spent the evening in a local house with some women, escaped capture by leaping from the structure along with his staff officers. Fighting continued through the next day, as Federal forces fell back, fighting from one hastily constructed barricade to another.[53] The next day, Kilpatrick found himself being attacked by Wheeler again. Squadrons of cavalry found themselves in pistol and sabre clashes throughout the day. When fighting ceased, Wheeler reported that 200 Federal cavalrymen were wounded, killed, or captured from the action.

The Rangers left Waynesboro and opposed Federal advances by Kilpatrick on November 28 at Buckhead Church. Wheeler's cavalry corps attacked Kilpatrick, who was accompanied by only one regiment (9th Michigan Cavalry). The besieged Union forces sent a report, containing a plea for help to Union Maj. James Connolly. The report also stated that fighting occurred day and night more than three days and that they (Union cavalrymen) were surrounded by Confederate cavalry.[54] Finally, on December 4, Kilpatrick drove the Confederate cavalry out of their positions using the new repeating rifles. When it was over, the Confederates captured 200 men, horses, and arms before withdrawing. The engagement caused Kilpatrick to abandon his raid on Augusta.

Before the war was out, the Rangers would have several more battles with Gen. Judson Kilpatrick. His own men eventually called him "Kill Cavalry" due to his wearing men out and getting them killed in charges. Kilpatrick featured large sideburns, cursed incessantly, and womanized.[54] One observer described him as having thin light hair, almost bald, sloping forehead, and large Roman nose. Kilpatrick was ambitious,[56] in that he hoped eventually to attain governorship of New Jersey and afterwards attain the presidency. Sherman's opinion of him was: "I know that Kilpatrick is a hell of a damned fool, but I want just that sort of man to command my cavalry on this expedition."

On December 2, Hood ordered Shannon to report to him

in Tennessee. Shannon's report claimed the activities of the thirty-man unit during Sherman's "March to the Sea" included capturing or killing 459 Yankees between October and December of 1864.[57] The Confederate cavalry could not stop Sherman, only slow him down.

The service in Georgia was challenging and difficult. General Wheeler knew the difficulties and acknowledged the challenges in an address to his cavalrymen on New Year's Eve.[58] Sherman and his forces stayed at Savannah that winter, but even he admired the fighting ability of his opponents.[59]

CHAPTER 7

The Road to Surrender
(1865)

"It was the most formidable cavalry charge I ever saw."
—Gen. Judson Kilpatrick

During January 1865, the Rangers were in winter quarters in Grahamville, South Carolina.[1] The harsh weather limited the frequency and severity of military activities. Sherman seemed poised for a new campaign.

With the war dragging on, changes came frequently and quickly. On January 17, Gen. John Bell Hood was relieved of command of the Army of Tennessee. With his removal, Shannon's Scouts began reporting to Gen. Joseph Wheeler. Wheeler then augmented the scouts with twenty men from the 11th Texas Cavalry and fourteen from the 51st Alabama Cavalry.[2]

Further command changes occurred in February, when the 8th and 11th Texas Cavalry regiments were combined in a joint brigade. This new brigade was under the leadership of corps commander Gen. Wade Hampton rather than Joseph Wheeler.[3]

Previously, Hampton led all of Gen. Robert E. Lee's cavalry after J.E.B. Stuart's death.[4] The brigade was quickly put to work. The two Texas cavalry regiments under Hampton, along with Shannon's Scouts, continued harassing Sherman. Part of the harassment consisted of killing Sherman's bummers on sight, even when they requested a surrender. The Rangers had become increasingly harsh in dealing with Sherman's bummers. They had seen firsthand what happened at farms and homes of fellow southerners. The bummers continued their atrocities against civilians even through the cold winter months, often leaving them without adequate protection from the cold weather. The bodies of killed bummers were often left on the roadside, as a warning to regular Federal troops as they passed through. It seemed that Sherman was fighting against the southern people more than the southern armies. In a letter home, Sherman wrote, "They regard us just as the Romans did the Goths and the parallel is not unjust."[5]

After capturing Savannah, Georgia, Sherman once again sent Union commander Judson Kilpatrick on a mission. This time he headed for Augusta, Georgia, in command of the cavalry troops. The Confederate command prepared for General Kilpatrick's arrival. General Wheeler learned of Kilpatrick's assignment and began preparing a surprise for him.

On February 17, twenty miles north of Augusta, in the town of Aiken, South Carolina, Joe Wheeler deployed his 2,000 cavalrymen (including the Rangers) in an ambush. The Confederate cavalry hid themselves along the side streets of Aiken. Kilpatrick brazenly charged into town, leading his Federal cavalrymen. Once in town, some of the Alabama troops fired sooner than planned, thus alerting the Federals. The Confederates then surged into the streets, producing a wild melee. Horses, swords, and bullets were hitting, clashing, and firing at close range.

One Federal sergeant described the fight as "a crash of horses, a flashing of sword blades, five or ten minutes of blind confusion and then those who have not been knocked out of their saddles by their neighbours horses, and have not cut off their own horses' heads instead of the enemy, find themselves they know not how, either running away or being run away from."[6]

General Kilpatrick escaped from the melee, although he

lost his hat during the ambush. Within a few minutes of fierce hand-to-hand fighting, the Confederates gained the upper hand. Capitalizing on their momentum, the Confederates then pursued the Federals. A sabre charge by the Federals turned back the initial pursuit. A subsequent Confederate pursuit chased the Federal troops out of town. Once out of town, the Federal troops finally stood their ground. They erected a barricade on a steamboat, approximately five miles north of the town, and held off the pursuing Confederates. Among the prisoners captured by Confederates were many Illinois troopers, including the color bearer. Confederate commanders expressed relief in the saving of Augusta.[7]

In mid-February, after Confederates retreated from Columbia, South Carolina, Sherman's troops occupied the city of Columbia. With the city's capture, the invading Yankee troops began terrorizing the citizens.[8] General Sherman pledged assurances to Mayor Goodwyn of the safety of Columbia. Despite the assurances, the city suffered from looting and pillaging. Eventually, troops under Sherman set fires at locations throughout the city. Libraries, private homes, and churches were burned indiscriminately. Sherman blamed the retreating Confederates, although residents blame Sherman for the burning of the city. Among the homes burned was Confederate Gen. Wade Hampton's residence. In early March, Wade Hampton was placed in command of Wheeler's cavalry.[9]

Two days after the burning of Columbia, an incident occurred which began a grim retribution between Yankees and the Confederate cavalrymen. Some of Wheeler's cavalry came across a home in shambles. The mother raved insanely about seven Yankees who had invaded the home. Her teenage daughter had been bound hand and foot, raped, then left for dead. The Confederate troops took immediate action. Spurring their horses forward, they overtook the Yankee troops, cut their throats, and left their bodies on the roadside with a sign: "These are the Seven." Thus began a series of retributions between Yankee bummers and the Confederate cavalry.[10] This was not the first rape incident reported, nor would it be the last atrocity.[11]

Shannon's Scouts were known for their exceptional brutality in dealing with Federal troops, especially the bummers. In one incident, attributed to Shannon's Scouts, the message "Death to all Foragers" was carved into some of the bodies left on the roadside. The incident enraged Kilpatrick to the point of threatening to hang eighteen of Wheeler's men as a reprisal.[12] On hearing of the violent deaths of Federal troops, Kilpatrick immediately accused Texans of the acts. He wrote General Wheeler, claiming the act was done by 300 men with Spencer rifles and commanded by a lieutenant colonel.[13] Wheeler denied his two Texas regiments (8th and 11th cavalry) had anything to do with it, that both regiments were commanded by captains and that neither had Spencers. The reality was that the Rangers were commanded by Col. Gustave Cooke, and the regiment had held fifty Spencer rifles since June 1864.[14]

At one point, Union Gen. Henry W. Slocum reported finding twenty-one bodies dumped into a ravine with their throats cut.[15] As violent reprisals continued, General Kilpatrick then went so far as to offer a $5,000 reward for Shannon's capture. Shannon later acknowledged the offer and countered with, "I want to thank you [Kilpatrick] for the signal honour, but I'm going to go you one better. I'm gonna get you for nothing."

In the closing days of February, in a rare truce, General Kilpatrick and Alexander Shannon finally met face to face. Kilpatrick allegedly complained that Shannon and his men were "fighting under the black flag." Kilpatrick threatened public execution for any of Shannon's men he captured. Shannon countered by pointing out that Kilpatrick had been unable to capture his men, and that if Kilpatrick's threats were carried out he would take revenge on captured Federals.[16]

The harassment of Federal troops by the Confederate cavalry intensified to the point where Sherman complained that "the actions of the Rangers were not in accordance with the rules of warfare, but uncivilized slaughter." The Rangers viewed their actions as protecting helpless civilians. Sherman's own attitude toward Confederate prisoners suggests hatred, if not cruelty. In one meeting with his staff during the March to the Sea, he said, "Prisoners would be better off if they were killed on the battlefield." He added, "I'm almost satisfied that it would be just as well to kill all prisoners. They would be spared all the atrocities. And the more awful you can make war, the sooner it will be over

. . . war is hell, at best." Sherman went on to threaten killing prisoners in retaliation for Ranger activities.[17] Gen. Wade Hampton, the corps commander to which the Rangers were attached, responded to the threat by offering to kill two of Sherman's men for every Confederate prisoner killed, with officers receiving preference.[18] Neither Hampton's nor Sherman's threats were carried out.

Fighting between Federal and Confederate troops moved from Georgia and centered in the Carolinas. One of the soldiers described the countryside of the Carolinas as "poor country, with predominately pine," although much had been burned by "bummers." Destruction of portions of the piney woods areas was severe. Bummers often burned the pine areas to prevent their use by Confederates. In places, the hot flames from the burning pine heated the nearby streams enough to singe the hair from horses' legs as they crossed streams through the pine country. Eyewitnesses told of how the Confederate troops were blackened from the many pine smoke fires.

Around March 8, Shannon's Scouts passed through a village leading to Fayetteville, North Carolina. When the closely pursuing Yankees entered the village, they rounded up the "'home guard." They then threatened them and the town for allegations of shooting at Federal troops. The "home guard" was then taken prisoner and sent to General Kilpatrick's camp.[19]

Early March, in one of the many skirmishes between Confederate cavalry forces and "Little Kil," the Federals captured Lt. H. Clay Reynolds, a member of Shannon's Scouts. After his capture, he was tied to the rear of Kilpatrick's Victoria (wagon). From that vantage point, he witnessed unheard of excesses for a military campaign. He grew angry at "Little Kil's" display of lavishness, which included using a French chef for preparing the cavalrymen's mess. Supplies on the wagon included wine, brandy, spices, herbs, bags of coffee beans, and sugar. Kilpatrick also maintained an attractive female in his Victoria. The female companion was Marie Boozer. Lieutenant Reynolds also observed that Kilpatrick had split up his cavalry forces. The two forces were situated about twelve miles apart.[20]

Kilpatrick's men camped in and about a local farmhouse to shelter themselves from the rain. The Yankee troops killed all the

livestock owned by the family whose farmhouse they comman-
deered. That night, after the fog set in, Reynolds escaped. He
made his way through the fog and rain to the Confederate calvary
forces under Wade Hampton's command and told Hampton what
he had observed. Upon hearing of the situation, including the location of Kilpatrick's headquarters and Confederate prisoners,
Hampton prepared an attack and broke camp that night. The
Rangers and other forces marched all night in readying for the attack. Members of Shannon's Scouts first infiltrated the Yankee
camp with orders to capture Kilpatrick.[21] One of Kilpatrick's lieutenants accidentally rode into Confederate lines, enabling them
to identify the exact location of Kilpatrick's headquarters and
Confederate prisoners. As part of the fruits of the scouting efforts,
Shannon's men removed the camp guards, and captured thirty
prisoners and a stand of colors.[22]

Near Fayetteville on March 9, a fog bank still covered
Kilpatrick's camp. In the early morning hours, while the
Federals slept and the guards removed, the main body of
Confederate cavalry moved into attack position. Just as the
Yankee bugler began sounding his trumpet for wake-up,
Confederate cavalrymen poured into the camp. Instead of a
trumpet call, the Federals woke to the infamous "Rebel yells."
With the guards removed, the Confederates charged into the
camp unhindered. The charge quickly confused the Federal
troops. In the midst of the confusion, the Confederate prisoners
overran their guards and rushed toward the attacking
Confederate cavalry. Among the prisoners were the home guard
captured the day before near Fayetteville. One witness said,
"The Yankee camp looked like a cyclone had struck all at once.
Their blankets were flying in the air and the men were flying in
the air and the men were running about in every direction in
their night clothes. . . . If this was not a stampede on foot, I
never saw one."[23] Some of the Confederate cavalrymen attempted hitching the artillery located in the center of camp to
horses, while others plundered the supplies.

Some of the Federals finally managed to organize resist-
ance. Members of the 1st Alabama (U.S.), 5th Kentucky. and 5th
Ohio managed to regroup and began opening fire into the
Confederates with their Spencer carbines.[24] The newer weapon

provided firepower superior to most Confederate weapons. The two sides engaged in a heated gun battle for several hours. Around 8:00, a Federal infantry brigade arrived, reinforcing the resistance. With the arrival of fresh troops and the success of a Union artilleryman who crawled through the battlefield and unlimbered a fieldpiece, the Confederates withdrew.[25] Kilpatrick did not even order his men to pursue their attackers. As a result of the action, 350 prisoners were taken and 175 Confederates freed. Kilpatrick later said, "It was the most formidable cavalry charge I ever saw." This episode was later known as "Kilpatrick's shirttail skedaddle" or the Battle of Monroe's Cross Roads.

The next day in a chilly rain, General Hampton rode with the combined cavalry into Fayetteville, North Carolina. Federal troops followed quickly behind them. Some of the Confederate cavalry broke off and offered resistance to their pursuers. A party of sixty-seven Federals briefly broke through and managed to get into town on March 11. After a brief melee between the advance Federal troops and Confederate cavalry, the Federal cavalry left. The Federals soon returned with an infantry column for additional support. The combined Federal force then captured the town.

After taking the town, Sherman began a five-day occupation of the town.[26] He ordered the destruction of the armory located there, and said, "I hope the people of Washington have the good sense never to trust North Carolina with an arsenal again." Destruction of the armory began on Monday morning. Sherman managed to turn his act of destruction into a grand spectacle, complete with a military band. Rams made from railroad iron were used to batter the walls. Once the walls weakened from the rams, the roof fell, and the band began playing. Amidst the rousing tunes, Federal soldiers began their rampage of the armory and town. After the collapse, the buildings which occupied more than 100 acres were burned. In addition, five cotton factories, a bank, a newspaper building, eleven warehouses, and some private residences were burned. Federal troops also hung some of the citizens by their thumbs until they revealed the location of Confederate troops and valuables. Other atrocities included one Federal drummer who confiscated a family Bible from a citizen, spread it on his mule's back, and used it as a saddle.[27]

At one point, Gen. O. Howard approached Sherman regarding Rebel sharpshooters who continued firing on the Federal troops, and said he believed them to be Texans.

Sherman replied, "Then shoot some Texas prisoners."

Howard replied, "We've got no Texans."

"Then shoot others, any prisoners. I will not have my men murdered," Sherman replied.[28]

On March 15, Kilpatrick's cavalry, while skirmishing with Confederate cavalry (including the Rangers) on the road to Raleigh, ran into General Taliaferro's Confederate infantry about six miles south of Averasboro, North Carolina, on Cape Fear River. In a short period of time, after being pressed by Confederate troops, Kilpatrick's men threw up crude breastworks in the swampy woodland. Rebel forces blocked the road to Raleigh. The swamps on either side of the road made any flanking move by the Federals difficult, if not impossible. Kilpatrick found he could not maneuver out of his situation, so he sent for help. Kilpatrick's men were reinforced by infantry (including Hawley's brigade, 129th Illinois, and 123rd New York). The infantry coming to Kilpatrick's aid fought in ankle-deep swamp water, and reported that everything was dripping wet.[29] After a stubborn fight, the Federals eventually broke through the line on March 16. Down the road from Averasboro lay the town of Bentonville, where the next major action occurred.

On March 19, Gen. Henry W. Slocum's column ran into waiting Confederate troops in the dense pine and turpentine forests at Bentonville, North Carolina. In the initial day's fighting, the Confederate cavalry were on the right flank. The initial Union assault that morning pushed the Confederates back. In the afternoon a Confederate counterattack was organized and executed. The attack drove the Yankees back until General Sherman arrived with reinforcements. Both armies remained on the battlefield at day's end. The first day's fighting ignited the surrounding woods. Flames leaped up and across the rosin-soaked pine trees. Limbs from the burning trees often landed on the wounded, causing screams and death.

In the second day of action at Bentonville on March 20, the cavalry forces were on the left side of the line. After halting a brutal Union attack, they charged. In their first charge, the

Rangers lost every field officer they had to wounds. The Rangers suffered major losses to their command structure in fighting that day.[30] The loss of field officers put Doc Matthews, the senior captain, in charge of the unit. The men ended the second day nursing wounds and looking for new leadership.

The next day, General Hardee's sixteen-year-old son, Willie Hardee, had run away from school to join the Rangers. Willie had run away from school several times before, and his father returned him to the school. Each runaway episode, he attempted to join the Rangers. That morning, on the third day of battle, he tried to join his father's staff. His father refused, saying, "He would not have rank unless he earned it." By the afternoon, his father changed his mind. This time his father relented and allowed him to join the Rangers. Just hours prior to the charge, while the men and horses were feeding, General Hardee approached the Rangers.[31] He pulled aside a Ranger captain and said, "Swear him [Willie] into service in your company as nothing else will satisfy him."

That afternoon at Bentonville two brigades of Federal infantry (including the 64th Illinois), commanded by Joseph A. Mower, threatened taking the bridge over the Neuse River, over which supplies arrived. Federal artillery supported the advancing infantry. As the Federals came upon a swampy area, the brigades in the advance separated.[32] At this time, the Rangers were sheltering themselves from artillery, wondering what the meaning of the cannon fire was. Then Gen. Joseph Wheeler rode up, asking for the commander of the Rangers. Wheeler had earlier committed the 11th Texas and the 3rd Arkansas into action. Wheeler finally found Doc Matthews and told him, "Captain, mount up your men, go as fast as you can and charge whatever you find at the bridge." The unit (then about 100 men) and the 4th Tennessee Cavalry assembled and took off for the front.[33]

Upon reaching a rise about 500 yards from the bridge, the Confederate cavalrymen stopped briefly to close up the column. While regrouping, Gen. William Hardee approached the men. Captain Matthews saluted Hardee, who inquired what troops they were and their orders. Upon being informed of the unit and orders, he told them, "Then execute your orders." The Rangers deployed to the right and the 4th Tennessee on the left.

General Hardee joined the cavalry force, as his son had recently joined the Rangers.

Upon reaching an open area, the troops halted briefly while General Hardee surveyed the situation. He observed the Federals fearfully throwing up breastworks across the highway leading to the bridge. He said, "There they are, boys, charge them." Doc Matthews then gave the orders, "Close order and reserve fire. Charge right in front." [34] The Rangers loosed a Rebel yell and rode across the open field into Slocum's 17th Corps.[35] The Rangers formed on the right side of the line, the 4th Tennessee Cavalry on the left. Along the way, Brown's division of Tennesseans (containing Vaughn's, Strahl's and Maney's brigade along with some South Carolinians and Georgians) joined in the charge. After discharging their weapons, they threw them to the ground, began using their revolvers, and spurred for the center of the Federal line.[36]

The charge was a grand spectacle as it crashed into the Yankee line. Within minutes, the Federal line broke. The Federals were routed, and the bridge was cleared.[37] Before the Federals could regroup, the Rangers disappeared into the nearby charred piney woods. The charge split the line between the 39th Ohio and the 32nd Wisconsin regiments. Unfortunately, General Hardee's sixteen-year-old son was mortally wounded in the action and died March 24. Ironically, the Union commander, Maj. Gen. Oliver Howard, had been Willie Hardee's Sunday school teacher at West Point.[38]

General Lafayette McLaws, who witnessed the charge, said he had served with J.E.B. Stuart in his exploits and never witnessed a charge equal in efficiency and effect.[39] General Hardee, who also witnessed the charge, turned to a fellow officer and remarked that he "had seen many a charge of cavalry, infantry and artillery on the plains of Mexico and elsewhere, and had seen the old United States dragoons charge, and the Comanches charge, but never witnessed the equal of the charge just made." [40]

During the night, the weather turned to a chilly rain. In the rain storm, the remainder of the Army of Tennessee fell back, through the mud, crossing the same bridge fought over earlier in the day. Neither army was allowed to have camp fires. The cold, wet soldiers shivered during their retreat. The only light that rainy night came from the burning pine forest near Bentonville, which cast an eerie light on the battlefield.[41] The Army of Tennessee continued its journey through the shadows to Smithfield, North Carolina.

During this time, Shannon received orders that he was chosen to lead a group of cavalry troops on a special mission. This special mission was to escort President Davis westward, across the Mississippi.[42] Unfortunately, President Davis, his escort, the 9th Kentucky Cavalry (who fought with the Rangers at Dug Gap), and Francis Lubbock (who had been on Wharton's staff in Texas) surrendered at Irwinville, Georgia, prior to Shannon reaching them.

In North Carolina the Rangers covered Johnston's retreat from April 12 through the 14th,[43] when 200 Federal cavalry attacked them. The Rangers quickly mounted and counterattacked. The counterattack succeeded in driving the Federals from the field. By April 15, surrender of the army seemed inevitable. Rumors abounded about whether General Johnston would surrender. When some of the Rangers approached General Wheeler about the rumors, he neither confirmed nor denied their authenticity.[44] After receiving such responses, many of the men discussed leaving the Army of Tennessee for Gen. Edmund Kirby Smith's command in Texas.

Shortly before Johnston's surrender at Greensboro, North Carolina, the Rangers camped on the Haw River. During the night, pickets were removed without the Texans becoming alerted. At sunrise, Federal cavalry charged the Ranger camp. The few Rangers that had risen early that morning alerted the others, and the unit armed themselves and counterattacked. The Rangers' stand sent the Federal cavalry back down the road they originally came in on. This action was the last the Rangers participated in as an organized unit.[45]

Outside of Greensboro, General Hardee summoned the regimental commander of the Rangers to his quarters. He held a special place in his heart for the Rangers. General Hardee advised young Captain Matthews of the pending situation. He advised him to join Dick Taylor's forces in Mobile, and added, "I don't want to see your regiment surrendered to the enemy."

Matthews returned to the Ranger camp and held a council with each of the company commanders. During the council he submitted his resignation as regimental commander. He advised the company commanders to "hold a council to determine your course, and each company decide and act for themselves regardless of what others may do." [46] The company commanders of the regiment then allowed all the men who wished to leave without being paroled to do so. The suggested intention of those leaving was joining Kirby Smith in Texas to continue the fight. In Shannon's Scouts, it was decided that there would be "no surrender"; instead they would "disband and in small squads strike for home and later we can reassemble west of the Mississippi River with General E. Kirby Smith." [47]

Of the 248 Rangers reporting for duty the previous morning, only 90 surrendered the next day, April 19. On that day, Joe Johnston formally surrendered the 89,000 troops stationed in North Carolina, South Carolina, Georgia, and Florida. The remainder escaped in pursuit of their own course of action. Capt. Tom Weston surrendered the 90 Rangers present at the North Carolina surrender site. The surrender of Ranger companies was thereafter known to the men as "the break up." It was at the surrender that Sherman informed Confederate commanders of President Lincoln's assassination.

One company of Rangers went south through Greensboro and rode up on an ambulance. On investigating, they found it carried Brig. Gen. Thomas Harrison, who was recuperating from wounds received at Bentonville. The wounded Harrison commended the men and expressed regrets that he could not join them. Harrison wished the men godspeed and then told them farewell. [48] Harrison himself surrendered on April 26. One squad of the Rangers consisting of approximately thirty men made it as far as New Orleans when the Department of the Trans Mississippi surrendered.

David Smith Terry left the Rangers sometime in 1863 and had been given his own cavalry regiment ("Terry's Regiment") in the Department of the Trans Mississippi. Terry and his cavalry unit made their way to Mexico, where they served under the Emperor Maximilian until he was removed from power in 1867.

Back in Texas, General Wharton had enjoyed some military

successes in the Red River campaign under Gen. John G. Walker.[49] The campaign successfully halted a Union offensive aimed at Texas with victories at Mansfield and Pleasant Hill. Wharton was eventually promoted to chief of cavalry for the Departments of Texas, New Mexico, and Arizona.

In early April, Wharton headed out with Gen. James Harrison to inspect the troops stationed at Hempstead, Texas. Desertion had recently become problematic, leading to irritability among the commanders. While on the way to Hempstead, Wharton saw Col. George Whythe Baylor, and harshly criticized him for not being where Wharton thought he should be. The situation quickly became heated. Baylor and Wharton then began striking each other. The accompanying officers, including Gen. James Harrison (Tom Harrison's brother), intervened by pulling the arguing men apart. Wharton then ordered Baylor to Magruder's headquarters in Houston, Texas, under arrest. Baylor made accusations about Magruder. Wharton then responded to Baylor, calling him a "liar." General Harrison finally had to forcibly take Wharton away from the scene.

Baylor obeyed Wharton's order to report to Magruder's headquarters in Houston. Upon arriving at headquarters, General Magruder was out, so Baylor went to Magruder's private residence at "Fannin House." Baylor was so shaken by events that he cried uncontrollably. Magruder finally arrived and sent him to a private room to compose himself. When Wharton arrived at Fannin House, he set about to find General Magruder. While searching the rooms, he found Baylor. After some exchange of words, the men began swinging at each other. Baylor soon produced a pistol. As General Harrison was reaching for the firearm, it went off, fatally killing Wharton. Baylor was later tried for the crime and acquitted.[50]

By June, Brig. Gen. James E. Harrison joined former Texas Ranger Maj. Thomas McKinney Jack and other members of the Confederate delegation for the somber duty of surrendering Texas to Federal troops in Galveston at the end of the fighting.[51] Thus members of Terry's Texas Rangers participated in the war from the early secessionist activity, to Manassas, and finally to the very act of surrendering the Confederate forces in Texas.

CHAPTER 8

Symbols and Folklore

"The banner is our glory, 'tis sacred in our eyes."
–From "The Texas Ranger War Song"

Symbols

Anthropologist Erika Bourguignon said of symbols: "It is assumed that a narrative or graphic style expresses basic psychological themes shared by its creator and the community, and that the appeal of the product lies precisely in the symbolic expression of themes or feelings that generally are not acknowledged explicitly." [1] Given that graphic symbols express themes common to the creator and the community (i.e., regiment), a closer look at the symbols and common themes is warranted. [2]

The most prominent symbol of a regiment was its flag. Terry's Texas Rangers used at least four different flags. [3] Besides being trophies when captured, flags (or colors) represented and symbolized who a military unit was, what they stood for, and often which battles they fought in. On the battlefield, the loca-

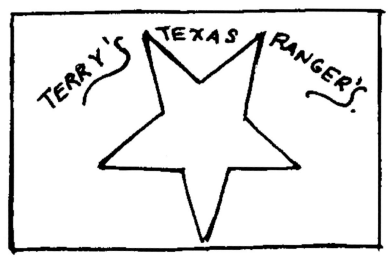

First flag design of Terry's Texas Rangers.

tion and identity of units was accomplished by observing the flags. These flags also helped stragglers from the unit identify a rallying point. Many of the unit flags were sewn by women in the members' hometowns and were presented to the men upon their departure for war. The flags represented the themes important to that community, and held a place of importance and pride for the Rangers, as evidenced by references to it in "The Texas Ranger War Song."

The first flag reportedly used by the Rangers is the Bonnie Blue flag design with an upside-down star in the center (a dark blue rectangle with an upside-down, five-pointed star in white). The name "Terry's Texas Rangers" was woven in gold-colored thread. Although most flags captured in combat from Confederate units were returned to southern states after reconstruction, the first Terry flag has not been returned to Texas and is located in the Decorative and Industrial Arts Collection of the Chicago Historical Society.

Eliza Groce and Annie Jefferson of Hempstead, Texas, made the Rangers' second flag. The flag was parallelogram in form. The ground was composed of deep-red French merino, having two broad bars of blue silk running crosswise on either side. Upon these were twelve white stars, and a large one where they met at right angles in the center. It was ornamented with a

Third flag of Terry's Texas Rangers.

tasseled border. A graceful blue streamer flew from the top of the flagstaff, bearing on one side the inscription "we conquer or die" and on the other, "Terry's Rangers," with the two words separated by a five-pointed star continuing the word "Texas" printed between the points.[4] This flag was carried into the Kentucky campaign of 1862, then was retired and reportedly sent to the state archives when they were presented with the third flag. The flag referred to in "The Texas Ranger War Song" is most likely the second regimental flag.

Mary McIverland and Robbie Woodruff of Nashville, Tennessee, made the third Rangers' flag and presented it to them near Tuscumbia, Alabama, on September 20, 1864. The blue silk was from one of McIverland's dresses, with the white silk from her wedding dress.[5] Unfortunately, it was lost less than a month later on October 13, 1864. The flag contained a red Maltese cross consisting of broad bars in the center field surrounded by a circle containing inscriptions. Each bar contained six five-pointed stars. The cross was placed within the circle on the center of the flag. The phrase "God defend the right" was on the top interior of the circle, and "Terry's Texas Rangers" was stitched along the bottom interior of the circle in blue silk floss. On the other side was written, "Ducit Armor Patriae" ("For the

Love of Country" or "Love of Country Leads Us") and "Terry's Texas Rangers" in blue silk floss.[6]

The symbol of the cross, combined with the motto "God defend the right," created an image associated with moral or holy crusades.[7] Joseph Wheeler in his farewell address referred to the war as "the holy cause."[8] "The Texas Ranger War Song" also refers to the banner as being "sacred." Placement of such symbols in the center of the flag suggests that the moral/holy crusade was a foremost concern, rather than the attainment of military honors, as seen in other unit flags containing references to battles and or trophies obtained. The moral/holy crusade aspect also shows up in the designations given to each company. Use of the terms "guards" and "Rangers" in company names connotes a protective, defensive mindset given by its originators.

The fourth flag was reported to have been torn up by the men at the time of surrender in order to prevent its capture. It is unclear what design this flag may have been. A flag destined for the unit was purchased and sent to them from supporters in the Houston, Texas, area by the editor of a Houston newspaper. This flag, purchased in Havana, Cuba, by Captain LaBlache, was made of silk with silver tassel. It is not known if the flag purchased in Cuba made it to the regiment via blockade runner.

When art therapy techniques are applied to the symbols associated with the Rangers, the results reveal insight concerning the men, the cause, and the mindset of the time. When reviewed as a sequential progression, the symbols reveal notable changes in attitudes regarding "the cause."

The first regimental flag was the "Bonnie Blue" design. The dark blue connotes a deep conflict with the mother. The use of blue can also suggest a sensitivity to rejection. The star suggests aspirations. Together, they indicate a conflict with the "mother country," stemming from a sensitivity to rejection and an aspiration for something different. The common meaning is that the lone star represents secession. Its placement on a field of blue represented independence. The origin likely had association with similar flags used in the War for Texas Independence and an earlier movement in the independence of West Florida, where the flag was first used.[9]

The second flag was the "St. Andrew's Cross" design. The

red connotes "lusts, blood and atavistic emotions associated with killing and assertiveness." The large amount of red in the background may indicate these feelings are to the point of anger and vindictiveness. The blue against the red suggests an attempt at liberation from the great mother and her dominance. The cross connotes a point of decision and sacrifice. Thus, together this flag is a symbol of assertiveness. The assertiveness has turned into anger and vindictiveness, along with such anger representing a time of decision and possible sacrifice. Once again, the assertiveness is related to liberation from the "mother country."

The third flag, with its unique design and mandala-like quality, is associated most often with the Rangers at reenactments. The large amount of blue shows the repeated "conflict with the mother country" theme. The white circle/mandala containing the cross continues the theme of sacrifice, as seen in the second flag. The cross itself within a mandala offers an integration point.

Symbolically, the third flag communicates a continuing struggle with the "mother country." Hostility is present, although more subdued than seen previously. The sense of "sacrifice" for the cause is now a focal point for them. The sacrifice is no longer for "the cause," but now is a form of self-assertion.

In other symbols used, some of the men wore a single five-pointed silver star on their hats (some sources report these as gold). The star had the name of the state written on it, in capital letters, with one letter on each of the five rays of the star. Some of the men painted the star emblems on their hats.[10] As the war progressed, some changes were made in the design. In 1863 the design changed due to other Texas units calling themselves "Rangers" as well. The new design, according to Chaplain Bunting, was "a five pointed star with the word TEXAS in between the star, the name TERRY on the star with the letter R in the center." The star is similar to those used by the law enforcement agency of the Texas Rangers, whose badge consists of the five-pointed star enclosed within a circle.[11, 12]

The wearing of the lone star occurred in other Texas units, showing close identification with the state. Units from other southern states also wore pins containing symbols of their states. The use of "TERRY" in the stars worn by the Rangers further highlights the close identification with the regimental name-

Star emblem association with Terry's Texas Rangers.

sake. "The Texas Ranger War Song" clearly indicates the close association with Terry ("Our star-crossed banner flashes, bearing Terry's name"). The lone star is seen in the available photographs of members of the unit from that time.

Folklore

Many folktales exist concerning the Rangers. Some of these tales began with the men themselves. The men told stories to fellow soldiers and others who would listen.[13] The oral tradition of the Rangers contains a mixture of fact and entertainment. The storytelling of the Rangers was not unique to their subculture, but rather shared with the oral traditions of Texans, long known for telling tall tales.

Reverend Bunting's letters to the papers, personal letters, and memoirs written after the war have served to create an image of the unit that makes separation of fact from folklore difficult. Creation of a factual accounting involves comparing personal letters written by the soldiers and surviving official records, although even these leave some gaps in the regimental account. The major Ranger accounts (e.g., Giles, Blackburn, etc.) are reminisence-oriented, which lend them to embellishment. Anthropologist Erika Bourguignon said of folktales: "Folktales and religion serve as a means of preserving aspects of a culture. Besides preserving a culture, they also serve to create a culture."[14]

In examining the Rangers, the folktales and religion preserve aspects of the original culture and also create a secondary or modified culture in its aftermath. The transformed culture romanticizes the Rangers' reputation and fighting ability.

Separating folklore and fact proves difficult, since many folklore elements are based on factual events.

Some of the major folklore themes involve the number of battles, personal anecdotes involving members of the regiment, and the regiment's fighting abilities. Some collaborative evidence exists concerning the large number of engagements in which the regiment participated. Other folklore tales include:

• the story of how after the war a former member of the regiment captured the man who reportedly killed Frank Terry and allowed Terry's son to kill the captive;

• the story of how General Wheeler destroyed many of General Wharton's reports sent to him, thereby keeping him from promotion;

• the story of Terry and his regiment flying "the black flag" in battles;

• the mystery of whether B.F. Terry was buried at Oakland plantation or Sandy Point Cemetery;

• the mystery of a ghost at the B. F. Terry mausoleum in Fort Bend County (this mystery also reports the image of a face appearing in the bricks comprising the mausoleum).

In addition to the folklore are the songs about the regiment, written by the Rangers themselves. The two songs are "The Texas Ranger War Song" and "Song of the Texas Rangers" by J. D. Young.

The Texas Ranger War Song
(Sung to the tune of "Bonnie Blue Flag")

We are a band of brothers from home and kindred fair,
The glory of old Texas in Southern border war,
For like a fiery billow we dash upon the foe,
And well the music of our carbines the Yankee troopers know.

Chorus
Through the blinding smoke of battle, like a red hot glare of flame,
Our star-crossed banner flashes, bearing Terry's name,
Leading us to our first battle, at Woodsonville he fell,
But since on many a field we have avenged him well.

Chorus
The banner is our glory, 'tis sacred in our eyes,

And we guard it like an Amulet on every field it flies,
Like a light from home 'twas sent us by our noble Texas girls,
And we seem to feel their eyes upon us when Count[15] its stars
unfurls.

Chorus

All Mississippi's borders are teeming with our fame,
On the hills of Alabama they love the Rangers' name,
In fettered land of Boone we unlinked the Despot's Chain,
And roused to life and energy her chivalry again.

Chorus

But the State, boy, of all others, this side of home we know
Where they give us hearty welcome and cheer us when we go,
With her spirited fair daughters, is proud old Tennessee,
And while a Yankee pollutes her soil, her Champions we shall be.

Chorus

Then let us throw our Kisses to the girls who hold us dear
With their fairy hands they beckon us in glory's dear career
True to our Southern honor—the Texian hearts we bear
We'll brighten still the star of our hopes—the proud old "Texas Star."

Chorus

Away! Away! To the battle front away,
Away! To the Enemy's lines,
We lead the fight to day.

(From the Batchelor-Turner letters)

Song of the Texas Rangers
(Sung to the tune of "The Yellow Rose of Texas")

The morning star is paling; the camp fires flicker low;
Our steeds are madly neighing; for the bugle bids us go:
So put the foot in stirrup and shake the bridle free,
For today the Texas Rangers must cross the Tennessee.
With Wharton for our leader, we'll chase the dastard foe,
Till our horses bathe their fetlocks in the deep, blue Ohio.

'Tis joy to be a Ranger! To fight for dear Southland!
'Tis joy to follow Wharton, with his gallant, trusty band!
'Tis joy to see our Harrison plunge, like a meteor bright,

Into the thickest of the fray, and deal his deadly might.
O! Who'd not be a Ranger and follow Wharton's cry!
And battle for his country, and, if needs be, die? [16]

In Memoriam of Col. Benj. F. Terry
By W. M. Gilleland—January 4, 1862

The war steed is champing his bit with disdain,
    And wild is the flash of his eye
As he waves to the wind his dark, flowing mane,
Stars, neighs, while the scouts and bugler's refrain
    proclaim the battle is nigh.

Charge! Charge! And the Ranger flies on his steed
    Bold Terry! the fearless and the brave;
His troops on his trail are moving with speed
And each has crowned his name with a deed
    That story or song will engrave!

He swept to the field with an eye of delight,
    At the head of his brave, chosen band,
As a meteor's course, 'mid the storms of the night,
So splendidly shone his form in the fight,
    And sunk down with a glory as grand.

He fought for the land of his kindred and birth,
    Not for fame—though his laurels are won;
His thoughts had a higher, a holier worth
Than the trumpet's acclaim, which tells to earth
    "Of the man!" not the deeds he has done.

The lightning that burst on the warrior's head,
    From the foe that outnumbered his band
Deterred not his course, as thro' columns he sped—
And left on his pathway the dying and dead,
    That yielded their breath to his band.

The thunders of battle are hush'd on the plain,
    And the wild cry of carnage is o'er,
Dark vultures are gazing from high at the slain,
And the earth drank the blood from the dark purple vein
    That thrilled to life's passions before.

But tear-drops of grief dim the eyes of the brave,
    For their lion in death is laid low,
Their banners in sable above him they wave,
And muffle their drums in his march to the grave,
    To the music and language of woe.

The Magnolia City laments for the dead,
    Through streets his gay banner he bore
To a far distant land—but low lies his head,
Yet columns shall rise on the fields where he bled,
    And freemen his memory adore.

O calm in the tomb is the conqueror's rest!
    For his labors of life are well done,
And though quenched is the light of his generous breast,
With heroes immortal his spirit is blest,
    Who o'er death have the victory won.

CHAPTER 9

How They Died

> *"Self-preservation is the first law of nature and people who would not defend their homes and property are not worthy of freedom or respect. . . . I am ready to offer my life, my fortune and sacred honor in her defense."*
> –Ranger J. K. P. Blackburn

In the nineteenth century, how someone died and the remembrance of them was often as important as how they lived. Remembrance of the dead also served to aid the mourning process for the families and friends of those who died. Death rituals were very important.

One of the popular ways that remembrance took form was in the erection of monuments. There are several monuments commemorating Terry's Texas Rangers. The most prominent monument is located at the south entrance to the Texas State Capitol in Austin. The monument, unveiled on June 26, 1907, consists of an equestrian statue with a mounted rider. True to form, the rider carries two pairs of six-shooters and a rifle. The statue won praise from critics across the country. The Terry's Texas Ranger Association presented the statue to the State of Texas. The statue

𝕿𝖍𝖊 𝕮𝖊𝖗𝖊𝖒𝖔𝖓𝖎𝖊𝖘 𝖔𝖋 𝖙𝖍𝖊 𝖀𝖓𝖛𝖊𝖎𝖑𝖎𝖓𝖌
𝖔𝖋 𝖙𝖍𝖊
𝕸𝖔𝖓𝖚𝖒𝖊𝖓𝖙 𝕰𝖗𝖊𝖈𝖙𝖊𝖉 𝖙𝖔 𝕮𝖔𝖒𝖒𝖊𝖒𝖔𝖗𝖆𝖙𝖊
𝖙𝖍𝖊 𝖁𝖆𝖑𝖔𝖗 𝖔𝖋

𝕿𝖊𝖗𝖗𝖞'𝖘 𝕿𝖊𝖝𝖆𝖘 𝕽𝖆𝖓𝖌𝖊𝖗𝖘

(8𝖙𝖍 𝕽𝖊𝖌𝖎𝖒𝖊𝖓𝖙 𝕿𝖊𝖝𝖆𝖘 𝕮𝖆𝖛𝖆𝖑𝖗𝖞 𝕮. 𝕾. 𝕬.)

𝖂𝖎𝖑𝖑 𝖈𝖔𝖒𝖒𝖊𝖓𝖈𝖊 𝖕𝖗𝖔𝖒𝖕𝖙𝖑𝖞 𝖆𝖙 𝖙𝖜𝖔 𝖔'𝖈𝖑𝖔𝖈𝖐 𝖕. 𝖒. 𝕵𝖚𝖓𝖊 𝖙𝖜𝖊𝖓𝖙𝖞-𝖘𝖎𝖝𝖙𝖍,
𝖓𝖎𝖓𝖊𝖙𝖊𝖊𝖓 𝖍𝖚𝖓𝖉𝖗𝖊𝖉 𝖆𝖓𝖉 𝖘𝖊𝖛𝖊𝖓
𝕬𝖚𝖘𝖙𝖎𝖓, 𝕿𝖊𝖝𝖆𝖘,

Program cover from the dedication ceremony of the monument to Terry's Texas Rangers. From the Weems collection.

— Courtesy of The Museum of Southern History, Sugarland, Texas

Ribbon from the dedication of the monument to Terry's Texas Rangers in Austin, Texas, June 25–26, 1907.
— Courtesy of The Museum of Southern History, Sugarland, Texas

was sculpted by Italian-born sculptor Pompeo Coppini[1] and faces east.

Around the base are quotations regarding the unit's performance from various Confederate leaders. Quotes include Gen. Albert Sidney Johnston, Gen. William Hardee, Gen. Joseph Wheeler, Gen. Braxton Bragg, and President Jefferson Davis. Some of the quotes are further embellished with fasces and a wreath. The statue also contains the last charge given the unit from General Wheeler on the day of formal surrender.[2] Another monument to the unit is located in Houston, Texas. The monument in Houston consists of a granite memorial located near the emergency room entrance of Ben Taub Hospital. The memorial was erected October 19, 1909.

As a tribute to Benjamin F. Terry, a county in northwest Texas and a high school in Richmond, Texas, are named after him. Thomas S. Lubbock also has a county named after him in the South Plains of northwest Texas. Terry's body lies in Glenwood Cemetery in Houston, Texas.[3] The grave, located to the southwest of the main building, is indicated with a large granite marker.

The grave of John A. Wharton, who commanded Terry's Texas Rangers is located in Austin at the Texas State Cemetery. The grave contains a bust of Wharton and brief synopsis of his career, including leadership of the unit and later military activi-

Memorial to Terry's Texas Rangers in Houston, Texas. The monument was erected October 19, 1909.

—From author's collection

Headstone and grave marker for B. F. Terry in Glenwood Cemetery, Houston, Texas.

—From author's collection

Memorial to John A. Wharton located in Alvin, Texas, at the Confederate Cemetery.
—From author's collection

ties. Wharton's grave is located to the south of Albert Sidney Johnston's grave. Another monument dedicated to John A. Wharton is located in Alvin, Texas.

The grave of Thomas Harrison is in the First Street Cemetery in Waco, Texas. His brothers and fellow generals are also buried there. They are the only trio of Texas brothers who served as generals in the Confederacy.

After the war, veterans held reunions sporadically in cities throughout Texas. The Terry's Texas Ranger Association was open to those who served with the regiment in their campaigns, including the servants.[4] The first organized meeting of veterans occurred in Houston, on December 17, 1867, the anniversary of Terry's death. Gustave Cooke was one of the original members of the organization formed. Photographs were often taken at these meetings. The annual reunions occurred at various cities in Texas (Houston, Fulshear, Galveston, and Gonzales) and in Nashville, Tennessee. The meeting in Nashville shows that special affections were associated with the city and its residents, being that they held the event so far from their native state. At the 1899 meeting in Dallas, the third regimental flag was returned to the members of the regiment. Some group photographs were taken at the reunions. At the 1909 reunion at Fulshear, Texas, members posed with a Patrick Cleburne divisional flag. Attendees at the reunions also included soldiers who fought alongside the Rangers in their campaigns.

Many of the Rangers made successes of their lives after the war. They returned to law and medical practices. Some excelled in ranching, railroads, and banking. Several involved themselves in politics and assumed elective offices. Although the regiment ceased, the influence of its members continued into the twentieth century. Examples follow.

Alexander M. Shannon. Federal authorities never pardoned Alexander M. Shannon. He was originally with Company C and later commanded a separate scouting unit. After the war, Shannon resided at his ranch on the San Antonio River. He later moved to New Orleans, where he went into the insurance business with Confederate Gen. John Bell Hood in 1869. After the business prospered, he moved to Galveston to open a Texas branch. He

1913 reunion of Terry's Texas Rangers in San Marcos, Texas.
– Courtesy of The Museum of Southern History, Sugarland, Texas

1905 reunion of Terry's Texas Rangers in Austin, Texas.
— Courtesy of The Museum of Southern History, Sugarland, Texas

1909 reunion of Terry's Texas Rangers in Fulshear, Texas. Note the display of Cleburne type regimental flag.

— Courtesy of Old South Plantation, Richmond, Texas

married while in Galveston. By 1880, his business expanded to include building public works and operating a line of tugs and barges. He proposed the building of a seawall for the city in 1886, and became postmaster of Galveston in 1893. Shannon later served as general manager of the Galveston and Western Railway. He died in Galveston 1906 and was buried in the Episcopal cemetery there.[5] Federal authorities never pardoned any of the men in his unit, known as "Shannon's Scouts." After the war, he spoke very little of his scout unit and their activities.

John B. Rector of Company D, a graduate of Yale (1859), and practicing lawyer, served as district attorney in Travis County (Austin) from 1866 to 1867. After being removed from office, as an impediment to reconstruction, he later served as judge of the 31st Judicial District from 1871 to 1876. He then returned to private practice. In 1884 he ran for Congress and was defeated. In 1892, John was appointed U.S. judge of the Northern Judicial District of Texas by President Benjamin Harrison, where he served until his defeat in 1896. He was buried in Oakwood Cemetery with Episcopal rites.[6]

Rufus Y. King, an original captain of Company A, became superintendent of the Confederate Home for Men, 1899–1903.[7]

Gustave Cooke was a county judge in Fort Bend prior to enlistment as a private in the Rangers' Company H. After the war, he returned to private law practice in Houston. Governor Coke appointed him judge of criminal court for Harris and Galveston counties, 1874–1888. After resigning, he was later an unsuccessful candidate for the Democratic nomination for governor against James S. Hogg, who went on to win the office. Gustave Cooke gave the first eulogy for Terry at the Oakland (Sugarland) Cemetery (the family burial site). Statements in the eulogy were instrumental in initiating the moving of Frank Terry's grave from Oakland to Glenwood in Houston. Cooke left Houston for health reasons, moving to San Marcos, Texas.[8]

Tom Harrison served with Jefferson Davis in the 1st Mississippi Rifles in the Mexican War. He left his law practice in

Waco to join the Rangers. After the war, he returned to private law practice. In 1866 he was elected district judge for the Nineteenth District of Lampassas and McClennan counties, but later he was removed. He was also active in affairs of the Baptist church and served two terms as trustee at Baylor University. Described as being "unreconstructed to the end," he died on July 14, 1891, and was buried in Waco at the First Street Cemetery.[9][10]

Robert Franklin Bunting graduated from Princeton Theological Seminary (1852) and moved to Texas as a missionary when he was twenty-three years old. He became chaplain of the Rangers. He has the distinction of being the first regularly commissioned chaplain in the Confederate army. While serving as chaplain, he operated a private carrier postal service for Texas troops and was correspondent for Houston and San Antonio newspapers. He also obtained leave of the regiment to form an institution called "The Texas Hospital" located in Auburn, Alabama.

After the war, he pastored the 1st Presbyterian Church in Nashville (1865–1869). He returned to Texas to pastor in Galveston (1869–1882). During the time he was in Texas, he was employed as a state agent for a "commercial house," where he engaged in business dealings with former Confederate general Braxton Bragg. His dealings included correspondences for business with the Russian monarchy. After leaving Galveston, he pastored in Rome, Georgia, from 1882 to 1883 and finally in Gallatin, Tennessee (1889–1891), where he died. He is buried at Gallatin.[11]

George Washington Littlefield of Company I graduated from Baylor and served as a major in the regiment. After the war, he opened a mercantile business in Gonzales, Texas. After some success at this, and accumulating land holdings, through purchasing farms in bankruptcy, he entered the cattle business. In 1871 he began leading cattle drives which earned him great revenues. He then founded the American National Bank in Austin, where he served as president. He also served as a member of the board of regents for the University of Texas. He established a fund to promote the study of Southern history at the university. George Littlefield also provided gifts to the university which allowed them to acquire the Wrenn library building, Alice Littlefield Dormitory, a fountain, the main building, and an entrance dedicated to Southern statesmen. Littlefield was a life-long Democrat and Presbyterian. Even after the war, he prided himself on his association with the Rangers and his promotion to major while in the regiment. He died November 10, 1920, and was buried at Oakwood Cemetery between his wife and life-long servant and former slave, Nathan Littlefield Stokes.

William R. Friend of Company E graduated from Princeton and was a lawyer by profession. He was also a member of the special detachment known as Shannon's Scouts. After being paroled at Demopolis, Alabama, he returned to Texas. In 1875 he was elected a state senator.

Mort Royston of Company K, who served as a lieutenant colonel in the regiment, was elected state treasurer in 1866. The occupational military commander later removed him as "an impediment to reconstruction." Royston later moved to Galveston, where he received an appointment as a clerk in the criminal district court there. Mort died in 1890. His son, Mort Royston, Jr., played a prominent role in assisting with Galveston's recovery from the 1900 hurricane. Most of his sons' efforts were in the fifth ward area of the city.

James Francis Miller graduated from Rutersville College and was admitted to the state bar in 1857. After the war, he engaged in law and banking ventures. He went on to become the first president of the Texas Live Stock Association and Texas Bankers Association. James also served as a congressman from 1883 to 1887.[12]

James Love served as first judge of the Harris and Galveston County Criminal Court. He was later removed as "an impediment to reconstruction." Judge Love was acclaimed by peers as an eminent jurist. He died in Galveston on June 12, 1874.[13]

David S. Terry returned to California, after his time in Mexico serving Emperor Maximilian ended in 1867. While in

California, he resumed his law practice. He was nominated to but declined a seat on the California Supreme Court. He was tragically killed by an angry client in 1898.[14]

Thomas McKinney Jack was a lawyer in private practice prior to the war. He joined Company B of the Rangers. He later became an aide-de-camp of Gen. Albert Sidney Johnston and was holding him when he died. He was promoted and transferred to the staff of Gen. Leonidas Polk, and was beside General Polk when he died at Pine Mountain, Georgia. After the war, he returned to law practice in Galveston. He died August 26, 1880.[15]

William Henry Pope studied law at the University of Virginia at the conclusion of the war. He returned to Texas, serving as county attorney for Harrison County. After three terms in office, he was elected state senator. He served ten years, then returned to private practice in Marshall, Texas. He later moved to Beaumont, where he was elected judge of the 58th Judicial District.[16]

Samuel Swann Ashe enlisted as a private in Company B. After the war, he entered the mercantile business. He then married Sallie Anderson from Lebanon, Tennessee. In 1870 he was elected justice of the peace of Harris County and subsequently was elected sheriff and then tax collector. From 1893 through 1897, he served as clerk of the district criminal court in Harris County.[17]

William Andrew Fletcher joined Company E. After the war, he wrote of his experiences in *Rebel Private, Front and Rear.* He involved himself in the lumber business. His business activities included a partnership in Village Mills Company. At one point, he owned 1,000 acres in Orange County, along with several other properties.[18]

Fergus Kyle joined Company D and eventually received promotion to captain. After the war, he served in the Texas House of Representatives. He also served in the Texas Senate. Among his accomplishments was the co-sponsorship of the Alamo purchase bill of 1905, which saved the Texas shrine. The town of Kyle, Texas, is named for him. One of his sons, Edwin

Amputation kit belonging to Dr. Robert Nathaniel Chapman Tate of Company I of Terry's Texas Rangers. The kit was owned by him at the time of the war.
— Courtesy of Gonzales County Historical Museum

Jackson Kyle, became the dean of Texas A&M, for whom Kyle Field is named.[19]

Dr. Robert Nathaniel Chapman Tate joined Company I of the Rangers. He later left the regiment due to the medical needs of his hometown, Gonzales, Texas. During and after the war, he continued his medical practice for fifty years. He also served as president of the County Medical Society. His amputation kit from before the war is displayed in the Gonzales County Historical Museum. He died September 4, 1911.

Samuel Maverick, Jr., originally joined Henry McCulloch's regiment, then left and joined Company B of the Rangers. After the war, he ran a family farm that is now Breckinridge Park in San Antonio, Texas. He studied and became a lawyer, then built the Maverick Bank in 1884. He involved himself in building San Antonio's first streetcar line and founded Maverick

Lithographing Company. Samuel later donated Maverick Park to San Antonio. He died February 27, 1936.[20]

David St. Clair Combs originally enlisted in Company D. After the war, he was one of the early traildrivers. For thirteen years he drove cattle and horses. By 1900, he established Combs Ranch in Brewster County. He played an important role in getting L. B. Giles to write his history of the regiment, *Terry's Texas Rangers*.[21]

Archelus M. Cochran completed his medical degree in 1861 and enlisted as a lieutenant in the regiment. After the war, he served as a state legislator, 1866–67, and then was elected to the Dallas City Council. In 1879 he was appointed postmaster of Dallas. He died on August 4, 1910, in Columbia, Tennessee.[22]

James Knox Polk Blackburn had been in San Antonio with Gen. Ben McCulloch's troops at Gen. David Twiggs' surrender. He later enlisted in the Rangers, Company F. He was separated from the regiment at the Battle of Farmington due to a severe wound, but recuperated and rejoined the unit. After the war, he returned to Tennessee, where he further recuperated. He owned a plantation and later was elected to the Tennessee state legislature. He wrote "Reminiscences of the Terry Rangers," which was published in 1918. He died on July 6, 1923.[23]

L.M. Kokernot joined his brother in the ranching business after the war. The Kokernot ranch eventually covered 500,000 acres in Pecos, Brewster, and Jeff Davis counties in Texas.

Terry's Texas Rangers have been portrayed in various works of art. Some of the more notable artists who produced works with the Rangers as subject matter include Carl G. Iwonski, Jack Amirian, Don Troiani, Bruce Marshall, Mort Kuntsler, and Raymond Desvarreux Larpenteur.[24]

The centennial of the War Between the States in the 1960s marked the beginnings of reenactors, or what is now called "living history." One of the early units formed was the 8th Texas Cavalry, Terry's Texas Rangers, formed in the 1950s. Guy Airey of Vidor, Texas, served as its first colonel. The reenactment regiment has companies in Texas, Georgia, North Carolina, Arizona, and an affiliated company in California. The new unit patterns itself on its predecessor. Those individuals in the unit furnish their own equipage and participate in living history demonstrations and reenactments of military engagements. The Terry's Texas Ranger regiment has appeared in several movies. Uniforms are often handmade and patterned after those in museums. Historical accuracy is emphasized in uniforms and equipment. As Edgar Hood of the reenactment group says, they try to "talk the talk and walk the walk." These living historians labor at preserving the customs and culture of the original units. Interest in reenacting has increased yearly since its inception.

Such reenactment activity indicates a revitalization of a former culture. Anthropologist Anthony F. C. Wallace defined revitalization movements such as this as "deliberate and conscious efforts by members of society to construct a more satisfying culture during periods of heightened stress." [25] Although this revitalization constructs the military forms, the political and social cultures are not revitalized. Some groups are focused on partial, if not full, revitalization of southern culture and politics. For southerners, the period from the centennial of the war in 1861 through the year 2000 placed considerable stress on a people whose national culture, identity, and nationalism were received with contempt, disdain, and hate by their critics. This reaction to southern identity occurred simultaneously while other cultural and identity groups received positive reactions, if not full independence. [26]

Nevertheless, the legacy of Terry's Texas Rangers has left a vivid imprint on the annals of history.

The first elected wartime governor of Texas, Francis R. Lubbock, said of the Rangers:

"No better soldiers ever drew battle-blade in freedom's cause than Terry's Texas Rangers."

In the years after the war, this stanza was written by an unknown poet concerning the Rangers:

> *Their shivered swords are red with rust,*
> *Their plumed heads are bowed;*
> *Their proud banner, trailed in dust,*
> *Is now their martial shroud.*

Eulogy for Benjamin Franklin Terry

Eulogy delivered by Jeffrey D. Murrah at the dedication of the Confederate Memorial to B.F. Terry on April 19, 1997, at Glenwood Cemetery in Houston, Texas.

BENJAMIN FRANKLIN TERRY

[Surrender] means that the history of this heroic struggle will be written by the enemy; that our youths will be trained by northern school teachers, will learn from northern schoolbooks their version of the war, will be impressed by all the influences of history and education to regard our gallant deed as traitors, [and] our maimed veterans as fit subjects for derision.
—Gen. Patrick R. Cleburne

Who is Benjamin Franklin Terry? Several months ago, this question was asked of me by a health care worker, who recently visited B.F. Terry High School in Richmond (Texas). She claimed no one there could answer her question. Four generations ago, Benjamin Franklin Terry was well-known to all Texas school children. His exploits and accomplishments were re-

143

Author delivering eulogy to B. F. Terry on April 19, 1997, at Glenwood Cemetery, Houston, Texas.

quired reading, alongside other patriots such as Travis, Crockett, Fannin and Bowie. We are here on this Confederate Memorial Day to remember the deeds of our patriot fathers, and honor Benjamin Franklin Terry.

Benjamin Franklin Terry was born in Russelville, Kentucky, on February 18, 1821. When he was ten years old, his family moved to Brazoria County, Texas, where his uncle, Ben Fort Smith, lived. (His father died during the journey, and his mother died shortly after reaching the Republic of Texas.)[1] His uncle then raised Terry and his brothers on the Brazoria plantation. Terry was home schooled on the plantation. B.F. Terry, known to his friends as Frank, grew into a big man. At six feet tall, with broad shoulders and a muscular frame, he towered above other men of his time. He rode tirelessly for long distances and was an unerring shot. It was in Brazoria County he befriended local hero and resident Albert Sidney Johnston.

Among his other friends was William Jefferson Kyle. In 1849, when gold fever swept America, Terry and Kyle joined a wagon train headed from Austin to California. Along the way, the men fought with Indians. While in California, Terry and Kyle found gold. The two returned to Texas in 1852 and purchased Oakland Plantation in Fort Bend County. Terry then changed the name to Sugar Land and began enlarging and modernizing the sugar plantation there. The two men had a vision for the Fort Bend area. Modernizations included negotiating with Sidney Sherman and William Marsh Rice to bring the railroad right in front of the sugar mill. They also enlarged local roads and made the river more navigable. In a few years the plantation covered 8,000 acres, and Terry was considered one of the richest men in the state.

Eventually, Terry married Mary Bingham, the daughter of Sir Francis Bingham, one of Stephen F. Austin's original 300 settlers. Terry and his wife built a two-story brick home on Oyster Creek in what is now the Covington Woods subdivision. It was here that he and his wife entertained local notoriety with horse races, dancing, and hunting. Their home became the social center of Fort Bend County. While in Fort Bend County, he became close friends with John Austin Wharton.

Frank Terry loved freedom and was prepared to fight for it.

When talk occurred of Mexican nationals pushing Americans from the Rio Grande to the Nueces River, Terry joined in the efforts to round up the Mexican bandit Juan Cortina. In the Cortina War, he fought alongside his friend Wharton, "Rip" Ford, and Robert E. Lee. Cortina was eventually chased across the border into Mexico and successfully contained there.

Freedom was threatened once again in the fall of 1860. Special interest groups consisting of Communists, women's rights advocates, and abolitionists succeeded in getting their candidate, Abraham Lincoln, elected president, despite not having a majority of the votes. Citizens all over the state held countywide meetings to consider their next course of action: secession. Frank Terry was elected as Fort Bend County's delegate to the secessionist convention. Frank loved freedom, and secession was the only way to preserve it.

In February 1861, at the secession convention, he adamantly supported the secession proposal. It was on the way home in the stagecoach, with his friends Wharton and Thomas S. Lubbock, that they decided to raise a cavalry regiment. By the end of the month, Terry was in the thick of the action, being part of an expedition headed by Ford to secure Fort Brown on the Rio Grande River.

In April, after events at Fort Sumpter, Terry and his friends hurried to Montgomery, Alabama, seeking permission to raise troops from Texas. They were denied. They met this denial with determination. Their determination paid off, finally securing positions on Gen. James Longstreet's staff as volunteer aides and scouts.

During the Battle of Manassas, Terry distinguished himself by shooting down the Union flag from the Fairfax Courthouse. The flag was presented to Longstreet, and then given to Gen. P.G.T. Beauregard. The event so impressed the War Department that Terry and his friends were given authorization to recruit a cavalry regiment.

Upon returning to Texas, recruiting captains were selected and volunteers poured in to join the regiment. I am proud to say, my great-great-grandfather was one of those volunteers. Twenty-one days after the call went out, the regiment was full, and sworn into service. On his way to mustering, Frank donned his new uniform and his uncle's sword. The sword was used in the Battle of New Orleans against the British, and at the Battle of San Jacinto against the tyrant Santa Anna. It was now called upon against the tyrant Abraham Lincoln and his imperial troops. He proceeded telling all of his slaves goodbye. As he was getting ready to go, a nanny ran up carrying his young son who was crying for his father. That was the last time the son saw his father alive.

Upon reaching New Orleans, his friend Gen. Albert Sidney Johnston sent word that the regiment was needed in Kentucky. Terry and the regiment changed their plans and went to Kentucky. Once there, his men, in true democratic style, elected Terry as their colonel. This regiment eventually became known as Terry's Texas Rangers.

On one of their earliest missions, on December 17, they were scouting along Green River near Woodsonville, Kentucky. Confederate General Hindman was called away, and he delegated command of all the Confederate forces in the area to Terry. Terry was told to decoy the enemy into attacking the Confederate positions. The decoy worked, and the Federals attacked. Once the Federals began attacking, Terry ordered his men to charge, emphasizing this with an oath. In leading his men in the charge, the forty-year-old Terry was mortally wounded.

Upon hearing of his master's death, Terry's slave became belligerent and sought to arm himself and avenge his master's death. Several Rangers then had to restrain the slave. Ranger Tom Downey claims that there was a large reward offered for Terry's body and that several men were killed fighting over his body in the battlefield.

From the fields of Woodsonville, the body was taken to Cave City, then to Nashville, Tennessee. There, the State Legislature adjourned for two days to pay respects. Respects were also paid in New Orleans, before his final return to Texas. Upon hearing of Terry's death, the Senate Chamber was draped in black, and state senators wore mourning badges for the next thirty days. Once in Texas, he was buried at his plantation.

His regiment did honor to his name by distinguishing themselves in over 100 engagements, including Shiloh,

Perryville, Chickamauga, Murfreesboro, the Atlanta campaign, and Bentonville.

In 1880, after a remembrance ceremony led by Ranger Gustave Cooke, his body was moved to its present location here at Glenwood. The State of Texas honored him by naming a county in northwest Texas and a high school after him.

Who is B.F. Terry? A true hero and model for our youth, rising from being a parentless child to one of the richest men in the state— without government schools or federal aid.

Who is B.F. Terry? A man who gave his blood, treasure and sacred honor in the righteous cause of free people choosing their own government.

Who is B.F. Terry? A visionary, entrepreneur, friend, and patriot who gave his life for his country and the freedom of its people.

Regimental Roster

Roster of members of Eighth Texas Cavalry, CSA (Terry's Texas Rangers). The roster contains the place of birth and county of residence where known.

REGIMENTAL STAFF

Benjamin F. Terry
b. KY; Ft. Bend Co.

Thomas S. Lubbock
b. SC; Harris Co.

Thomas Harrison
b. MS; Waco

Martin H. Royston
Galveston Co.

Benjamin H. Botts
b. MS; Houston

Robert H. Simmons
b. MS; Gonzales

John McQuinney Weston
b. AL; Ft. Bend Co.

R. E. Hill
b. AL; Bastrop Co.

William B. Sayers
b. MS; Gonzales Co.

M.F. de Bagligethy
b. Hungary; Houston

James Edmonson
b. MS; Brazoria

Thomas J. Potts
b. England, Bastrop Co.

Robert F. Bunting

COMPANY A

Thomas Harrison
b. MS; Waco

Rufus Y. King
Burleson Co.

William H. Jones
b. AL; Falls Co.

Marcus L. Gordon
b. GA; Bosque Co.

T. C. Freeman
b. KY; Bell Co.

Dan Neil
Bosque Co.

Charles F. Reavill
Burleson Co.

Jack Randal
Bosque Co.

Edward H. Ross
Milam Co.

Thomas A. Porter
Burleson Co.

A. Arundle
Burleson Co.

Charles A. Allday
b. GA; Burleson Co.

James M. Allen
Falls Co.

R.C. Arendel
Washington Co.

W. B. Arendel
Burleson Co.

Bryant Aycock
Burleson Co.

John Aycock
Falls Co.

A.C.A. Baker
b. KY; Washington Co.

149

C.F. Baker
Washington Co.

Preston Calvert Baker
b. KY; Washington Co.

S.M. Baker
b. KY; Washington Co.

J. William Baldridge
Milam Co.

Gabe B. Beaumont

Rufus M. Beavers
Coryell Co.

Walter Bennett

L.S. Bowen

J.F. Brown

Joseph W. Brown
b. GA; Falls Co.

Thomas W. Cade
Burleson Co.

W.A. Callaway
Baton Rouge

John C. Capehart
Falls Co.

Thomas W. Carson
b. NC; Coryell Co.

W.G. Carson

J.J. Carter

Elijah F. Davidson
b. MS; Falls Co.

John Davidson

B.F. Denton
Falls Co.

W.N. Dobbs

L.D. Douglass
Grimes Co.

Thomas Jeff Dubose
b. AL; Burleson Co.

Robert Elgin
Washington Co.

W.H. Evans
Falls Co.

James Foak
Falls Co.

William A. Gill

W.C. Glasco

D.M. Gordon
Milam Co.

W.H.H. Gordon
b. TN; Burleson Co.

A.M. Gott
b. IL; Falls Co.

Sam S. Gott
b. IL; Falls Co.

Daniel W. Graham
Bell Co.

R. Grantham

Robert W. Gray

D.J. Greech
Panola Co.

Henry Gregg
Burleson Co.

D. Grouthouse
Milam Co.

John A. Hanna
b. AR; Bosque Co.

William Harmon

J. Harris

Richard H. Holdsworth
Milam Co.

B.D. Holland
Panola Co.

David Hooks

Josiah Jackson
b. NC; Brazos Co.

B.R. Johnson
Milam Co.

D.C. Jones
b. TN; Burleson Co.

H.H. Jones
b. TN; Burleson Co.

James N. Jones
Montgomery Co.

M. Jones
b. TN

John H. Keen
b. TN; Bosque Co.

John T. Kelly
b. Ireland; Burleson Co.

L.C. King
Burleson Co.

H. C. Kingsbury
b. GA; Erath Co.

A.W. Kirk
Washington Co.

B.B. Lacy
Panola Co.

John M. Lane
b. TN; Burleson Co.

James Langan
b. Ireland; KY

George Laxson
Bell Co.

Daniel Lindermann

Thomas D. Lineard
McLennan Co.

John C. Lowe
Erath Co.

Robert H. McCann

Peter L. Martin
Burleson Co.

Walter B. Martin
Burleson Co.

Albert Medford
Bosque Co.

A.C. Mims

J. Thomas Mitchell
Milam Co.

M.M. Moake
b. TN; Burleson Co.

Daniel P. Moser
Burleson Co.

John S. Moser
Burleson Co.

R.H. Mumford
Milam Co.

Charles W. Nash

William Nash

C.W. Neel
Burleson Co.

Thomas R. Owens
Washington Co.

S. H. Pate
Rusk Co.

Charles B. Pearre
McLennan Co.

Charles M. Pearre
McLennan Co.

A.V.B. Pierson

John H. Pierson
b. KY; Falls Co.

J.B. Pool
Falls Co.

M.H. Porter
b. TN; Burleson Co.

G.W. Price

Thomas J. Pruett
Falls Co.

G.W. Randal
Bosque Co.

John T. Randal
Washington Co.

James J. Rawles

Gaston Rayner
Comanche Co.

James T. B. Richards
Milam Co.

Samuel L. Richards
Milam Co.

W. C. D. Richards
Milam Co.

William F. Richards

James F. Roberts

A.R. Robinson
Falls Co.

C.W. Rogers

J.F. Rogers

Pat H. Rogers
b. AL

Lafayette Roselle

Routt
Washington Co.

Thomas D. Sanders
Burleson Co.

Jobe Simmons

A.T. Skinner
Bosque Co.

Wiley Smith
Washington Co.

Frank Smoker

James F. Stewart
Milam Co.

S.A. Stiles
Harris Co.

James Stoneham
Grimes Co.

Albert Stoneham
Grimes Co.

A.A. Stovall
Burleson Co.

D.B. Suddeth

S.G. Sypert

James K. Terry

D.G. Thompson
Falls Co.

J. William Thompson
Washington Co.

J.H. Todd
McLennan Co.

Lawson Turner

Miles S. Turner
b. AL; Robinson Co.

G.B.W. Vaughn
Milam Co.

John H. Wallace
Brenham, TX

John Walter

A.J. Weaver

John Williams

A.A. Winston
Burleson Co.

W.H. Wood
Nashville

COMPANY B

John Austin Wharton
Brazoria Co.

George W. McNeel
Brazoria Co.

William Henry Sharp
Brazoria Co.

Theo. J. Bennet
Brazoria Co.

J.C. Herndon
Brazoria Co.

William W. Groce
Austin Co.

C.J. Gautier
Brazoria Co.

William W. Nance
Matagorda Co.

E.A. Hearndon
Harris Co.

Jule W. Manor
Brazoria Co.

William B. Maxey
Brazoria Co.

Sam Mims
Brazoria Co.

Isaac Dunbar Affleck
Washington Co.

W. H. Aldrich
b. Columbia, TX;
Brazoria Co.

P. Archer
Brazoria Co.

J.C. Ashcom
Brazoria Co.

Rowland A. Allen
Harris Co.

R. Gaston Ashe
Harris Co.

Samuel S. Ashe
Harris Co.

William L. Ashe
Harris Co.

E.J. Baker

T.J. Barker
Houston Co.

Green A. Ballinger
Brazoria Co.

Joseph S. Bates
Brazoria Co.

Joseph L. Baughn
Calhoun Co.

Ben M. Bennett
b. TN; Austin Co.

Charles S. Bennett
Brazoria Co.

J. M. Bowen

Henry C. Bradbury
Calhoun Co.

James L. Bradshaw
Wharton Co.

William J. Bridges
Brazoria Co.

Robert Bruce
Brazoria Co.

J. Terry Bryan
Brazoria Co.

Sam A. Bryan
Brazoria Co.

S. F. A. Bryan
Brazoria Co.

J.P. Burkhart
Matagorda Co.

John H. Burney
Brazoria Co.

Robert A. Burney
Brazoria Co.

W.K. Burney
Brazoria Co.

James Bush
Brazoria Co.

E.M. Bussey
Brazoria Co.

William J. Bussey
Brazoria Co.

Robert Campbell
Lavaca Co.

W.W. Cannon
Brazoria Co.

Ed Chambers
Austin Co.

A.G. Champion
Brazoria Co.

Richmond Champion

Tom Champion
Brazoria Co.

K.K. Chatham
Austin Co.

R.W. Chatham

George Cheesman
Matagorda Co.

W.P. Churchill
Brazoria Co.

C.H. Cleveland

William D. Cleveland
Austin Co.

John D. Cocheran
Austin Co.

George M. Collingworth
Matagorda Co.

J.L. Compton
Washington Co.

C.O. Cossay
Austin Co.

J. M. Crain
Calhoun Co.

T. F. Crain
Calhoun Co.

A.S. Crisp
b. MS; Colorado Co.

Richard C. Crisp
Colorado Co.

Samuel S. Crisp
Colorado Co.

William Cuiston
Brazoria Co.

H.T. Curiton

Robert H. Curiton
Brazoria Co.

B.H. Davis
Brazos Co.

Joseph J. Davis

N.B. Davis
Brazos Co.

W.P. Dever
Washington Co.

John T. Dial
Brazoria Co.

James William Duncan
Brazoria Co.

W.W. Eckols
Burleson Co.

F.C. Edney
Washington Co.

G.H. Edwards
Washington Co.

John Eisle
Brazoria Co.

John B. Estes
Brazoria Co.

T.J. Estes
Brazoria Co.

William Fleming
Guadalupe Co.

Henry O. Flourney
Brazoria Co.

A. Frank
Austin Co.

Isaac Fulkerson
Washington Co.

James David Freeman
b. AL; Ft. Bend Co.

Henry A. Garland
Brazoria Co.

R.F. Garnett
Brazoria Co.

J.M. Gates
Brazoria Co.

Ramon Garza
San Antonio

S. Gillaspie
Burleson Co.

A. S. Gillett
Walker Co.

S. Girard
Brazoria Co.

Henry W. Graber
b. Germany; Hempstead

Jared E. Groce
Austin Co.

T. Groce
Austin Co.

J.W. Gullick
Washington Co.

W. S. Gwinn

James Hagerman
Harris Co.

John C. Haines
Titus Co.

A.F. Hammond

Willie B. Hardee

D. Hardeman
Matagorda Co.

J. W. Harper
Austin Co.

A.J. Harris
Washington Co.

J. Coffee Harris
Washington Co.

D. Harris

Joe P. Harris
Colorado Co.

M.A. Harvey
Austin Co.

Amos Haynes
Calhoun Co.

Arthur Haynes
Calhoun Co.

C. Haynes
Calhoun Co.

H. Haynes
Washington Co.

C.W. Hearndon

W.R. Hendricks
Austin Co.

T.A. Hicks
TN

John W. Hill
Brazoria Co.

A.R. Howell
Brazoria Co.

John S. Hubbard
Lavaca Co.

G.C. Hungerford
Uniontown, AL

J.C. Hungerford
AL

J.P. Hutchinson
Calhoun Co.

Ike Hutchinson

Thomas M. Jack
Galveston

John C. Jackson
b. SC; Brazoria Co.

Andrew Jackson
Brazoria Co.

William R. Jefferson
Austin Co.

A.C. Jones
Matagorda Co.

J.T. Joyce
Austin Co.

T.H. Kent
Travis Co.

Tom King
Murfreesboro, TN

Louie LeGercie
Calhoun Co.

T.J. Levine
Harris Co.

C.B. Lewis
Washington Co.

Joseph Lewis
Burleson Co.

I.E. Lipscomb
Washington Co.

William Little
Washington Co.

Antonio Lopez
San Antonio

S. C. McBroom
Wharton Co.

J. D. McCann
Austin Co.

A. McDonald
Harris Co.

John McIver
TN

R.M. McKay
Harris Co.

J.A. McKenzie
b. KY; Brazoria Co.

Caynean McLeod
Galveston

Benjamin McNeal
Brazoria Co.

J.G. McNeal
Brazoria Co.

L.H. McNeal

Pleasant D. McNeel
Brazoria Co.

E.N. McNeil

Leander McNeill
Brazoria Co.

Dan McPhail
Washington Co.

Henry Madideu
b. AL; Brazoria Co.

W. P. Massenburg
Brazoria Co.

C.F. Maxey
Walker Co.

F.C. Maxey

G.F. Maxey

William B. Maxey

D. Mims

N. Monks
Austin Co.

E.R. Moore
Brazoria Co.

C.A. Morgan
Washington Co.

Ruben Morris
Austin Co.

Eugene D. Munger
Austin Co.

I.H. Muse
Washington Co.

W. S. Oldham
Washington Co.

J.M. Onins
Washington Co.

James Patterson
TN

A. Pennington
Washington Co.

Virgil H. Phelps
Brazoria Co.

J. B. Picket
Brazoria Co.

Ben C. Polk
Leon Co.

T.S. Reneau
Austin Co.

F.Y. Rhoades
Washington Co.

Jesse Rice
Austin Co.

Mat G. Roberts
b. AL; Brazoria Co.

Vick W. Rogers
Harris Co.

C.C. Rosie

A.J. Royel

J.D. Rugeley
Matagorda Co.

Robert Rugeley
Matagorda Co.

William Fort Smith
Brazoria Co.

William L. Springfield
Austin Co.

A.G. Stansbury
Austin Co.

James M. Staten
b. NC; Brazoria Co.

Ire Stewart

Joe A. Stewart
Austin Co.

Joseph S. Stewart

William S. Stewart
Washington Co.

Joe Stuart

Mat Talbott
Matagorda Co.

E.R. Terrell
Harris Co.

E.B. Thomas
Galveston

Elijah Thomas

Elisha Thomas
Galveston

Theo K. Thompson
Galveston

Samuel Tillery
b. NC; Washington Co.

O. Tilghman
Austin Co.

J.A. Trumbull
Washington Co.

James M. Tucker
Washington Co.

John B. Tucker

Joseph L. Walker
Matagorda Co.

William Ward
Brazoria Co.

W. R. Webb
Austin Co.

Ben F. Weems
Brazoria Co.

J. King White
b. GA; Austin Co.

J. K. White

John W. Wiggins
Matagorda Co.

Irwin G. Wilson
Brazoria Co.

Samuel Woodburn
Burleson Co.

Joseph Yearby
Brazoria Co.

COMPANY C

Marcus L. Evans
Gonzales Co.

Alexander M. Shannon
Karnes Co.

James M. Dunn
b. AL; Karnes Co.

John W. Baylor
Karnes Co.

Benjamin F. Batchelor
Gonzales Co.

E.S. Alley
Fayette Co.

R.A. Byler
b. AL; Gonzales Co.

Daniel L. Russell
Fayette Co.

Tom J. Oliver
b. TN; Limestone Co.

Isaac T. Lane
b. AL; Gonzales Co.

A.D. Walker
Gonzales Co.

G.G. Kibbe
Bee Co.

John McDonald

B.F. Burriss
Karnes Co.

F.M. Adams

W.S.J. Adams
Dallas Co.

George W. Archer
Limestone Co.

John L. Aycock
b. GA; Falls Co.

James Baker
Ft. Bliss, TX

James A. Baker
Gonzales Co.

L.H. Barlow
Dallas Co.

James E. Bartlett
Gonzales Co.

V.A. Bond
b. AL; Limestone Co.

J.R. Brooks

R.W. Brooks
b. KY; Limestone Co.

W.R. Brooks
b. TN; Limestone Co.

A.P. Burnham
Gonzales Co.

Thomas S. Burney
b. AL; Limestone Co.

G.F. Byerly

W.T. Campbell
Fayette Co.

L. John Carlton
Karnes Co.

Jacob Chesney
Gonzales Co.

C. Davis

Isham Davis
Karnes Co.

J.B. Davis
Williamson Co.

W.H. Dromgoole
b. MS; Karnes Co.

A.W. Dunn
b. AL; Karnes Co.

H.F. Dunn
Karnes Co.

H.V. Dunn
b. AL; Karnes Co.

G.L. Eslinger
Fayette Co.

Dr. A.D. Evans
b. AL; Gonzales Co.

Henry Clay Evans
Gonzales Co.

John Ferguson

W.H.H. Forrester
Gonzales Co.

Samuel Garrett
Ft. Bliss Co.

J.H. Glasco
Fayette Co.

W.F. Glasco
Fayette Co.

N.W. Grant
b. VA; Limestone Co.

Phil P. Hale
b. AR; Fayette Co.

W.N. Hodge
Fayette Co.

John Holloway

N. Holt
b. TN; Limestone Co.

J.C. Johnson
Fayette Co.

P.L. Kendall
b. TN

G.B. Kennedy
b. TN; Limestone Co.

Felix G. Kennedy
b. TN; Limestone Co.

J.P. Kennedy

J.C. Kirkner
Ft. Bliss

John Lattimer
Gonzales Co.

Michael Lomax
b. MO; Gonzales Co.

C.W. Love
Limestone Co.

S.M. Lowrie
Karnes Co.

J.M. Lynch
Limestone Co.

W.A. Lynch
Limestone Co.

J.M. McCallom
Bee Co.

James McGill
Washington Co.

M. Y. McGuyre
Bee Co.

Charles H.C. Maigne
Colorado Co.

J.R. Mangham

J.M. Mangum
Gonzales Co.

D. E. Miller

J.W. Moore
Karnes Co.

W.T. Moore
Bee Co.

A.L. O'Neal

M.H. O'Neal
Limestone Co.

William Owens, Sr.
Limestone Co.

William M. Owens, Jr.
Limestone Co.

J.D. Pace
Karnes Co.

R.W. Parham

Bulger Peeples
Limestone Co.

William M. Perry
Limestone Co.

E.J. Pitts
Gonzales Co.

D. Pope

G.W. Posey
Limestone Co.

Uriah Posey
Limestone Co.

J.C. Pybas
Franklin, AL

Henry Rennick
b. KY; Ft. Bliss, TX

J.M. Rogers
Limestone Co.

Thomas G. Sanders
Washington Co.

R. Scarborough
Gonzales Co.

Sol. K. Scruggs
b. AL; Limestone Co.

W. H. Shannon
Karnes Co.

W. H. Sikes
b. AL

W.M. Slaughter
Ft. Griffin

J. M. Stinnard
b. VA; Colorado Co.

C.K. Stribling
Ft. Griffin

George E. Stubblefield
Austin Co.

E. Taiff
b. South Wales;
 Colorado Co.

E. C. Tatum
Bee Co.

J. E. Thornton
Limestone Co.

George Hugh Turner

Gus Walker

J.B. Webb

John G. Wheeler
b. AL

Terry W. Wylie
Limestone Co.

G. W. Williams
Goliad Co.

John E. Wilson

Walter S. Wood
Limestone Co.

James B. Woodley
Lavaca Co.

M.V. Wright
Bee Co.

COMPANY D

Steven C. Ferrell
b. AL; Bastrop Co.

Charles Leroy Morgan
Bastrop Co.

J.F. Burditt
b. TN; Travis Co.

William R. Doak
b. MS; Burleson Co.

George M. Decherd
b. TN; Bastrop Co.

R. T. Hill
Washington Co.

J. Milam Duty
Travis Co.

John H. Morgan
b. TN; Bastrop Co.

J. B. Cowan
b. VA; Bastrop Co.

George Bacon Burke
b. MD; Bastrop Co.

Ed Harris
b. MS; Bastrop Co.

J. H. Cheshier
b. NC; Bastrop Co.

Samuel W. Green
b. AL; Bastrop Co.

W. A. Allbright
b. TN; Bastrop Co.

George R. Allen
Bastrop Co.

Hugh E. Allen
b. TN; Bastrop Co.

N.J. Allen
b. TN; Bastrop Co.

C. P. Autrey
b. TN; Bastrop Co.

Thomas B. Banks
Travis Co.

W. W. Beall
Bastrop Co.

J.P. Billingsley
b. TN; Bastrop Co.

Elisha W. Black
Bastrop Co.

William R. Black
b. MS; Houston

Richard Burger
Travis Co.

Fenton A. Bott
b. MS; Travis Co.

B. L. Bludworth

James M. Brannan
Weberville, TX

James H. Bunton
Bastrop Co.

Joel D. Bunton
Bastrop Co.

Aaron J. Burleson
b. Bastrop Co.; Travis Co.

Jeff W. Burleson
Travis Co.

W. H. Caldwell
Bastrop Co.

C. G. Caldwell
Bastrop Co.

J.B. Campbell
b. TN; Bastrop Co.

G. W. Camper

Volney Catron
b. VA; San Antonio

John M. Claiborne

David S. Combs
b. AL; Hayes Co.

James W. Connor
b. AL; Bastrop Co.

Felix H. Corbell
b. AL; Caldwell Co.

John F. Creain
b. OH; Bastrop Co.

J. Davidson
Travis Co.

W. R. Davis
Travis Co.

J.J. Doak

E.S. Dodd
b. KY; Travis Co.

D.A. Dotey
b. AL; Bastrop Co.

Joseph R. Ford
Travis Co.

Sigman (Sam)
  Friedberger
b. Europe; Bastrop Co.

John A. Gage
Bastrop Co.

Jesse L. Garth
b. VA; Bastrop Co.

James H. Gault
b. TN; Bastrop Co.

L.B. Giles
b. TN; Travis Co.

L.L. Giles
b. TN; Travis Co.

Thomas A. Gill
b. TN; Bastrop Co.

Perry Green
b. GA; Burleson Co.

Wayne Hamilton
Travis Co.

Joseph Harris

G.R. Harrison

Thomas Hart
Travis Co.

John R. Henry
Travis Co.

D. O. Hill
Bastrop Co.

E. D. Hill
Bastrop Co.

F.M. Hill
Travis Co.

John W. Hill
b. AL; Travis Co.

R.E. Hill
b. AL; Bastrop Co.

T.A.W. Hill
b. AL; Travis Co.

R.R. Holton

E.R. Hopper
b. TN; Bastrop Co.

Isaac V. Jones
Travis Co.

John C. Judson

Ed R. Kennedy
b. MS; Bastrop Co.

Peyton R. Kennedy
b. AL; Bastrop Co.

A.J. Kyle
Hayes Co.

Curran Kyle
b. MS; Hayes Co.

Fergus Kyle
Hayes Co.

P.R. Kyle
Hayes Co.

William Kyle
b. MS; Hayes Co.

L. Lasher

Robert M. Lewis
Bastrop Co.

Frank Loften
b. NC; Bastrop Co.

Alonzo T. Logan
Travis Co.

N.H. Lovell
Hayes Co.

James McArthur
Travis Co.

M. G. McCannon

Charles McGehee
Hayes Co.

George T. McGehee
Hayes Co.

John G. McGehee

F.W. McGuire
b. AL; Washington Co.

James F. McGuire
b. AL; Washington Co.

George Beardy Miller
b. KY; Burleson Co.

Jefferson J. Miller
b. AR; Travis Co.

Woods S. Miller
b. TN; Bastrop Co.

William C. Moore
b. TN; Burleson Co.

J. Milt Morin
b. MS; Burleson Co.

P.M. Mullin
Burleson Co.

J. W. Neely
b. KY; Bastrop Co.

James Nicholson
b. England; Bastrop Co.

William Nicholson
b. NY; Bastrop Co.

James T. Nolen
b. TN; Bastrop Co.

D.D. Nunn
b. GA; Bastrop Co.

Charles Pelham
b. AR; Travis Co.

Thomas G. Peterson
b. MS; Bastrop Co.

James C. Pickle
b. VA; Travis Co.

H.B. (Sam) Piper
Travis Co.

T.B. Poe
Travis Co.

Thomas J. Potts
b. England; Bastrop Co.

John B. Rector
b. AL; Bastrop Co.

Kenner K. Rector
b. AL; Bastrop Co.

T. Mason Rector
b. AL; Bastrop Co.

W.P. Rice
b. VA; Bastrop Co.

William H. Roberts
b. VA; Bastrop Co.

Joe B. Rogers
Travis Co.

Jesse B. Rowe
Travis Co.

Jo M. Royston
b. TN; Bastrop Co.

Richard C. Royston
b. TN; Bastrop Co.

Roland Rucker
Travis Co.

W. T. Rucker

William B. Sayers
b. MS; Bastrop Co.

G. Schmeltzer
San Antonio

Samuel H. Screws
Bastrop Co.

Oliver H. Shipp

Robert H. Shipp
b. MS; Bastrop Co.

J.W. Sims

William Tarrant Sims
Bastrop Co.

Reuben Slaughter
b. MS; Caldwell Co.

D.P. Smith
Bastrop Co.

M.A. Smith
Bastrop Co.

William Cicero Smith
Bastrop Co.

W. A. Standifer
Bastrop Co.

A.K. Stewart
Burleson Co.

Charles W. Stone
Travis Co.

Reuben Stroud
b. SC; Bastrop Co.

J. V. Sutton

Thomas J. Taylor
b. GA; Bastrop Co.

M. E. Thomas
b. VA; Austin

M.H. Thomas
b. AL; Burleson Co.

Thomas J. Vardin
b. TN; Bastrop Co.

Felix Vaughn
b. LA; Bastrop Co.

Carroll Walton
b. MS; Bastrop Co.

John H. Washington
Travis Co.

Paul J. Watkins
b. AL; Hayes Co.

Sam M. Watkins
b. AL; Hayes Co.

W. Walker Wheeler
Austin Co.

Jerry C. Wilkins
b. KY; Bastrop Co.

J.S. Wynn
b. GA; Burleson Co.

James Joseph Young
b. NC; Bastrop Co.

George B. Zimpelman
b. Europe; Austin

COMPANY E

Leander M. Rayburn
b. MS; Gonzales Co.

William L. Foster
Gonzales Co.

H. E. Storey
Gonzales Co.

Phil A. Coe
Gonzales Co.

Mark A. Hunter
Gonzales Co.

Thomas B. Key
Gonzales Co.

C.C. Littlefield
Gonzales Co.

C.E. Littlefield
Gonzales Co.

William W. Wells
Gonzales Co.

J.T. Bratton
De Witt Co.

James M. Hunt
Gonzales Co.

J.P. Caldwell
De Witt Co.

John G. Pipkin

G.D. Mitchell
Gonzales Co.

Dr. Charles Spath
Gonzales Co.

A.T. Ardry
De Witt Co.

Nathan Arms
De Witt Co.

H. C. Alley
Gonzales Co.

A.A. Amonett
Gonzales Co.

B.E. Anderson
Gonzales Co.

J.A. Barnett
Gonzales Co.

William Augustine
DeWitt Co.

George W. Baker
Gonzales Co.

W.H. Baldwin
Gonzales Co.

J.P. Barnett
Gonzales Co.

W.L. Barnett
Gonzales Co.

D.B.F. Bird

John Bratten
Gonzales Co.

A.T. Brown
Gonzales Co.

E.G. Bigelow

O.H.F. Boren

James A. Brace
DeWitt Co.

A.P. Browning
DeWitt Co.

John M. Brownson
Gonzales Co.

T.J. Brownson
DeWitt Co.

G.H. Bruce
b. VT; Gonzales Co.

S.R. Bruce
b. VT; Gonzales Co.

Samuel D. Calhoun
DeWitt Co.

John G. Callison
DeWitt Co.

Hayes A. Carson
DeWitt Co.

R.H. Carson
Gonzales Co.

J.P. Caldwell
Gonzales Co.

Mike Cassady
b. Ireland; DeWitt Co.

D. G. Castings

W.H. Chapline
b. VA; DeWitt Co.

Stephen Chenault
Gonzales Co.

Aaron Compton
DeWitt Co.

N. Contraras
b. Mexico; DeWitt Co.

P.H. Coe
Gonzales Co.

J.J. Coulter
b. MS; DeWitt Co.

George W. Cuppett
b. MS; Gonzales Co.

F. M. Clairy
Gonzales Co.

Robert S. Davis
Gonzales Co.

William M. Davis
DeWitt Co.

W.F. Dickey
DeWitt Co.

A.J. Duren
DeWitt Co.

J.F. Ernest

William H. Fisher
DeWitt Co.

Thomas Ellis
Gonzales Co.

B.J. Denmark
Gonzales Co.

William Andrew Fletcher

C.C. Floyd
b. SC

Robert H. Floyd
DeWitt Co.

William F. Floyd
DeWitt Co.

G.W. Fogg

William R. Friend

J.L.W.D. Gibson

W.L. Giddens

R.L. Gill

William A. Gill

Perry Grice

J.C. Grady
Gonzales Co.

W.P. Gwynn

M.D.L. Hairgrove

David J. Hall

J.M. Hall

H. Hampton

J.T. Hayes

E.T. Hendley

Thomas B. Hill

W.P. Hull

F.M. Hunt
b. GA

J.M. Hunter
Gonzales Co.

N.B. Key

James P. King

J.M. Kirkland
Gonzales Co.

John W. Littlefield

Robert Littlefield

William Washington Lock

Emmett Lynch

J.W. Lemmond

C.M. Lemmond

Jason W. Ivy

W.S. Lowry

A.H. McClure

C.M. McGarrity

John W. McGarrity

W.P. McGarrity

W.T. Mahan

G.H.G. May

Joseph Metze
b. Prussia

Nick Mitchell

S.S. Morris

James T. Mathieu

A.O. May

Morris May

F. Morrison

W.S. McAda

A.K. Neal
b. TN

Richard Newsom

J.T. Nixon

Ferd Noelke

William J. Nash

E.M. Patterson

D.C. Price
Gonzales Co.

J.T. Price

J.H. Ranft

Thomas S. Richie

A.H. Robertson

J.B. Roberts

A.H. Sample
b. AL

J.M. Sample

Thomas S. Sanson
Guadalupe Co.

M. B. L. Schrier

Charles M. Sherman
DeWitt Co.

D.B. Shuler

George W. Shuler

Glen W. Shuler

H.E. Shuler

Joab Shuler

W.A. Smith

Munroe Sullivan

Johnson Squirrel

J.F. Stockton

H.C. Thomas

H.M. Trammell

R.E. Trammell

M.H. Talley

Robert M. Wallace

L.T. Ward

R.Mc. Ware

J.M. Wheat

G.A. White

James K. White

William Wilson

L.C. Wright

T.J. Wingate

G.A.W. Wright

John P. York

COMPANY F

Louis M. Strobel
Fort Bend Co.

William R. Jarmon
b. TN; Fayette Co.

Phocion Pate
Fayette Co.

William N. Tate
Fayette Co.

A.J. Murray
b. SC; Fayette Co.

Volney F. Cook
b. KY; Fayette Co.

C.D. Barnett
Fayette Co.

J.T.J. Culpepper
Lavaca Co.

A.G. Ledbetter
Fayette Co.

Burr E. Joiner
Fayette Co.

L. Watson
b. SC; Lavaca Co.

J.W. Rabb
Fayette Co.

O.W. Alexander
Fayette Co.

J.B. Allen
b. TN

S.L. Anderson
Fayette Co.

J.H. Andrews
Colorado Co.

P.H. Arnold
Lavaca Co.

A.M. Beall
Lavaca Co.

Theo C. Bennette
Fayette Co.

J.K. Polk Blackburn
Lavaca Co.

Robert Bracey
Austin Co.

Henry Brown
Fayette Co.

Benjamin F. Burke
Fayette Co.

H.G. Burton
Fayette Co.

J.E. Carlton
Colorado Co.

G.L. Chandler
Fayette Co.

N.P. Cheatham
b. KY; Fayette Co.

G.G. Clark
Colorado Co.

James A. Cook
b. AL; Fayette Co.

W.H. Coffman
Burleson Co.

D.P. Craft
Fayette Co.

L.K. Crockett
Fayette Co.

R.R. Crockett
b. AL; Fayette Co.

R.A. Dandridge

Samuel B. DeHart
Colorado Co.

Charles Dirr
Fayette Co.

Samuel C. Drake
Colorado Co.

William E. Drisdale
Fayette Co.

C.M. Dunnaway
Lavaca Co.

Ed H. Eans
Fayette Co.

William T. Fitz
Fayette Co.

J.K. Flewellyn
Lavaca Co.

L.P. Gordon
b. FL; Fayette Co.

T.J. Groce
Colorado Co.

F.A. Green
Lavaca Co.

Sam H. Grover
Fayette Co.

G.L. Gwynn
Fayette Co.

M.G. Harbour
Fayette Co.

A.P. Harcourt
b. KY; Fayette Co.

J.L. Harris
Fayette Co.

Thomas Harris

W.H. Harris
Lavaca Co.

John G. Haynie
Fayette Co.

O.E. Herbert
Colorado Co.

J.R. Hester
Colorado Co.

W.J. Hill
Fayette Co.

J.A. Holman
Fayette Co.

Nat Holman
Fayette Co.

F.F. Hooper
Austin Co.

Charles H. Howard

John P. Humphreys
Lavaca Co.

J.D. Hunt
Fayette Co.

James P. Hutchins
Fayette Co.

Charles L. Izard
Fayette Co.

R.A. Jarmon
Fayette Co.

S.L. Jarmon
Fayette Co.

J.F. Jenkins
Colorado Co.

A. Jones
Lavaca Co.

C.B. Jones
b. GA; Lavaca Co.

Redding Jones
b. AL; Jackson Co.

R.H. Jones
Lavaca Co.

Thomas B. Jones
Fayette Co.

J.C. Justice
Fayette Co.

Edward Kaylor
Lavaca Co.

R.P. Kirk
Lavaca Co.

A.Kuykendall
Lavaca Co.

B.P. Lewis
Lavaca Co.

William M. Lewis
Fayette Co.

Fritz Lindenburg
Lavaca Co.

John B. Long
Fayette Co.

R.D. McClellan
Fayette Co.

H.H. McCrary
Fayette Co.

D.A. McGonigall
b. MS; Lavaca Co.

T.G. Mercer
Fayette Co.

H.C. Middlebrook
b. MS; Lavaca Co.

J.E. Middlebrook

J.G. Middlebrook

W. H. Middlebrook
Fayette Co.

J.H. Moore
Fayette Co.

W.S. Morton
Colorado Co.

R.L. Nevill
Fayette Co.

S.B. Noble
b. SC; Lavaca Co.

William N.A. Norton
NC

F.C. Patman

A. Patton
Fayette Co.

D.C. Payne
Lavaca Co.

William M. Penn
Fayette Co.

J.T. Pettus
Colorado Co.

J.P. Phillips
Fayette Co.

A. Ponton
Lavaca Co.

James W. Pope
Fayette Co.

J.E. Priest
Fayette Co.

N.C. Rives
Fayette Co.

William B. Rives
Fayette Co.

M.H. Sanders
Fayette Co.

S.W. Scallorn
Fayette Co.

A.G. Seals
Lavaca Co.

F.C. Shipin

C.O. Simpson
Fayette Co.

W.B. Simpson
b. AL; Lavaca Co.

S.W. Slack
b. GA

O.P. Smith

J.H. Stevenson
Fayette Co.

S.A. Street
Fayette Co.

J.R. Stewart
Fayette Co.

Henry Terrill
Colorado Co.

S.C. Thigpen
Lavaca Co.

William L. Thornton
Fayette Co.

S.R. Tutwiler
b. VA; Fayette Co.

William Wallace
Fayette Co.

W. J. Ware
Lavaca Co.

B.R. Watson
b. SC; Lavaca Co.

W.T. Webb

W.S. White
Fayette Co.

T.H. Wood
Montgomery Co.

S.K. Woodward
Fayette Co.

J.W. Yarborough
Fayette Co.

COMPANY G

William Y. Houston
b. AL

William M. Ford
b. NY; Bexar Co.

Martin L. Mitchell

William Ellis
b. MO

Egbert F. Lilly

Arthur Pue

John M. Tanquary
b. VA

John B. Briscoe

Edward R. Tarver
b. MS

Thomas H. Berry
Wilson Co.

Thomas E. Drinkard
b. VA

William H. Jenkins
b. TN

J.L. Akridge

Osceola Archer
b. MD

Thomas Archer
b. MD

Louis Barho
b. Germany

Emory C. Barker
b. AL

Joseph Barker

T.H. Barrett
b. OH

John Beard
Harrison Co.

James M. Bennett
b. KY

William H. Bigelow
b. Canada

David J. Blair
b. Victoria Co.

A.H. Bogart

Joseph C. Booth

Travis Bowles
Travis Co.

Daniel A. Bradshaw

James L. Bradshaw

James T. Bradshaw

Andrew C. Buford

Robert D. Burns
b. MD

F. Lucius Campbell
b. SC

James K. Polk Childress
b. TX

Samuel T. Colman
b. KY

Jeptha H. Cotton
b. Jefferson Co.

Robert B. Cotton

Thomas A. Diviney
b. VA

James Farrell
b. Ireland

William T. Gainer
b. KY

Edward P. Gallagher

James L. Gonzales
Corman

Joseph C. Hacguin
b. AL

William Hacguin

Silas B. Harmon

Thomas Harris

David H. Houston
b. AL

Robert C. Houston
b. AL

James M. Howell
b. VA

Levi Humphreys

James W. English

Claiborne Jarmin

James P. Johnson

Albert T. Kibbie

F.M. Kiddo

Miles L. Kimball
Bosque Co.

Alverado M. Knowles

William C. Kroeger
b. Germany

Joseph C. Kuykendall
b. KY

W.C. Lillard
b. TN

William E. McAndrews
b. GA

Thomas P. McCampbell
b. TN

Charles W. Marshall
b. NY

Samuel Maverick

John Newbrand
b. MD

Darius C. Newton
b. AL

David D. Nunn

Meredith L. Ogden
b. NY

Edwin M. Phelps
b. IO

Anson K. Presnell
MA

James Pryor
b. KY

James W. Pyron
b. Franklin, AL

David Rice

Charles Rieber

Francis Rome
b. NY

Alfred K. Rosell
b. San Augustine Co.

William E. Scull

William M. Seever
b. KY

John T. Scott

William J. Shirkey
b. VA

Andrew J. Smith
b. NC

Hugh J. Smith
b. LA

John D. Smith

John M. Smith
San Antonio

William L. Smith

George Stormfelz
b. PA

Hugh L. Tally
b. GA

Benina Thomas

John A. Thomas
b. TX

John Tynan
b. Ireland

Pope Vaught

James M. Waddell
b. SC

Joseph L. Walker

Robert McE. Weir
b. KY

Charles J. Wells
b. England

James Z. Young
b. MD; El Paso Co.

COMPANY H

John T. Holt
b. MS; Fort Bend Co.

Tom S. Weston
b. AL; Fort Bend Co.

Robert Calder
Fort Bend Co.

William D. Adams
b. GA; Fort Bend Co.

Gustave Cook
b. AL; Fort Bend Co.

Robert J. Hodges
Fort Bend Co.

Jesse Thompson
b. GA; Fort Bend Co.

Johnson C. Williams
b. MS

James Edmondson
b. MS; Fort Bend Co.

Eugene Griffin
b. AL; Fort Bend Co.

Edward A. Bolines
b. MO; Fort Bend Co.

Thomas D. Barrington
b. FL; Brazoria Co.

David S. Terry
b. TX; Fort Bend Co.

Benjamin Franklin
   Adams
b. AL; Fort Bend Co.

Jack Adams
b. AL; Fort Bend Co.

Robert Grooves Adams
Robertson Co.

William H. Albertson
b. NC; Wharton Co.

W.J. Alexander

F.M. Arnold
b. AL; Fort Bend Co.

Joseph F. Asher
b. KY

Lock Wilson Atwell

Adam George Autry
b. TX; Fort Bend Co.

George Henry Bailey
b. GA; Fort Bend Co.

Ballinger

Clement Newton Bassett
b. TX; Fort Bend Co.

William Albert Bestwick
b. MO

Drury Budd Bohannan
b. AL; Fort Bend Co.

Milam Borden
b. TX; Fort Bend Co.

G.R. Brom
b. TN; Fort Bend Co.

A. Brown
Washington Co.

I.H. Brown

James H. Brown
b. TN; Fort Bend Co.

Thomas B. Brown

Edwin Bryan
Grimes Co.

Frederick Zachariah
 Buckley
b. TX; Fort Bend Co.

E.H. Byne
b. GA; Fort Bend Co.

William Henry Byne
b. GA; Fort Bend Co.

O.M. Callis
b. VA; Fort Bend Co.

Benjamin Louis Caloway
b. AL; Wharton Co.

Lemuel Luneford
 Caloway
b. AL; Wharton Co.

David H. Cook
b. Ireland; Fort Bend Co.

J.L. Cox
b. NC; Wharton Co.

G.H. Chambers
b. AL; Fort Bend Co.

Lytle Crawford
b. TX; Galveston

P.D. Crume

William Moore Darst
b. TX; Fort Bend Co.

D. G. Davis
b. TX; Fort Bend Co.

N.C. Davis
b. MS; Fort Bend Co.

Jesse Dean
b. AL; Fort Bend Co.

James Doris
b. KY; Washington Co.

Hubbard Drake

Robert A. Drane
b. GA; Wharton Co.

P. Dyre
Fort Bend Co.

Charles Henry
 Edmonson
b. DC; Wharton Co.

W.B. Ernest
b. VA

Stephen Ethetton
b. Wharton Co.

G.W. Farnsworth
Davidson Co., TN

Benjamin B. Fatheree
b. VA; Liberty Co.

John H. Ferguson
b. LA; Fort Bend Co.

A. Ferris
b. TX; Fort Bend Co.

R.C. Ferris
b. MO

David Campbell Fielder
b. TN; Wharton Co.

John Fisher
b. England;
 Fort Bend Co.

Morgan L. Fitch
b. MS

John Thomas Fowler
b. KY; Fort Bend Co.

James David Freeman
b. AL; Fort Bend Co.

William Freeman
b. AL; Fort Bend Co.

James Lewis Gallaher
b. TX; Wharton Co.

Stephen Gallaher
b. TX; Wharton Co.

E.D. Gibbon

J.B. Gibbons

Samuel B. Glasscock
b. LA; Fort Bend Co.

John Shoemaker
b. VA; Gonzales Co.

M.B. Groce
b. FL

John Washington Hall
b. KY; Washington Co.

A.W. Hart
b. LA; Fort Bend Co.

Emil Hemmon
b. Germany; Galveston

Lafayette Herbert
b. AL; Fort Bend Co.

Arthur Hirshfield
b. Germany; Galveston

John S. Hirshfield
b. Germany; Harris Co.

Mazillon Houston
b. KY

E.D. John
b. TX; Galveston

James Jones
b. TX; Fort Bend Co.

Samuel Houston Jones
b. TX; Fort Bend Co.

C. Kemp
b. LA

F.W. Kimball
b. LA; Liberty Co.

R.W. Lawson

John Samuel Leneave
b. AK; Fort Bend Co.

C. Lewinton
Freestone Co.

James Archer Lilly
b. SC; Fort Bend Co.

Neil Livingston

G.A. Lockey

James Henry Lowther
b. NC; Fort Bend Co.

Alexander D. McArthur
b. KY; Jackson Co.

Floyd Marion McCarty
b. GA; Fort Bend Co.

E.H. McDaniel
b. AL; Fort Bend Co.

William McElroy

Isaac McFarland
b. Jamaica; Fort Bend Co.

James McFarland
b. Jamaica; Fort Bend Co.

B.F. McGlone

James McKenzie
b. KY; Brazoria Co.

J.C. McKethan
b. NC; Fort Bend Co.

C.H. McMahan

G.L. McMurphy
b. GA; Galveston

John Maxmillian
Sabine Parish, LA

Joseph Maxmillian
Sabine Parish, LA

John Thornton Maxwell
b. LA; Fort Bend Co.

John Washington Miles
b. KY; Fort Bend Co.

John Francis Miller
b. IN; Fort Bend Co.

Addison Moore
b. MO; Fort Bend Co.

Charles Albert Moore
Wharton Co.

Samuel G. Moore
b. TX

John Herryman Morgan
Fort Bend Co.

N.H. Morrow
b. NC; Fort Bend Co.

W.P.A. Murray
b. MS; Colorado Co.

C.D. Nelson
b. NY

Robert G. O'Brian
b. KY; Jackson Co.

Thomas O'Brian
b. KY

M.A. Page
b. NY

John Dale Palmer
b. SC; Austin Co.

Augustus Hardy Perry
b. GA; Fort Bend Co.

Joseph Edward Perry
b. GA; Fort Bend Co.

Pendleton Rector
b. TX

William L. Rhodes
b. GA; Fort Bend Co.

William Thomas Rives
b. AL; Wharton Co.

Samuel G. Houston
Roark
b. TX; Fort Bend Co.

R.A. Roberts
Sabine Parish, LA

Elisha Tarber Robinson
b. GA; Wharton Co.

R. Robinson

John Howard Rorie
b. AL; Fort Bend Co.

Samuel Jackson B. Rorie
b. AL; Fort Bend Co.

Edward Darnaby Ryan
b. KY; Fort Bend Co.

John Ryan
b. KY; Fort Bend Co.

J.S. Seriare

William Nelson Shaw
b. TX; Fort Bend Co.

Andrew Sheahan
b. Ireland; Wharton Co.

W.H. Silliman
b. TX; Fort Bend Co.

William Barker Spencer
b. VA; Fort Bend Co.

Alexander L. Steele
b. KY; Colorado Co.

John Stewart
b. TN; Galveston

W.J. Swilley
b. AL; Liberty Co.

Harrison Tankersley
b. AL; Brazoria Co.

H. Thompson
b. TX; Fort Bend Co.

R.A. Torrance
b. NC; Fort Bend Co.

Jonathon B. Van Houten
b. IL; Harris Co.

Edward Waldert

James T. Walker
b. TX; Fort Bend Co.

W.W. Waller
b. TX; Austin Co.

James Griffin Ward
b. MD; Wharton Co.

James McQuinney
Weston
b. SC; Fort Bend Co.

Henry Clay Wiley
b. AL; Fort Bend Co.

Clarence Williams
b. Jamaica; Fort Bend Co.

COMPANY I

Isham G. Jones
Gonzales Co.

William H.A. Harris
Gonzales Co.

Augustus D. Harris
Gonzales Co.

James H. Harramore
Gonzales Co.

James S. Harris
Gonzales Co.

J.C. Dilworth
Gonzales Co.

George W. Littlefield
Gonzales Co.

Charles W. Mason
Gonzales Co.

William E. Jones
Gonzales Co.

Benjamin F. Burr
Guadalupe Co.

H.M. Norwood
Gonzales Co.

Daniel E. Holcomb
b. NC; Gonzales Co.

James D. Bunting
Gonzales Co.

L.A. L. Lampkin
Gonzales Co.

N.B. Cotton
Gonzales Co.

George R. Allen
Gonzales Co.

J.D. McClure
Gonzales Co.

K.O. Dougherty
Gonzales Co.

R.F. Bostwick
Gonzales Co.

Thomas Miller
Gonzales Co.

J.Z. Walker
Gonzales Co.

James Tuton
Gonzales Co.

Robert N.C. Tate
b. NC; Gonzales Co.

Matthew D. Anderson
b. TN; Orange Co.

Samuel Andrews
Gonzales Co.

Thomas E. Balfour
b. MS; Guadalupe Co.

William H. Baltzell
Caldwell Co.

J. T. Bankhead
Gonzales Co.

Lem Barnett
Bee Co.

B.F. Batchelor
Gonzales Co.

D.J. Blain
Gonzales Co.

J.W. Blain
Gonzales Co.

Miles Biggs
b. AL; Gonzales Co.

A.Biggs
Caldwell Co.

H.H. Bobbett
Gonzales Co.

T.E. Bolling
Gonzales Co.

Texas P. Dimnet
DeWitt Co.

Henry Donnett
Liberty Co.

James B. Duff
Gonzales Co.

C. Britton
Gonzales Co.

D.W. Broadnax
Gonzales Co.

Robert Broadnax
Gonzales Co.

William H. Broadnax
Gonzales Co.

R. Brock
Gonzales Co.

A.A. Brooks
Gonzales Co.

John Bunting
Gonzales Co.

I.E. Campbell
Gonzales Co.

S. Chenault
Gonzales Co.

M.B. Cockran
Gonzales Co.

G.J. Booth
Jackson Co.

Walter Bourke
Gonzales Co.

C.M. Bradshaw
Gonzales Co.

A.G. Branch
Gonzales Co.

B. Branch
Gonzales Co.

Frank G. Brocker
Gonzales Co.

Jess L. Bunting
Gonzales Co.

W.M. Campbell
Fayette Co.

James Carruthers
McLennan Co.

James E. Carlton
San Patricio Co.

Robert D. Carpenter
DeWitt Co.

James H. Cobb
Gonzales Co.

L.R. Cockran
San Antonio

J.J. Colter
Liberty Co.

Volney R. Cook
Gonzales Co.

J.R. Cox
Guadalupe Co.

A. Cupputt
Gonzales Co.

Henry Donnett
Liberty Co.

J. L. Dunting
Gonzales Co.

L. Durry

Robert J. Eskridge
Gonzales Co.

Solomon Dartch
Gonzales Co.

Warren Davis
Gonzales Co.

Green DeWitt
Gonzales Co.

H.C. Doyal
Gonzales Co.

William M. Evans
Gonzales Co.

J. W. Eldridge
Gonzales Co.

R.J. Eldridge
Gonzales Co.

M.L. Evans
Gonzales Co.

H.C. Evans
Gonzales Co.

D.C. Evans
Gonzales Co.

Randolph Fields
Liberty Co.

William D. Fry
Guadalupe Co.

R. Fleniken
Gonzales Co.

John Floyd
Gonzales Co.

D.C. Ford
Gonzales Co.

Charles Foster
Gonzales Co.

Bennett Frank
Gonzales Co.

A.J. Frazier
Gonzales Co.

G.W. Fritch
Gonzales Co.

R. B. George
Guadalupe Co.

Robert Gilhorn
Gonzales Co.

J.D. Gilmore
Gonzales Co.

Joseph F. Hall
Victoria

William H. Hall
DeWitt Co.

Robert B. Hardeman
San Patricio Co.

James E. Hardy
Gonzales Co.

T. Harris
Gonzales Co.

William F. Holcomb
Gonzales Co.

Thomas J. Gilmore
Gonzales Co.

George Gregston
Gonzales Co.

Eli Halfin
Gonzales Co.

W.G. Jarvis
Gonzales Co.

James C. Jones
Gonzales Co.

T.W. Jones
Gonzales Co.

L.M. Kokernot
Gonzales Co.

W.H. Kyle
Calhoun Co.

J.C. Lattimer
Gonzales Co.

William C. Lillard

C.M. McDonald
San Patricio Co.

Thomas McGuffin

H.N. McKellar

Harvey Lewis
Gonzales Co.

Evan Lovett

George Littlefield

Pete M. McKellar
b. NC

James M. McKinney

Charles Mason

A.S. Miller
Gonzales Co.

Banquelle Miller
Banquet, TX

J.F. Miller
Gonzales Co.

Joseph Miller

M.E. Miller
b. AL

S.G. Miller
San Patricio Co.

B. Frank Mooney

Samuel Moore

B.F. Mooring

E.C. Minter

James Minter

O.Z. Mitchell

John Monroe

E.A. McCorkle

John T. Nelson
Gonzales Co.

T.H. Newby
b. TN; Gonzales Co.

John L. Norwood
Gonzales Co.

Mitch Norwood
Gonzales Co.

Milam B. Polk

Robert C. Pullen
b. NC; Gonzales Co.

W. M. Needham

F. Nelson

B.F. Norman

R.H. Ray
Lavaca Co.

Ed T. Rhodes
Guadalupe Co.

V.B. Ridley
DeWitt Co.

John N. Rodgers

James Randle

J.W. Rowley

R.H. Simmons
Gonzales Co.

A. Sloneker
b. VA; Colorado Co.

L.T. Snider
DeWitt Co.

William H. Snider
DeWitt Co.

T.L. Snider
DeWitt Co.

Enoch M. Steen
Gonzales Co.

Henry Stevens

Joseph E. Stevens
Gonzales Co.

William F. Stevens

H.D. Sullivan
San Patricio Co.

P.H. Swanton
Gonzales Co.

J.W. Still

L.M. Still

J.A. Strickland

C.C. Stutling

Robert Taylor
Victoria Co.

H.H. Thigpen
Lavaca Co.

Edward T. Thorn
Gonzales Co.

T.L. Witter
Gonzales Co.

A.G. Wood
Colorado Co.

William B. Wood
b. AL; Gonzales Co.

William A. Wrae
Lavaca Co.

Robert L. Young
b. AL; Gonzales Co.

William Young
St. Martin's Parish, LA

George White

Ben Weed, Jr.

William H. West

H.G. Zumwalt

COMPANY K

John G. Walker
b. AL; Harris Co.

A.W. Morris
Montgomery Co.

W. Henry Thomas
b. Harris Co.; Harris Co.

Samuel Pat Christian
Houston

J.M. Hottell
Montgomery Co.

A.L. Baines
Washtinton Co.

E. Morris

M.F. de Bagligethy
b. Hungary; Houston

H.J. Bearfield
Washington Co.

E.S. Coleman

C.C. Newhard
b. KY;

Michael Dunn

J.D. Alexander

J.H. Alexander
Erath Co.

William H. Ballentine
Washington Co.

D.K. Bannerman
Leon Co.

A.J. Barnett

James Bates
b. AL; Montgomery Co.

W.H. Billingsley
Washington Co.

P.B. Bloodgood
Harris Co.

T.J. Borrows
Montgomery Co.

Green Bouldin
b. AL

H. Bouldin

J.L. Bowers
Washington Co.

J.W. Bowers
Washington Co.

A.B. Briscoe
Harris Co.

D.H. Browning
Washington Co.

I.C. Buckley
Harris Co.

G.P. Burke
Harris Co.

S. Carter
b. KY

P.L. Cartwright
b. TX

Noah W. Chatham
Montgomery Co.

Thomas Chatham
Montgomery Co.

William Cheany
Washington Co.

A.M. Clay
Washington Co.

T.C. Clay
Washington Co.

J.C. Clepper

James D. Coates
Victoria Co.

John Cockburn

W.J. Coffield

James A. Collins
Dallas

Joseph Collins
Victoria Co.

L. Coleman
Harris Co.

R.M. Condron
Washington Co.

Silas P. Conway
New Orleans

L.S. Crump
Washington Co.

T. Cypert

A.J. Davis

Samuel M. Dennis
Harris Co.

M. V. Dillard
Washington Co.

A.M. Dunman
Harris Co.

H.R. Dunman
b. TX

R. L. Dunman
Harris Co.

C. Dunmap

F. M. Elam

W. H. Elkin

J.S. Ellidge
b. MS

J. W. S. Emerson

L.H.A. Emerson

S. Epperson

Samuel Everett

John Farmer

Ludus Folk

J.W. Forsgard

John Foster
Montgomery Co.

J.C. Fowler

Dekalb R. Freeman
Guadalupe Co.

Thomas Givens

John A. Glover

T.O. Calder

J.R. Grant

John D. Grissett
b. AL; Washington Co.

W.M. Grubb
Washington Co.

J.M. Hackney

A.L. Hammond

F. H. Hammond
Harris Co.

W. H. Harmon

J.W. Haskell

F.D. Haynes
b. MS; Washington Co.

A.B. Hill

Henry Hemnoff
b. Germany

Daniel Hoffman
Harris Co.

T.R. Hoxey

Harry Hunter

E.G. Jackson

John Jackson

Albert Jankes

Charles Jankes
Washington Co.

J.Cicero Jenkins

Ben F. Johnson
b. GA

W. Jones
b. Galveston

John A. Kachelor
b. Germany

J.H. Keating

John Keiskell

F.H. Kennedy

M.A. Lea

T.U. Lubbock
b. Harris Co.

J.W. McCormick

J.M. McDonald

Ed McKnight

E.L. McLendon
McLennan Co.

J.W. McMurrian
b. GA

A. McMurry

William McRoy

Edward Malone

J.W. Martin

J.F. Matthews

J.W. Matthews

P. Milton

Daniel Mitchell
Montgomery Co.

Jabez Mitchell
Montgomery Co.

William E. Moore

A.W. Morris, Jr.

William D. Morse

D.C. Muckle
Montgomery Co.

John Neal

A. Neils

J.D. Parks

M.T. Parks

W.E. Parks

J.S. Paul

Alexander Peddy
b. GA

J.H. Pinchback

J.B. Pinkston
Montgomery Co.

William M. Pitts

A.W. Proctor
Washington Co.

T.J. Proctor

Ira Proctor

Tom Reverly

H.G. Rice

William Robinson

J.W. Rogers

G.W. Routt

John W. Routt
b. AL; Washington Co.

S.R. Routt

Martin H. Royston

P.L. Sasser

William Sasser
b. NC

J.M. Shannon
Comal Co.

R.D. Simonton
Montgomery Co.

Joseph Smith

S.P. Soser

J.A. Steel

W.E. Stokes

T.J. Sypert

A.M. Thaxton
Washington Co.

James H. Thompson
b. Scotland

R.C. Tolbert

John Tynan
b. Ireland

C.M. Vaught

P.C. Walker
Harris Co.

Thomas Walker

W. H. Warren
Leon Co.

Frederick Weigan
b. Germany

J.H. West

R.M. West

Richard West
b. NC

T.P. Wayne
Kentucky

Thomas Williams

Charles Wilson

J.W. Woods

Hayes B. Yearington

COMPANY L

J.S. Anderson

J.S. Gordon
Gonzales Co.

Frank Bell

Fontain Winston

Edwin Hodges

Fred Sparks

Benjamin J. Sanford

G.W. Spencer

A. Kerr

F.M. Girand

W.B. Wilson

Van McClay

N. J. Smith

Thomas M. Blakely

J.K. Pilant

Charles Dennis

W.K. Joiner

H. Duke

A.S. Thornton

B. W. Bell

Joseph Blum

J.W. Brown

J.C. Bullington

John Clark

John L. Cox

Samuel Dennis

C.K. Finney

William Bigson

J.D. Hart

A.M. Hill

R.W. Hubbard

Charles Ingram

W.H. Jackson

J.H. Jenkins

Emet Jones

W.E. Lawrence

JM Lewis

R. Lawson

J.T. McGehee

James Mitchell

Robert P. Mitchell

Montgomery

M.A. Moore

Thomas Moore

Z.L. Nevell

D.M. Oliver

R.J. Price

George Quinan

R. Robinson

William Ryan

John Scott

A.J. Smith

R.A. Smith

Henry Stevens

J.W. Watson

Jacob Weiss

N.L. Williams

Alexander Wilson

Endnotes

Chapter 1

1. Jon L. Wakelyn, *Biographical Dictionary of the Confederacy* (Westport, CT: Greenwood Press, 1977), 529; Charlie C. Jeffries, *Terry's Rangers* (New York: Vantage Press, 1961), 59.

2. Wakelyn, 220.

3. Lester N. Fitzhugh, "Terry's Texas Rangers," *Soldiers of Texas* (Waco, TX: Texian Press, 1973), 79.

4. Marcus J. Wright, and Harold, B. Simpson (eds.), *Texas in the War, 1861–1865* (Waco, TX: Hill Junior Press, 1965), 80.

5. William Pitts Papers in the Papers of B. F. Terry, Archives, Rosenberg Library, Archives, Galveston, Texas.

6. Clarence R. Wharton, *History of Ft. Bend County* (San Antonio, TX: Naylor Company, 1939).

7. Margaret Swett Henson, "Smith, Obedience Fort," *The Handbook of Texas Online.*

8. Frank's father did not die in Texas; the parents divorced. His father, Joseph R., remained in Kentucky, remarried and lived to collect a War of 1812 pension. He died in 1874 in Cumberland County, Kentucky. His second wife, a widow (Bethenia Phelps), also received a pension. For some reason, many writers have claimed that his father died on the journey, suggesting that the divorce may have been a stormy one.

9. Ben Stuart Papers, Archives, Rosenberg Library, Archives, Galveston, Texas.

10. Maj. Francis Bingham is buried in the Sandy Point cemetery in Brazoria County, Texas, along with other members of Stephen F. Austin's original 300 settlers.

11. Oakland, or Sugarland as he called it, burned to the ground in 1875 due to a grass fire. Robert M. Armstrong, *Sugar Land Texas and the Imperial*

173

Sugar Company (Houston, TX: D. Armstrong, 1991), 22. William J. Kyle later commanded the 16th brigade of Texas State Troops. William M. Lubbock was a member of this unit, and fought with it at the Battle of Galveston.

12. Later, the city of Houston approved a one percent ad valorem tax for construction of a second rail line, the Houston Tap. The BBB&C was later taken over by the Galveston, Harrisburg and San Antonio Railway Company. That railroad eventually became part of the Southern Pacific line known as the "Sunset Limited." Russell Straw, "SP's Oldest Line" in *S-P Trainline*, 1996, No. 48, Southern Pacific Historical and Technical Society; R. M. Armstrong, *Sugar Land, Texas and the Imperial Sugar Company*, 1991, 16; George C. Werner, "Houston Tap Railroad," *The Handbook of Texas Online*.

13. Robert M. Armstrong, *Sugar Land Texas and the Imperial Sugar Company*, (Houston, TX: D. Armstrong, 1991), 16; Russell Straw, "SP's Oldest Line," *S-P Trainline 1996*, no. 48, Southern Pacific Historical and Technical Society.

14. Juan Cortina was notoriously antagonistic toward Americans. He once commented, "The sight of an American makes me feel like eating little kids." John S. Ford, *Rip Ford's Texas* (Austin: University of Texas Press, 1963).

15. Juan Cortina later maintained an influential position in the border area during the War for Southern Independence.

16. Ben Stuart Papers, Archives, Rosenberg Library, Galveston, Texas.

17. Wakelyn, 533.

18. Many prominent early Texas settlers, including Stephen F. Austin, consulted with Wharton's father at Eagle's Nest. William Wharton Groce, "Major General John A. Wharton," *Southwestern Historical Quarterly XIX* (January 1916): 273; Wakelyn, 220.

19. Groce, 272.

20. The Wharton family also possessed an original copy of Santa Anna's farewell to the Texas army that belonged to his uncle.

21. Wharton often quoted British and American poetry to others. His favorite was "Bingen on the Rhine." Francis R. Lubbock, *Six Decades in Texas: The Memoirs of Francis R. Lubbock, Confederate Governor of Texas* (Austin and New York: Pemberton Press, 1968); L. B. Giles, *Terry's Texas Rangers* (Austin, TX: Brasada Reprint Series, The Pemberton Press, 1967), 273.

22. Groce, 273.

23. Anna Marie Sandbo, "The First Session of the Secession Convention of Texas," *Southwestern Historical Quarterly XVIII*, number 2 (October 1914): 50.

24. James Masterson was later added to the practice. Groce, 271–274.

25. Wright and Simpson, 113–114.

26. Walter Prescott Webb, ed., *The Handbook of Texas* (2 volumes) (Austin, TX: The Texas State Historical Association, 1952) 727: Edith Lee Lubbock Steele, "The Five Lubbock Brothers" in *Heroes in Gray Glory,* Jefferson Davis Chapter #1637, (Houston, TX: United Daughters of the Confederacy, 1983), 114–115. The Lubbock brothers were Francis Richard, Thomas Saltus, William M., Henry S., and John Bell.

27. Sandbo, 170.

28. *Ibid.*

29. *Ibid.*

30. *Ibid.,* 162–163.

31. *Ibid.,* 171.

32. W. P. Rogers later served as commander of the Second Texas Infantry. Rogers died in the Battle of Corinth leading a charge on Union troops. A statue on the battlefield commemorates his regiment's actions.

33. Sandbo, 185.

34. Wright and Simpson, 175-181.

35. At this time, in Southern states, one was first a citizen of the said state and then secondarily a citizen of the United States. After the passage of the 14th amendment to the U.S. Constitution, order of priorities reversed.

36. Sandbo, 186.

37. Sandbo, 187.

38. Sandbo, 190–191.

39. Webb, 587.

40. Lubbock, *op. cit.*

41. Sandbo, 189.

42. Webb, 587.

43. Sam Maverick was also a member of the committee. His son, Sam Maverick, Jr., was a member of Terry's Texas Rangers. The term "maverick" originated in reference to Sam Maverick's horses.

44. Lester N. Fitzhugh, "Terry's Texas Rangers," *Soldiers of Texas* (Waco, TX: Texian Press, 1973), 75.

45. Jeanne Heidler, "Embarrising Situation: David E. Twiggs and the Surrender of United States Forces in Texas, 1861" in *Lone Star Blue and Gray,* edited by Ralph Wooster (Austin, TX: Texas State Historical Association, 1995), 32.

46. *Ibid.,* 39.

47. *Ibid.*

48. Although General Twiggs made the statement regarding surrender to McCulloch, the Committee of Public Safety had been in correspondence with General Twiggs since February 9.

49. Webb, 780.

50. Kevin R. Young, *To the Tyrants Never Yield: A Texas Civil War Sampler* (Plano, TX: Woodware Publishing, 1992), 52.

51. *Ibid.,* 68.

52. B. P. Galloway, ed., *The Dark Side of the Confederacy* (Dubuque, IA: William C. Brown Book Company, 1968).

53. Hiram Granbury was later the commander of "Granbury's Brigade." The town of Granbury, Texas, is named after him, and contains a statue of him.

54. Robert E. Lee had been instrumental in establishing Camp Cooper.

55. J. J. Bowden, *The Exodus of Federal Forces From Texas: 1861* (Austin, TX: Eakin Press, 1986), 70–71.

56. The vessels *General Rusk, Shark* and *Union* were used in this operation.

Maury Darst, "Robert Hodges, Jr. Confederate Soldier" in *East Texas Historical Journal IX*, no. 1 (March 1971): 20–47.

57. O. M. Roberts, and Clement A. Evans, eds., *Confederate Military History: Texas and Florida*, vol. XI, The Blue and Grey Press: 40.

58. Paul S. Scott, "Eighth Texas Cavalry Regiment, CSA," master's thesis, University of Texas at Arlington, 1977, 9.

59. Bowden, 86.

60. John S. "Rip" Ford gained his nickname from his responsibilities with the Texas Rangers. Ford's responsibilities included sending out death certificates and reports, which he concluded with "Rest In Peace" after his signature. This habit earned him the nickname, "RIP" or "Old Rip." Stephen B. Oates, "Recruiting Confederate Cavalry in Texas," *Southwestern Historical Quarterly* 65 (April 1961): 463–477.

61. Ford's was ordered by the Committee of Public Safety to recruit a volunteer force in the Houston area, then proceed to the lower Rio Grande and capture all United States property and munitions of war. Oates, "Recruiting Confederate Cavalry in Texas," 465.

62. Fort Brown contained four light 12-pounders, a battery wagon, two 24-pound howitzers, four 12-pound guns, and two 6-pound guns. Bowden, 20.

63. Bowden, 89.

64. Fitzhugh, *op. cit.*, 76.

65. *Ibid.*

66. Ben Stuart Papers, archives, Rosenberg Library, Galveston, Texas, 6–7.

67. Steele, *op. cit.*

68. Col. Earl Van Doren was assembling Confederate troops for an operation against the Federal camp and evacuation route through Indianola. Robert F. Bunting, "True Merit Brings Its Own Reward," in Wharton Papers, Archives, Rosenberg Library, Galveston, Texas, 1.

69. The oath of allegiance was administered either verbally or in writing. A sample oath was:

I, _____ of the County of _____, State of _____ solemnly swear that I will protect and defend the Constitution and the Government of the United States against all enemies, whether foreign or domestic; that I will bear true faith allegiance, and loyalty to the same, any ordinance, resolution or laws of any State, Convention or Legislature to the contrary notwithstanding; and further that I will faithfully perform all the duties which may be required of me by the laws of the United States; and I take this oath freely and voluntarily without any mental reservation whatsoever.

Subscribed and sworn before me, this ___ day of _____A.D. 18__.

70. Bunting, "True Merit Brings Its Own Reward."

71. G. T. Beauregard, "The First Battle of Bull Run," in *Battles and Leaders of the Civil War*, edited by Ned Bradford (New York: Meridian Press, 1984), 59.

72. Bruce Marshall, "Terry's Texas Rangers," *The Texas Star*, August 22, 1971, 2–3.

73. J. K. P. Blackburn, "Reminiscences of the Terry Rangers," *Southwestern Historical Quarterly XXII* (July 1918): 41. Goree remained in Virginia, serving

on the staff of Gen. James Longstreet. The Goree Unit of the Texas Department of Criminal Justice was named after him.

Chapter 2

1. Marcus J. Wright, and Harold B. Simpson (eds.), *Texas in the War 1861–1865* (Waco, TX: Hill Junior College, Texian Press, 1965), 113.

2. The authorization was worded as follows:

Having been authorized by the Secretary of War of the Confederate States of America to raise a regiment of mounted rangers for service in Virginia, we hereby appoint Captain _____ to raise and enroll a full company, to consist of one captain, one first lieutenant, two second lieutenants, four sergeants, four corporals, one blacksmith, two musicians and from sixty four to one hundred privates and to report the same to us on or before the 1st day of September next. Each man will be required to furnish equipment for his horse and to arm himself. The company will be transported free. The term of service will be during the war unless sooner discharged.

B.F. Terry
T. S. Lubbock

3. Formal college education in Texas included instruction in Greek and Latin, along with literature of western European civilization. Education was highly prized in Texas. Many present-day small towns in Texas held greater influence, wealth, and significance in the 1850–1865 period, including intellectual influence. Some of these smaller towns contained colleges (e.g., Galveston, Rutersville, La Grange, and Gonzales). These small-town colleges even granted advanced degrees. Most of the Rangers were college-educated either in those small-town institutions or universities on the East Coast (e.g., Princeton, Yale, University of South Carolina). Many men in the Rangers continued following their educational pursuits during the war, often borrowing books from libraries or private citizens during campaigns.

4. J. K. P. Blackburn, "Reminiscences of the Terry Rangers," *Southwestern Historical Quarterly,* XXII (July 1918): 38–77.

5. Stephen B. Oates, *Confederate Cavalry West of the River* (Austin, TX: University of Texas Press, 1992), 23–24.

6. Lester N. Fitzhugh, "Terry's Texas Rangers" *Soldiers of Texas* (Waco, TX: Texian Press, 1973), 75.

7. Stephen B. Oates, "Recruiting Confederate Cavalry in Texas," *Southwestern Historical Quarterly* 65 (April 1961): 473.

8. Many veterans of the War for Texas Independence were living at the time; Tom Lubbock had fought in it. Some of Lubbock's friends in the New Orleans Greys died at the Alamo. Members of the Rangers fought in Indian conflicts, the Mexican War, and the Cortina War. John Walker was reportedly a member of the legendary law enforcement group known as the "Texas Rangers." The concepts of independence and individuality were a greater part of daily existence for nineteenth-century Texans than was Washington D.C., the Union, and national American identity.

9. This company later changed its name to the "Lubbock Scouts."

10. Some documentation indicates this regiment was consolidated May 20, at Camp Bee, Harris County. Tom Lester, "Guide to 202nd Battalion, 2nd Military Police Group, Texas State Guard."

11. L. B. Giles, *Terry's Texas Rangers,* Brasada Reprint series (Austin: The Pemberton Press, 1967), 13.

12. Membership included alumni of Harvard, University of North Carolina at Chappel Hill, University of Edinburg, Yale, Princeton, Virginia, South Carolina, Baylor University and Texas Military Institutes. J. M. Claiborne, "Terry's Texas Rangers," *Confederate Veteran* V (June 1897).

13. Samuel Marion Dennis graduated from Princeton University and was a founding father of Sigma Alpha Epsilon fraternity. This was the first international fraternity founded in the Deep South. The fraternity was founded at the University of Alabama March 5, 1856.

14. Charlie C. Jeffries, "The Character of Terry's Texas Rangers" *Southwestern Historical Quarterly* 4 (April 1961): 457.

15. The men comprising the unit consisted mainly of single cowboys and college-educated men. Only about 40 of the original 1,100 were married. The unit contained physicians, lawyers, and other college-educated professionals. Of the regimental commanders, three were lawyers/judges (Gustave Cooke, Thomas Harrison, and John Wharton), one a planter (Benjamin Terry), one a financial stock raiser (T.S. Lubbock), and one was regular army (John G. Walker). As educated men, they would have easily identified fallacies in their cause if it were an unworthy one. This is especially true of the lawyers and judges who were trained to identify errors in law, logic, and constitutionality.

The common phrase used that the war was "a rich man's war and a poor man's fight" did not apply to the Rangers. The men comprising the unit were educated, monied, and owned land. Terry and Wharton were two of the richest men in the state at the time of the war (e.g. Wharton owning 11,700 acres). Thomas Lubbock himself was a man of considerable means. From the flag bearer, A. C. Jones who owned 6,000 acres, to Elam, who had fourteen of his own horses shot out from under him, the majority of the members were men of substance.

The men comprising the Rangers volunteered for service rather than serve under conscription or draft. Besides volunteering, they willingly opted for service lasting the duration of the war. The members of the regiment largely kept to their oath taken in Houston, as the regiment experienced few desertions during the war. Although some members had prior military experience, the Rangers were not comprised of disgruntled Federal servicemen. After the war, many returned to their professional lives, which for some included election to public office. Although some professionals comprised the Rangers, there was a cowboy contingent. This contingent displayed occasional rowdiness (e.g., the Nashville shooting incident). The cowboy contingent possibly helped create a "backwoods" or "uneducated hick" perception of the Texas Rangers. One lieutenant is credited with saying that the Rangers were not a regiment at all but a "damned armed mob." A. P. Harcourt, "Terry's Texas Rangers," *The Southern Bivouac* (November 1882); Giles, *op. cit.,* 90.

16. Charlie C. Jeffries, *Terry's Rangers* (New York: Vantage Press, 1961), 14.

17. Clarence R. Wharton, *History of Ft. Bend County* (San Antonio: Naylor Company, 1939).

18. Oates, *op. cit.,* 474.

19. Bruce Marshall, "Terry's Texas Rangers," *The Texas Star,* August 22, 1971, 2.

20. Stephen B. Oates, *Confederate Cavalry West of the River* (Austin: University of Texas Press, 1992), 24.

21. Lieutenant Sparks later served on the staff of Henry E. McCulloch. Henry McCulloch was the brother of Ben McCulloch. Both McCulloch brothers served the Confederacy and are buried at the Texas State Cemetery in Austin, Texas.

22. Thomas Cutrer, "McKinney, Thomas Jack," *The Handbook of Texas Online*.

23. Stephen B. Oates, *Confederate Cavalry*, 28.

24. Jeffries, 12.

25. Fitzhugh, *op. cit.,* 78.

26. Francis R. Lubbock, *Six Decades in Texas: The Memiors of Francis R. Lubbock, Confederate Govenor of Texas* (Ausitn and New York: Pemberton Press, 1968).

27. Fitzhugh, *op. cit.,* 4.

28. Lubbock, 325–326.

29. Fitzhugh, *op. cit.,* 78.

30. The fact that some of the Rangers attired themselves in frontier clothing added attention to the newly arriving Texans. Capt. John G. Walker was singled out for his dressing in buckskin and a sombrero. Fitzhugh, *op. cit.,* 4–5.

31. Fitzhugh, *ibid.,* 79.

32. Francis R. Lubbock claimed the dispatch arrived in Chattanooga, Tennessee. It was also in this location that he left Terry and continued on to Richmond, Virginia. Lubbock, 325–326; Giles, 16.

33. Fitzhugh, *op. cit.,* 79.

34. *Ibid.*

35. Claiborne, *op. cit.*

36. M. Darst, "Robert Hodges, Jr.: Confederate Soldier," *East Texas Historical Journal IX,* number 1 (March 1971): 28. Some of the women specifically identified included Mrs. Mary Ramage, Mrs. Felicia Grundy Porter, Mrs. James Knox Polk (widow of the former president), Mrs. Harriet Overton, Mrs. McCall, Mrs. Fogg, Mrs. Kukman, and Mrs. Porterfield. John Claiborne, "From Nashville, Tennessee to Corinth, Mississippi," *New Birmingham Times,* 1891, edited by Paul Scott.

37. Blackburn, 47–48.

38. Bruce Marshall, "Terry's Texas Rangers," *The Texas Star,* August 22, 1971, 2; Lester Fitzhugh, "Terry's Texas Rangers," an address given before the Houston Civil War Round Table, March 21, 1958, 4–5.

39. Blackburn, 48.

40. Giles, 17: Fitzhugh, *op. cit.,* 79.

41. One of Terry's brothers, David Smith Terry, was also later selected as a colonel leading a Confederate cavalry unit from Texas. This unit joined Confederate forces operating in Mexico after the War for Southern Independence officially ended.

42. Fitzhugh, "Terry's Texas Rangers," *Soldiers of Texas*, 81.

43. George Whythe Baylor gained notoriety from reportedly raising the first Confederate flag in Austin, Texas.

44. Stanley F. Horn, *The Army of Tennessee* (Norman and London: University of Oklahoma Press, 1993), 59.

45. Darst, *op. cit.*, 23.

46. Giles, *op. cit.*, 17.

47. H. J. H. Rugelugh, ed., *Batchelor–Turner Letters, 1861–1864* (Austin: The Steck Company, 1961).

48. Darst, *op. cit.*, 23.

49. Blackburn, *op. cit.*, 49.

50. Giles, 101.

51. Fitzhugh, *op. cit.*, 81.

52. Reports, B. F. Terry to William M. McKall, 30 October 1861, compiled service records, B. F. Terry file.

53. John S. Bowman, ed., *The Civil War Almanac* (New York: World Almanac Publications), 281.

54. A. P. Harcourt, "Terry's Texas Rangers," *The Southern Bivouac*, November 1882.

55. As the war progressed, armaments changed. Not only were the six-shooters of killed comrades utilized, but also weapons secured through combat. Evidence indicates the Rangers possessed as least fifty Spencer rifles acquired from Union troops as early as June 1864.

56. Woodsonville, Kentucky, is located in the county adjacent to Abraham Lincoln's birthplace county. Woodsonville is also near where Stephen Foster wrote "My Old Kentucky Home."

57. William T. Gainer, *Reminiscences of the Boys in Gray: 1861–1865*, M. Yeary (ed.) (Morningside, 1986), 249.

58. Ward McDonald, "Sensations in Kentucky Backwoods," *Confederate Veteran III* (May 1895).

59. Fitzhugh, *op. cit.*, 82.

60. Giles, 20.

61. O. M. Roberts, and Clement A. Evans, eds., *Confederate Military History: Texas and Florida*, vol. XI (The Blue and Grey Press), 157.

62. This regiment contained many seasoned Prussian veterans. The 32nd Indiana regiment was also known as the 1st German, 32nd Regiment Indiana Volunteer Infantry. Michael A. Peake, *Indiana's German Sons: A History of the 1st German, 32nd Regiment Indiana Volunteer Infantry* (Indianapolis, IN: Deutches Haus-Athenaeum, 1999), foreword.

63. Gen. August (von) Willich previously participated in the 1848 socialist uprising in Germany. During the uprising, Willich supported the socialists in their unsuccessful efforts to overthrow the government. Al Benson, *The Socialist*

Supportes of Honest Abe (Arlington Heights, IL: 1995); A. E. Zucker, "The Biographical Dictionary of the Fourty-eighters" in: Id., *The Fourty-Eighters: Political Refugees of the German Revolution of 1848,* (Columbia, NY: Columbia University Press, 1950), 355.

64. A. P. Harcourt, "Terry's Texas Rangers," *The Southern Bivouac,* November 1882.

65. Claiborne, *op. cit.,* 609.

66. Blackburn, *op. cit.,* 49–50.

67. Claiborne, *op. cit.,* 609.

68. Fitzhugh, *op. cit.,* 83.

69. Harcourt, November 1882.

70. Kate Scurry Terrell, "Terry's Texas Rangers," in Dudley Wooten, ed., *A Comprehensive History of Texas,* 2 vols. (Dallas: William G. Scharff, 1898).

71. Gainer, 249.

72. Claiborne, *op. cit.,* 609.

73. Gainer, *op. cit.,* 249.

74. This battle is also known as the Battle of Rowlett's Station or the Battle of Green River.

75. This is one of the few instances where a mounted cavalry unit attacked and overcame infantry in a kneel and parry position. It is likely that the first Ranger flag, now in the Chicago Historical Museum, was lost in this action.

76. Claiborne, *op. cit.,* 609.

77. Fitzhugh, *op. cit.,* 83.

78. Roberts and Evans, *op. cit.,* 157–158.

79. Jeffries, *op. cit.*

80. *Brazoria Bend County Museum Historical Bulletin,* November 1999.

81. Terry's body was moved to Glenwood Cemetery, Houston, Texas, in 1880. Gustave Cooke delivered the eulogy for his burial at that location. Some local stories in Sugar Land, Texas, claim that an unusual apparition of a face exists on one of the bricks of the original Terry family mausoleum located in Brazoria Cemetery.

82. Tom Curter, "Thomas McKinney Jack," *Texas Handbook Online.*

83. Terrell.

84. The Army of Tennessee contained several regiments of Texas troops. The state of Texas appropriated funds for regimental hospitals for the 2nd and 9th Texas Infantry and Terry's regiment, although little or no action occurred regarding the purchase of supplies to equip the hospitals. The communities from which the regiments originated provided the needed supplies for the men. The main hospital for Texas units was located in Quitman, Mississippi, in Clarke County, although some men were treated at hospitals in Corinth, Mississippi, and Rome, Georgia. These facilities existed at the time of the Battle of Shiloh. Hospitals were identified by the yellow flag flying outside of them. Since the germ theory had not been discovered, conditions at this and other hospitals were unsanitary by today's standards. Tetnus and dysentery were common. A common procedure to deal with severe wounds was amputa-

tion. Eight of ten amputations resulted in death. Due to unsanitary conditions, any wound was potentially fatal.

The following table shows how death via illness occurred more frequently than death on the battlefield for the companies in the regiment:

Company	Number Enlisted	Number Killed	Number Wounded	Number Died (via illness or natural causes)
A	117	26 (22.2%)	27 (23%)	18 (15.3%)
B	167	26 (15.5%)	38 (22.7%)	22 (13.1%)
C	87	11 (12.6%)	16 (18.3%)	16 (18.3%)
D	134	29 (21.6%)	33 (24.6%)	23 (17.7%)
E	105	14 (13.3%)	30 (28.5%)	14 (13.3%)
F	114	13 (11.4%)	33 (33%)	13 (11.4%)
G	87	12(13.7%)	14 (16%)	17 (19.5%)
H	133	19 (14.2%)	40 (30%)	21 (15.7%)
I	100	13 (13%)	33 (33%)	13 (13%)
K	123	13 (09%)	23 (20.6%)	19 (15%)
Total	1170	165 (14%)	280 (24%)	180 (15%)

Union troops under W. T. Sherman burned the Confederate hospital at Quitman during a raid in early 1864. Rev. R. F. Bunting of the Rangers initiated the establishment of another hospital for wounded and sick Texas soldiers in Auburn, Alabama, during 1864. Reverend Bunting eventually ran the "Texas Hospital" in Auburn. Hospitals were often a place soldiers "found religion." Here many soldiers experienced spiritual conversion experiences prior to dying. Colporters and army missionaries from the various denominations often visited hospitals to minister to the ailing soldiers housed there. Joseph E. Chance, *The Second Texas Infantry: From Shiloh to Vicksburg* (Austin: Eakin Press, 1984), 44; Stanley F. Horn, *The Army of Tennessee* (Norman and London: University of Oklahoma Press, 1993), 149; A. J. Sowell, *A History of Ft. Bend County* (Houston, TX: W.H. Coyle, 1964), 275; Walter Prescott Webb, ed., *The Handbook of Texas*, 2 volumes (Austin, TX: The Texas State Historical Association, 1952).

85. Marcus J. Wright, and Harold Simpson, (eds.), *Texas in the War, 1861–1865* (Waco, TX: Hill Junior College, Texian Press), 114.

Chapter 3

1. R. F. Bunting, "True Merit Brings Its Own Reward," John A. Wharton Papers, Archives, Rosenberg Library, Galveston, Texas.

2. Paul R. Scott, "Eighth Texas Cavalry Regiment, CSA," Master's Thesis, University of Texas at Arlington, 1977, 63.

3. Bunting, 2.

4. The party consisted of General Hindman, his staff, officers, and a detachment of the Rangers.

5. Scott, "Eighth Texas Cavalry Regiment, CSA," 65.

6. Batchelor Turner Letters, archives, Rosenberg Library, Galveston, Texas.

7. Bunting, 2.

8. *Ibid.*

9. Scott, "Eighth Texas Cavalry Regiment, CSA," 67.

10. L. B. Giles, *Terry's Texas Rangers,* Brasada Reprint series (Austin: The Pemberton Press, 1967), 27.

11. Bunting, 3.

12. Lester N. Fitzhugh, "Terry's Texas Rangers," an address given before the Houston Civil War Round Table, March 21, 1958, 10.

13. Lester N. Fitzhugh, "Terry's Texas Rangers," *Soldiers of Texas* (Waco, TX: Texian Press, 1973), 84.

14. Scott, "Eighth Texas Cavalry Regiment, CSA," 69.

15. Giles, 27.

16. Prior to statehood, residents of the Texas Republic referred to themselves as Texians. After statehood, the term used was Texans. Fitzhugh, "Terry's Texas Rangers," *Soldiers of Texas,* 84.

17. A. P. Harcourt, "Terry's Texas Rangers," *The Southern Bivouac,* November 1882.

18. Wiley Sword, *The Battle of Shiloh* (Eastern Acorn Press, 1982) 9.

19. Ulysses S. Grant, "The Battle of Shiloh," *Battles and Leaders of the Civil War* (New York: Meridian, 1989), 86.

20. Giles, 29.

21. George Whythe Baylor, "With A.S. Johnston at Shiloh," *Confederate Veteran V* (1897):609.

22. *Ibid.*

23. Leonidas Polk and Albert Sidney Johnston had been roommates at West Point.

24. John C. Breckinridge had previously served as vice president of the United States under President Buchanan.

25. Stanley F. Horn, *The Army of Tennessee* (Norman and London: University of Oklahoma Press, 1993),123–124.

26. Sword, *op. cit.,* 15.

27. Sword, *ibid.,* 13.

28. Harcourt; Giles, 30.

29. Baylor, 609.

30. *Ibid.*

31. Giles, 30–31.

32. Horn, 121.

33. Sword, *op. cit.,* 16.

34. Harcourt.

35. O. M. Roberts, and Clement Evans (eds.), *Confederate Military History: Texas and Florida,* vol. IX (The Blue and Grey Press), 262.

36. Tom Burney, Letter to Lucy Burney, "The Famous Terry Rangers," undated.

37. Harcourt.

38. Burney, Letter to Lucy Burney.

39. Roberts and Evans, 262.

40. Ulysses S. Grant, "The Battle of Shiloh," *Battles and Leaders of the Civil War* (New York: *Meridian*, 1989), 86.

41. Tom Cutrer, "Jack, Thomas McKinney," *The Handbook of Texas Online*; Baylor, 609.

42. J. K. P. Blackburn, "Reminiscences of the Terry Rangers," *Southwestern Historical Quarterly XXII* (July 1918), 55.

43. *Official Records*, vol. X:626.

44. Thayer's brigade contained the 1st Nebraska, 23rd Indiana, 58th and 68th Ohio regiments.

45. Blackburn, 58.

46. Bunting, "True Merit Brings Its Own Reward," 626.

47. Harcourt.

48. Jack Hurst, *Nathan Bedford Forrest: A Biography,* (New York: Vintage Books, First Vintage Civil War Library Edition, 1994), 94.

49. Harcourt.

50. *Ibid.*

51. Fitzhugh, *op. cit.*, 85; Blackburn, 60.

52. Fitzhugh, *op. cit.*

53. Blackburn, 60.

54. G. McWhinney and Perry D. Jamison, *Attack and Die: Civil War Military Tactics and the Southern Heritage* (University of Alabama Press, 1982),127.

55. Report by Major Harrison, *Official Records*, Series I, vol. X, Part 1: 923.

56. The general tactics of the Rangers combined their good horsemanship with the rapidity of fire offered by the revolvers and short range of shotguns. The men would ride into the enemy as quickly as their horses would carry them, open fire with shotguns, then deliver twelve shots with rapidity and reasonable accuracy. This action generally led to the enemy giving way. The rapidity of fire functioned like a "wall of lead" falling upon the enemy.

Shotguns played a vital role in some of the recorded charges made by the unit. Shotguns were used in the actions at Woodsonville, Fallen Timbers, and Murfreesboro. Formal cavalry tactics at the time emphasized use of the saber. The Ranger accounts contain few references to sabers, although evidence exists confirming that Rangers were issued and used sabers. Despite using sabers themselves, the Rangers made fun of Union cavalrymen who heavily relied upon them. Giles, 101; McWhinney and Jamison, 64.

In Thomas Harrison's report to Wharton, he wrote, "I cannot say more than they fully sustained the ancient fame of the name they bear." (Terrell.)

57. Roberts and Evans, 262.

58. Clinton Terry is buried at Sandy Point Cemetery in Brazoria County, Texas, along with William Jefferson Kyle (B.F. Terry's business partner).

Chapter 4

1. A. P. Harcourt, "Terry's Texas Rangers," *The Southern Bivouac*, November 1882.

2. L. B. Giles, *Terry's Texas Rangers*, Brasada Reprint series (Austin: The Pemberton Press, 1967), 34.

3. This is the town where Union General Phillip Sheridan obtained the horse "Reinzi," with whom he made his famous ride.

4. Lester N. Fitzhugh, "Terry's Texas Rangers," *Soldiers of Texas* (Waco, TX: Texian Press, 1973), 86.

5. Thomas G. Woodward to John Adams, May 10, 1862, *OR*, vol. X, Part 1:887–888.

6. Posey, in Mamie Yeary (ed.), *Reminiscences of Boys in Gray 1861–1865*, 137–138.

7. Letter, Robert Franklin Bunting, University of Texas Archives, 2–3.

8. Letter, Benjamin F. Burke to James and Martha Ogden Burke, June 14, 1862, *Letters of Private Benjamin F. Burke*, 16.

9. Gracy, "With Danger and Honor," *Texana*, 12

10. Robert Franklin Bunting, "True Merit Brings Its Own Reward," John A. Wharton Papers, Rosenberg Library, Galveston, Texas.

11. Henry W. Graber, *The Life Record of H. W. Graber, a Terry Ranger, 1861–1865*. Reprint. (Austin: State House Press, 1987), 64.

12. Letter, Dunbar Affleck to Mr. and Mrs. Thomas Affleck, June 29, 1862, "With Terry's Texas Rangers: The Letters of Dunbar Affleck," Robert W. Williams and Ralph A. Wooster (eds.), *Civil War History* IX (September 1963):308.

13. Graber, 144–145.

14. General William Brent to Nathan Bedford Forrest, June 9, 1862, OR, vol. X, Part 2: 602.

15. Fitzhugh, *op. cit.*, 86.

16. Giles, 35.

17. William H. King, "Forrest's Attack on Murfreesboro, July 13, 1862," *Confederate Veteran* XXXII (November 1924).

18. Letter, Cyrus Love to Jas. M. and T.A. Love, 1862.

19. At the start of the week, Crittenden's men held twelve citizens in jail, guarded by 200 troops. By Friday July 9, the number of incarcerated citizens was increased to 400. That Friday, Crittenden required all citizens to assemble in the city square. The citizens complained they were experiencing a hard time. Crittenden responded that now they were having a good time, on Monday (July 12), he would initiate "iron rule." (King); Jack Hurst, *Nathan Bedford Forrest: A Biography* (New York: Vintage Books, First Vintage Civil War Library Edition, 1994), 99.

20. Giles, 36; Bunting, "True Merit Brings Its Own Reward," 4.

21. Hurst, 98.

22. Frank Battle, "General Forrest's Order to Colonel Baxter Smith," *Confederate Veteran* V, no. 12: 609.

23. Paul R. Scott, "Eighth Texas Cavalry Regiment, CSA," 97.

24. Blackburn, 66.

25. The lieutenant colonel of the 9th Michigan Infantry stated in his report of the attack: "The forces attacking my camp were the First Regiment Texas Rangers, Colonel Wharton, and a battalion of the First Georgia Rangers, Colonel Morrison, and a large number of citizens of Rutherford County, many

of whom had recently taken the oath of allegiance to the United States Government. There were also quite a number of Negroes attached to the Texas and Georgia troops, who were armed and equipped, and took part in the several engagements with my forces during the day." (*OR*, series I, vol. XVI: 805).

26. Bunting, *op. cit.*, 5.

27. In Lieutenant Colonel Parkhurst's Report (9th Michigan Infantry) of the attack, he said: "The forces attacking my camp were the First regiment Texas Rangers, Colonel Wharton, and a battalion of the First Georgia Rangers, Colonel Morrison, and a large number of citizens of Rutherford County, many of whom had recently taken the oath of allegiance to the United States Government. There were also quite a number of Negroes attached to the Texas and Georgia troops, who were armed and equipped, and took part in the several engagements with my forces during the day." OR, series I, vol. XVI, part 1: 805.

28. Giles, 36.

29. Battle, 609; Andrew Nelson Lytle, *Bedford Forrest and the Critter Company* (New Jersey: J. S. Sanders and Company, Cranbury, 1975), 94.

30. Jeffries, 53.

31. Blackburn, 66; Giles, 37.

The text of the demand for surrender was as follows:

                                   Murfreesboro, July 13, 1862

Colonel:— I must demand an unconditional surrender of your forces as prisoners of war, or I will have every man put to the sword. You are aware of the overpowering force I have at my command, and this demand is made to prevent the further effusion of blood. I am Colonel, very respectfully, your obedient servant,

                                              N. B. Forrest

32. Lytle, 94.

33. *Ibid.*, 96.

34. Fitzhugh, *op. cit.*, 87.

35. This battery on new parrot 12-pounders was used by Forrest through the remainder of the war. Command was given to his chief of artillery, Capt. John W. Morton. The unit was thereafter known as the Morton battery. Battle, 609.

36. *Ibid.*

37. Blackburn, 67.

38. Stanley F. Horn, *The Army of Tennessee* (Norman and London: University of Oklahoma Press, 1993), 161.

39. Giles, 40.

40. *Ibid.*, 36.

41. Horn, 161.

42. *Ibid.*

43. A stockade consisted of logs twelve to fifteen inches in diameter and twelve feet long, set on end in trenches two feet deep, closely touching each other with portholes cut between logs as high as a man's head to shoot through. The logs were thoroughly tamped into place and a small door in one

side for passing in and out with a screen of like make was just inside. So one going in would pass in the door and turn to left or right to get inside the stockade. Blackburn, 65.

44. Federal forces captured a slave of one of the Rangers killed in the stockade assault. The slave provided important information to the pursuing Federals. *OR*, vol. XXVIII: 901.

45. Letter, Robert F. Bunting to editor, *Tri-Weekly Telegraph*, July 26, 1862, R.F. Bunting Papers.

In order to maintain military discipline, several forms of punishment were used. Among these were "marking time," "roots," "fatigue duty," and running in place. "Roots" consisted of digging holes followed by covering them up, then repeating the process. "Fatigue duty" was assigned to all horseless men. Until mounts were found, they dug graves, unloaded railroad cars and hauled wood and straw for the hospitals. Courts-martial were frequent, along with disciplinary actions. Discipline was strict in and out of camp, at least from the Rangers' perspective.

Despite questions raised concerning their discipline, the unit participated in the drills, reviews, and inspections held in camp. The Rangers frequently did well in these inspections, which indicates that discipline was enforced enough to secure favorable outcomes at inspections and reviews. Testimonies regarding Wharton's abilities also indicate the regiment was very disciplined when necessary.

46. Horn, 168.

47. *Ibid.*, 169.

48. Henry W. Graber, *The Life Record of H. W. Graber, a Terry Ranger, 1861–1865*. Reprint. (Austin: State House Press), 157.

49. Giles, 43.

50. Paul R. Scott, "Eighth Texas Cavalry Regiment, CSA," master's thesis, University of Texas at Arlington, 1977, 97.

51. William Wharton Groce, "Major General John A. Wharton," *Southwestern Historical Quarterly* 19, no.3 (January 1916): 276.

52. Bunting, "True Merit Brings Its Own Reward," 7. A historian wrote, "Of all the 292 engagements led by the Eighth Texas Rangers, Terry's Texas Rangers, the Battle of Bardstown would go down as their finest moment." Brian Bush, *The Battle of Bardstown, Kentucky.*

53. Groce, 276.

54. Giles, 46.

55. *Ibid.*, 145–146.

56. *OR*, vol. X, p. 898.

57. Fitzhugh, *op. cit.*, 88.

58. Horn, 189.

59. The *Official Records* shows skirmish and battle actions during the October portion of the Kentucky campaign as follows:

October 1 -Skirmish on the Louisville Pike, Kentucky
        2 -Skirmish at Shepherdsville Road, Kentucky
        4 -Action on the Bardstown Pike, Kentucky

6 -Skirmishes a Fair Grounds, Springfield, Burnt Cross-Roads, Beach Fork, and Grassy Mound, Kentucky

7-Skirmishes at Brown Hill and Perryville, Kentucky

8-Battle of Perryville, Kentucky

9 -Skirmishes at Mackville Pike and Bardstown Road, Kentucky

10-Skirmish at Danville Cross-Roads, Kentucky

11-Skirmish at Danville, Kentucky

12-Skirmish at Dick's Ford, Kentucky

14-Skirmishes at Lancaster and Crab Orchard Road, Kentucky

15-Skirmishes at Crab Orchard and Barren Mound, Kentucky

16-Skirmishes as Mountain Gap and Mount Vernon, Kentucky

17-Skirmishes at Valley Woods and Rocky Hill, Kentucky

18-Skirmishes at Cross-Roads, Big Hill, Little Rockcastle River, and Mountain Side, Kentucky

19-Skirmish at Wild Cat, Kentucky

20-Skirmish near Wild Cat, Kentucky

21 Skirmish at Pitman's Cross-Roads, Kentucky

60. Giles, 47.

61. Blackburn, 69.

62. E. A. Pollard, *The Lost Cause* (New York: Grammercy Books, 1994), 351.

63. Blackburn, 143.

64. Authority structure within military units follows according to rank. The Rangers comprised a regiment. A regiment was often led by a colonel. A regiment comprised ten companies of 100 men each. Each company was led by a captain. A brigade consisted of three or more regiments combined. (Although originally an independent command, the Rangers were eventually brigaded with other units. The unit operated as an independent command in many battles.) Brigadier generals were assigned command of brigades. Two or more brigades formed a division. Divisions were led by a major general. The combination of two or more divisions produced a corps, commanded by a lieu-tenant general. Two or more corps combined made up a field army, com-manded by a general.

In the early days of the war, the strength of a Confederate regiment was around 1,000 men; as the war progressed, 300–500 men was the typical strength of a brigade. In the last two years of the war, a normal strength brigade was 200–300 men.

65. Lester N. Fitzhugh, "Terry's Texas Rangers," an address given before the Houston Civil War Round Table, March 21, 1958, 13.

66. *Ibid.*

67. Horn, 193.

68. Pollard, 347.

69. Blackburn, 72.

70. *Ibid.,* 73.

71. Giles, 49.

72. Bunting, "True Merit Brings Its Own Reward," 8.

73. Pollard, 347; Horn, 198.

74. Bunting, *op. cit.,* 8.

75. Roberts and Evans, 166.

76. B. L. Ridley, "Echoes From the Battle of Murfreesboro," *Confederate Veteran* XI, no. 2 (February 1903).

77. *Ibid.* These papers indicate an army of 60,000 was defeated by Bragg's force of about 30,000.

78. Roberts and Evans, 166.

79. Bunting, *op. cit.,* 8–9.

80. Blackburn, 27–39.

81. This was one of the few times a cavalry charge with sabers was broken with shotguns.

82. Blackburn, 76.

83. Although standard cavalry training manuals at the time emphasized use of the saber, the Rangers did not initially want them. Although they disliked sabers, all were equipped with Bowie knives. Some historians report that this dislike of sabers was shared by their one-time commander, Nathan Bedford Forrest. Forrest's philosophy consisted of training his men to fight with revolver when mounted and with the rifle when on foot, which fit well with the Rangers' preferred style of fighting, which consisted of using shotguns followed by revolvers in close action. Later, they were no longer under Forrest and were equipped with and used cavalry sabers. McWhiney and Jamison, 64; Fitzhugh, "Terry's Texas Rangers," *Soldiers of Texas,* 81; Francis Trevelyan Miller, ed., *The Photographic History of the Civil War, Vol 4—The Cavalry* (New York: Castle Books, 1957), 145, 282.

84. Blackburn, 27–39.

85. Pollard, 350.

86. B. L. Ridley, "Echoes From the Battle of Murfreesboro," *Confederate Veteran* XI, no. 2 (February 1903).

87. Scott, "Eighth Texas Cavalry Regiment, CSA," 125.

88. Ridley.

89. Dr. Joseph Cross, and J. William Jones (eds.), *Christ in the Camp* (Harrisonburg, VA: Sprinkle Publications, reprint 1986), 541–542.

Chapter 5

1. Lester N. Fitzhugh, "Terry's Texas Rangers," *Soldiers of Texas* (Waco, TX: Texian Press, 1973), 89.

2. W. H. Davis, "Cavalry Service under General Wheeler," *Confederate Veteran* XI, no. 3 (1903):353–354.

3. Joseph Wheeler to George William Brent, February 1863, *OR,* vol. XXIII, Part 1: 39–41; L. B. Giles, *Terry's Texas Rangers,* Brasada Reprint series (Austin: The Pemberton Press, 1967), 53.

4. R. L. Dunman, "One of Terry's Texas Rangers," *Confederate Veteran* XXXI, no. 3 (March 1923): 103.

5. Jack Hurst, *Nathan Bedford Forrest: A Biography* (New York: Vintage Books, First Vinatge Civil War Library Edition, 1994), 113.

6. A. P. Harcourt, "Terry's Texas Rangers," *The Southern Bivouac* (November 1882).

7. L. B. Giles, *Terry's Texas Rangers*, Brasada Reprint series (Austin: The Pemberton Press, 1967), 54.

8. Dunman, 103.

9. Sam Maverick's father, S. A. Maverick, was a member of the Committee of Public Safety, which interacted with General Twiggs through correspondences asking for surrender of his men and the facilities.

10. Letter, George Q. Turner to Amasa Turner, February 20, 1863, *Batchelor-Turner Letters*, 46; *Letters of Private Benjamin F. Burke*, 25.

11. During the Donelson raid, several Rangers formally organized a specialized unit known as "Wharton's Scouts." The unit served as a spy company and personal bodyguard for Wharton. Sam Maverick, who burned a gunboat at Fort Donelson, was a member of this company. Members included men from the Rangers and the 11th Texas Cavalry.

12. Hurst, 114.

13. Randall Bedwell, ed., *May I Quote You General Forrest?* (Nashville, TN: Cumberland House Publishing, 1997), 20.

14. Letter, George Q. Turner to Amasa Turner, February 20, 1863, *Batchelor-Turner Letters*, 47. Amasa Turner organized and led some of the units at the Battle of San Jacinto during the War for Texas Independence.

15. Giles, 54.

16. *Diary of E. S. Dodd, Co. D, Terry's Texas Rangers & An Account of His Hanging as a Confederate Spy* (Austin: Ranger Press, 1979), 7.

17. Giles, 55.

18. Joseph Wheeler to George William Brent, April 11, 1863, *OR*, vol. XXIII, Part 1: 219–221; George P. Este to George E. Flynt, April 12, 1863, *OR*, vol. XXIII, Part 1:216.

19. Joseph Wheeler to George William Brent, April 11, 1863, *OR*, vol. XXIII, Part 1:219.

20. Letter, Benjamin Franklin Batchelor to Julia Turner Batchelor, July 7, 1863, *Batchelor-Turner Letters*, 60.

21. This brigade would later be named Granbury's Brigade.

22. James M. McCaffrey, *This Band of Heroes: Granbury's Texas Brigade, C. S. A.* (Austin: Eakin Press, 1985), 68.

23. Letter, George Q. Turner to Amasa Turner, July 7, 1863, *Batchelor-Turner Letters*, 59.

24. McCaffrey, 64.

25. Louis D. Watkins to George Lee, July 4, 1863, OR, vol. XXIII, Part 1:550.

26. Bragg's retreat occurred in close time proximity to the twin defeats of Vicksburg, Mississippi, and Gettysburg, Pennsylvania.

27. Giles, 56–57.

In the area of spiritual health, the Presbyterian Rev. R.F. Bunting served the Rangers as full-time chaplain. The chaplain served from November 1861 until sometime in 1864. Bunting was the first chaplain officially sanctioned by the CSA government. His duties included preaching and praying for the men

along with looking after the mail. Reverend Bunting regularly conducted services on Sundays for the men and often accompanied them on their missions.
Many of his sermons presented to the Rangers are contained in his papers.
With a full-time chaplain, the Rangers received constant religious training and
encouragement. In addition to services provided by Reverend Bunting, some
members of the regiment also attended other church services held in camps.

Religious fervor increased in intensity, reaching a peak in July–August
1863. During this time, Reverend Bunting conducted daily church meetings at
a Primitive Baptist Church near Rome, Georgia. During the revival of religious
fervor, Rangers "found peace in believing," some showed interests and several
confessed their sins. This culminated in over 100 conversions. Religious conversions were often referred to as "finding peace in believing" or "joining the
church." The religious revival was not limited to the Rangers, and occurred
throughout the Army of Tennessee. Reverend Bunting even preached services
for other troops (Ector's and Vance's brigades). As an outgrowth of the revival
in their regiment, the Rangers organized a "provisional church" and
"Christian association" among their members. During the time of the revival,
President Jefferson Davis called for a "day of fasting, humiliation and prayer."

There are also accounts of another preacher being one of the enlisted men
in the regiment. It is recorded that this pastor even performed a wedding for
one of the Rangers during one of their campaigns. As time permitted, the men
in the regiment who were Masons formed their own Masonic Lodge.

Among the commanders, Gen. John A. Wharton and Maj. George Littlefield
were Presbyterian and Gen. Thomas Harrison, a Baptist. Harrison maintained active involvement in the Baptist church following the war. Their brigade commander during the Knoxville campaign, Gen. Alexander Stewart maintained regular religious services. Blackburn, 152; J. William Jones (ed.), *Christ in the Camp*
(Harrisonburg, VA: Sprinkle Publications, 1986), 573, 577.

28. About this time, similar spiritual revivals occurred in the Army of
Northern Virginia.

29. Wharton owned the saddle prior to the presentation. The saddle was
later destroyed in a fire at the home where Wharton's belongings were kept.

30. Many Texans resented the Georgians. The Texans claim the Georgians
had raised the prices on their goods when the Army of Tennessee arrived in
their state.

31. Fitzhugh, "Terry's Texas Rangers," *Soldiers of Texas*, 90.

32. Jefferson Davis, in J. William Jones (ed.), *Christ in the Camp*, 46–47.

33. Fitzhugh, *op. cit.*, 91.

34. Joseph Wheeler to George William Brent, October 30, 1863, *OR*, vol.
XXX, Part 1:520–521.

35. Blackburn, 144.

36. John Allen Wyeth, in Miller, *The Photographic History of the Civil War,*
158.

37. Giles, 60.

38. Blackburn, 144.

39. John McIntyre was also a schoolmate of Texas Ranger John Claiborne.

Another version of McIntyre's quote is "The Rangers killed and wounded my men faster than ships could bring them from Europe." (Claiborne.) On another occasion, Captain McIntyre was ordered to "drive the enemy before them." Being that he was facing the Rangers, he replied to his commander that that was "easy to order, but hard to fulfill, they are Terry Rangers, and for three years I have been trying to drive them, and there are a thousand Fourth Ohio graves made by these fellows; they don't drive worth a cent." John Claiborne, "Various Complimentary Remarks and Excerpts from different general orders read out to the army of Tennessee," *New Birmingham Times,* 1891, edited by Paul Scott, 2000.

40. John Allen Wyeth, in Miller, *op. cit.,* 160.
41. Blackburn, 145.
42. Edward G. Longacre, *Mounted Raids of the Civil War* (Cranbury, NJ: A.S. Barnes and Company, 1975), 210.
43. Wyeth, in Miller, *op. cit.,* 160.
44. *Ibid.,* 164.
45. *Ibid.,* 160–164.
46. Longacre, 216.
47. *Ibid.*
48. *Ibid.*
49. Scott, "Eighth Texas Cavalry Regiment, CSA," 157.
50. Longacre, 217.
51. Giles, 66.
52. Blackburn, 147.
53. Longacre, 222.
54. Gustave Cooke was referred to as a "living lead mine" due to the number of wounds received in battles. John M. Claiborne, "Terry's Texas Rangers," and Paul R. Scott, ed., *New Birmingham Times,* 1891.
55. Longacre, 223.
56. Giles, 72.
57. Wheeler's report is in *OR,* series I, vol. XXX, Part 2: 722–725.
58. W. H. Davis, "Cavalry Service under General Wheeler," *Confederate Veteran* XXI, no. 3 (March 1923):353.
59. Letter, Joseph Wheeler to G. Moxley Sorrel, Dec. 31, 1863, *OR,* vol. XXXI, Part 1:541.
60. *Ibid.,* 540–541.
61. *Ibid.,* 541.
62. Giles, 68.
63. Henry S. Burrage, "Burnside Holds out at Knoxville," in Henry Steele Commager, *The Blue and the Grey* (The Fairfax Press, 1982), 916.
64. Giles, 69–70.
65. McWhiney and Jamison, 90–91.
66. Roberts and Evans, 179.
67. Fitzhugh, "Terry's Texas Rangers," an address given before the Houston Civil War Round Table, March 21, 1958, 17.

68. William T. T. Martin to Moxley Sorrel, January 8, 1864, *OR,* vol XXXI, Part 1:546.

69. Oscar Hugh La Grange to John S. Pratt, January 20, 1864, *OR,* vol. XXXII, Part 1:90–91.

Chapter 6

1. William B. Stokes to Burn H. Polk, March 28, 1864, *OR,* vol. XXXII, Part 1:494.

2. Paul R. Scott, "Eighth Texas Cavalry Regiment, CSA," master's thesis, University of Texas at Arlington, 1977,174.

3. It was shortly after the Battle of Dalton that a writer wrote of Johnston's army: "It is wonderful to see with what patience our soldiers bear up under trials and hardships. I attribute this in part to the great religious change in our army. Twelve months after this revolution commenced, a more ungodly set of men could scarcely be found than the Confederate army. Now the utterance of oaths is seldom and religious songs and expressions of gratitude to God are heard from every quarter. Our army seem to be impressed with a high sense of overwhelming Providence. They have become Christian patriots with a sacred object to accomplish—an object dearer than life." J. William Jones (ed), *Christ in the Camp* (Harrisonburg, VA: Sprinkle Publications, 1986), 556.

4. Scott, *op. cit.,* 173.

5. Hiram Granbury assumed command of the Texas Brigade in November 1863. His previous command had been surrendered with him at Fort Donelson. Granbury maintained a law practice in Waco, Texas, prior to the war.

6. The 9th Kentucky saw action the previous day against the 119th New York Infantry. James M. McCaffrey, *This Band of Heroes: Granbury's Texas Brigade, C.S.A.* (Austin, TX: Eakin Press) 103.

7. *Ibid.*

8. Oliver Howard, "The Struggle for Atlanta," in *Battles and Leaders in the Civil War* (New York: Meridian), 495.

9. O.M. Roberts, and Clement Evans, eds., *Confederate Military History: Texas and Florida,* vol. IX, The Blue and Grey Press, 495.

10. L. B. Giles, *Terry's Texas Rangers* (Austin TX: The Pemberton Press, 1967), 79–80. Colonel La Grange initially refused surrendering his arms to his captor, John Haynie of the Rangers, claiming he would not surrender to anyone of inferior rank. John told him that "All Rangers rank Colonels in the Yankee army." La Grange replied, "I think you are correct," and then surrendered his weapon and followed the Ranger. John Claiborne, "Various Complimentary Remarks and Excerpts from different general orders read out to the army of Tennessee," *New Birmingham Times,* 1891, edited by Paul Scott, 2000.

11. *Ibid.*

12. John A. Wharton commanded the regiment during much of the war and influenced the authority structure of the Rangers. In his military advancement, Wharton exhibited astute political acumen and possessed great ability as an orator. His oratory contained force of argument and conviction,

although he avoided popular approval or notoriety. Wharton also required his commanders to be responsible for depredations committed by troops under them. Through his leadership, "his troops are warmly attached and feel the utmost confidence in his capacity: well assured he will care for their wants." The recommendations by fellow generals testifies of his leadership abilities by peers, although Andrew Lytle's biography of Forrest cast some doubts on Wharton's abilities and presented the regiment as being "green." Had Wharton survived the war, accounts regarding his leadership would likely be more flattering.

Although unsuccessful in some of his political activities, the successes he enjoyed were notable. Wharton's attempt at obtaining a transfer of the unit was a disappointing failure. In the aftermath of the setback, Wharton received a transfer for himself and his bodyguard. He also secured several letters of recommendation from fellow officers, which he presented to Generals Kirby Smith and John Magruder. Unfortunately, Wharton struggled politically against Joseph Wheeler, whose star was also rising. Some researchers of the regiment suspect that Wheeler pigeon-holed many of Wharton's reports. It is suspected that Wheeler rewrote battle reports and edited them to make himself look good and minimize the influence of Wharton. Wheeler's political connection included fellow Georgian Braxton Bragg and through Bragg to Jefferson Davis. Although Francis Lubbock joined Davis' staff in the latter part of the war, it was too late to help Wharton in crucial political decisions at critical times.

Wharton's loss was noted in Maj. Gen. Alexander Stuart's letter to Kirby Smith: "I have frequently been thrown with him on 'the front' and have always found him vigilant- active and ready.... His removal from here is a great loss to this army and a decided gain to yours." Letter, General Alexander Stewart to General Kirby Smith, John A. Wharton Papers, Archives, Rosenberg Library, G.

13. Holman in Mamie Yearie (ed.), *Reminiscences of Boys in Gray 1861–1865*, 345.

14. Lester N. Fitzhugh, "Terry's Texas Rangers," *Soldiers of Texas* (Waco, TX: Texian Press, 1973), 92.

15. Giles, 81.

16. John M. Claiborne, "Terry's Texas Rangers," Paul R. Scott, ed., *New Birmingham Times*, 1891.

17. O.M. Roberts, and Clement Evans, eds., *Confederate Military History: Texas and Florida*, vol. IX (The Blue and Grey Press), 187.

18. *Ibid.*, 188.

19. Joseph E. Johnston, "Johnston Halts Sherman at New Hope Church" in Henry Steele Commager, *The Blue and the Gray* (The Fairfax Press, 1982), 934.

20. *Ibid.*, 935.

21. *Ibid.*

22. Stanley F. Horn, *The Army of Tennessee* (Norman and London: University of Oklahoma Press, 1993), 329–330; G. McWhiney, and D. Perry, *Attack and Die: Civil War Military Tactics and the Southern Heritage* (University of Alabama Press, 1982), 116.

23. John B. Hood, "The Defense of Atlanta" in *Battles and Leaders of the Civil War* (New York: Meridian, 1989), 517.

24. Paul R. Scott, "Shannon's Scouts Combat Reconnaissance Detachment of Terry's Texas Rangers," *Military History of Texas and the Southwest* XV, no. 3:6.

25. *Ibid.*

26. Hood, "The Defense of Atlanta," 520.

27. *Ibid.*

28. The historical marker on the courthouse square in Newnan, Georgia, reads as follows: "On July 27, 1864, Brig. General E. M. McCook with 3,660 Federal cavalry began a raid to destroy railroads south of Atlanta and release 32,000 Federal prisoners at Andersonville. Three miles south of Newnan, on July 30th, Major General Joseph Wheeler with some 1,400 Confederate cavalry caught and routed the Federals, captured about 2,000 men, several ambulances, a full battery, and released 500 Confederate prisoners. Here General Wheeler whipped the 'pick' of the Federal cavalry and saved Newnan from capture and possible destruction."

29. Edward McCook to William T. Sherman, August 3, 1864, *OR,* vol. XXXVIII, Part 2:762.

30. Journal of Brigadier General Asbury Soup, CS Army, Chief of Staff of Operations, July 25–Sept. 7, 1864, *OR,* vol. XXXVIII, Part 3:688–689.

31. Hood, "The Defense of Atlanta," 520.

32. *Ibid.*

33. Joseph Wheeler to A. P. Mason, October 9, 1864, *OR,* vol. XXXVIII, Part 3:957–958; Hood, "The Defense of Atlanta," 521.

34. Diary of Jim Hill, unpublished manuscript, 1907.

35. Giles, 87.

36. James B. Eustis to Joseph Wheeler, September 18, 1864, *OR,* vol. XXXIX, Part 2:844.

37. Tom Burney, "Shannon's Scouts," *Groesbeck Journal,* Thursday December 9, 1909.

38. Giles, 90–91.

39. Jeffries, 103. On hearing of the loss of the flag, supporters in Texas took up a collection for a fourth flag. The flag was a four-foot-square battle flag purchased in Havana, Cuba. Scott, "Eighth Texas Cavalry Regiment, CSA."

40. Daniel Oakey, "Marching Through Georgia and the Carolinas," in *Battles and Leaders of the Civil War* (New York: Meridian, 1989), 592.

41. Some researchers report the Rangers' participation in over 1,000 armed engagements within a four-year period. In the event those reports are true, it is likely that members developed an affinity to aspects of warfare. Rangers routinely volunteered for dangerous missions, suggesting that the large number of actions did not deter volunteering for further actions. Exposure to such high numbers of combat situations would doubtlessly affect the soldiers, desensitizing them to aggression and associated hostilities seen late in the war. If such exposure to combat occurred in the 1990s, many members of the regiment would likely develop symptoms of post-traumatic stress disorder. As the brutality of war-

fare escalated in Sherman's "March to the Sea," the aggression exhibited suggests possible symptoms of post-traumatic stress disorder.

Numerically, the frequency of actions indicates that over 60% of the duration of the war was in combat for the Rangers. Although the numbers seem extremely high, Wharton's contemporary, Maj. Gen. Patrick Cleburne, attested to many of the actions. "(Wharton). . . has done more constant hard fighting than any other east of the Mississippi." Cleburne himself witnessed many battles, and his testimony carries high credibility.

42. Joseph Wheeler to Thomas Benton Roy, December 24, 1864, *OR*, vol. XLIV: 406–407.

43. *Ibid.*

44. Griswoldville was the location of the largest producers of revolvers for the Confederacy during the war.

45. Thomas Jefferson Jordan to James Biggs, November 22, 1864, *OR*, vol. XLIV:386; Joseph Wheeler to Thomas Benton Roy, December 24, 1864, *OR*, vol. XLIV:407.

46. Clem Bassett, "Clem Bassett" in Mamie Yeary (ed.), *Reminiscences of Boys in Gray 1861–1865*.

47. Oakey, 595.

48. Gen. W. T. Sherman wrote to Gen. U. S. Grant: "The amount of burning, stealing and plundering done by our own army makes me ashamed of it. I would quit the service if I could, because I fear that we are drifting to the worst sort of vandalism. I have endeavored to repress this class of crime, but you know how difficult it is to fix guilt among the great mass of an army. In this case I caught a man in the act. He is acquitted because his superior officer ordered it. The superior officer is acquitted because I suppose, he had not set fire with his own hands and thus you and I and every commander must go through the war justly chargeable with crimes at which we blush." *OR*, Part 3:574.

49. Oakey, 598.

50. Burney, *Groesbeck Journal*, December 9, 1909.

51. W. H. Davis, "Cavalry Service Under General Wheeler," *Confederate Veteran* XXXI, no. 3 (March 1923): 353–354.

52. Joseph Wheeler to Thomas Benton Roy, December 24, 1864, *OR*, vol. XLIV: 353–354.

53. Burke Davis, *Sherman's March* (New York: Random House, 1980), 83.

54. *Ibid.*

55. *Ibid.*, 254.

56. Earlier in 1864, Kilpatrick led a raid aimed at Richmond, Virginia. The true intent of the raid remains debated, although captured papers (Ulric Dahlgren's papers) indicate it was to "kill the traitor Davis and his cabinet."

57. Paul R. Scott, "Shannon's Scouts," 12.

58. Wheeler sent this address to his cavalrymen:

Head Quarters, Cavalry Corps
December 31st, 1864

My brave Soldiers,

The close of the year terminates a campaign of eight months, during which you have engaged in continuous and successful fighting.

From Dalton to Atlanta you held the right of our army. Opposed almost continuously by a force on infantry ten times your number, you repulsed every assault, inflicting upon the enemy a loss in killed and wounded numerically greater than your entire strength. Every attempt on the part of the enemy to turn or strike our right flank was met and repulsed by your valor and determined courage. It should be a proud reflection to you all, that during the entire campaign, the Army of Tennessee never lost a position by having the flank turned which it was your duty to protect.

During every movement of our line, you have been between our infantry and the enemy hurling back his exulting advance, and holding his entire army at bay until our troops had quietly prepared to receive and repulse his gigantic assaults. Having failed by other means to drive our army from the positions in front of Atlanta, he sends three heavy columns of cavalry to destroy our communications, to release prisoners of war, and march in triumph with them through our country. You promptly strike one column and drive it back discomfited; then quickly assailing the two others, you defeat them and complete their destruction and capture. This, alone cost the enemy more than five thousand men, horses, arms and equipment, besides material, colors and cannon. This was due to your valor, and is without parallel in the history in this war.

Having been detached and sent to the rear of the enemy you captured his garrison, destroyed his stores and broke his communication more effectively and for larger periods than any other cavalry force, however large has done.

During Sherman's march through Georgia you retarded his advance and defeated his cavalry daily, preventing his spreading over and devastating the country.

During the last five months you have traveled nearly three thousand miles, fighting nearly every day, and always with success. You must have been victorious in more than fifty pitched battles, and a hundred minor affairs placing a number of the enemy hors du combat fully four times the greatest number you ever carried into action.

I desire, my brave soldiers, to thank you for your gallantry, devotion and good conduct. Every charge I have asked you to make, has been brilliantly executed. Every position I have asked you to hold, has been held until absolutely untenable. Your devotion to your country has filled my heart with gratitude. You have done your full duty to your country and to me; and I have tried to do my full duty to you. Circumstances have forced upon you many and great deprivations. You have been deprived of the issues of clothing and many of the comforts and conveniences and have borne all without a murmur.

Soldiers of Kentucky, Tennessee, Texas and Arkansas! You deserve special commendation and fortitude. Separated from your homes and families you have nobly done all that gallant devoted men could do. Soldiers from Alabama and Georgia! Your homes have nearly all been overrun and destroyed, yet without complaint you have stood to your colors like brave and patriotic men. Your country and your God will one day reward you.

The gallant Kelly whom we all loved so well is dead. Many other brave spirits whose loss we deeply feel sleep with him. They fell—the price of victory.

Allen, Humes, Anderson, Dibbrell, Hagan, Crews, Ashby, Harrison, and Breckinridge, and my other brave men whose gallantry you have so often witnessed are here still to guide and lead you in battles to be fought and victories yet to be won.

Another campaign will soon open in which I only ask you to fight with the same valor I have always seen you exhibit upon many fields where your determined courage has won victory for our cause.

J. Wheeler
Major General

Joseph Wheeler, in Richard B. Harwell (ed.), *The Confederate Reader: How the South Saw the War* (New York: Dover Publications), 198.

59. Sherman wrote in a letter home, "Their devotion is wonderful. Men of immense estates of 30 to 50,000 dollars have given up all and now serve as common soldiers in the Ranks. Why cannot we inspire our people with the same ardor. . ." W. T. Sherman, in Joseph H. Ewing, "The New Sherman Letters," *Civil War Chronicles* (1994): 20–31, 34–35.

Chapter 7

1. Letter, John W. Rabb to Mary C. Rabb, January 11, 1865, Rabb Letters.

2. Paul R. Scott, "Shannon's Scouts Combat Reconnaissance Detachment of Terry's Texas Rangers," *Military History of Texas and the Southwest* XV, number 3:14.

3. O. M. Roberts, and Clement A. Evans, eds., *Confederate Military History: Texas and Florida,* vol. XI (The Blue and Grey Press), 192.

4. Francis Trevelyan Miller, ed., *The Photographic History of the Civil War, vol 4–The Cavalry* (New York: Castle Books, 1957), 287.

5. William T. Sherman, "General Sherman Thinks His Name May Live," in Henry Steele Commager, ed., *The Blue and the Gray* (The Fairfax Press, 1982), 967.

6. Burke Davis, *Sherman's March* (New York: Random House, 1980),151.

7. *Ibid.,* 150–151.

8. Atrocities included pillage, breaking into stores, robbing citizens at gunpoint, soldiers defecating on and in beds and cookery, and graves robbed. E. A. Pollard, *The Lost Cause,* Reprint. (New York: Grammercy Books, 1994), 666–667.

9. William Preston Mangum, "Kill Cavalry's Nasty Surprise," *America's Civil War* (November 1996).

10. Davis, *Sherman's March* (New York: Random House, 1980), 187.

11. *Ibid.,* 152.

12. Judson Kilpatrick to Lewis Mulford Dayton, February 22, 1865, *OR,* vol. XLVII, Part 2:533.

13. Scott, "Shannon's Scouts," 3:15.

14. *Ibid.*

15. Davis, *Sherman's March,* 187.

16. Scott, *op. cit.,* 3:16.

17. James Knox Polk Blackburn, "Reminiscences of the Terry Rangers," *Southwestern Historical Quarterly* XXII (October 1918):165.

18. *Ibid.,* 165–166; *OR,* vol. XLVII, Part 2:546, 596.

19. Edward Kennedy, "The Mills of the Gods," *Confederate Veteran* XXII (April 1924):126.

20. Mangum.

21. *Ibid.*

22. *Ibid.*

23. Davis, *Sherman's March,* 213.

24. Mangum.

25. *Ibid.*

26. Davis, *Sherman's March,* 215–216.

27. Mrs. John H. Anderson, "What Sherman Did to Fayetteville, North Carolina," *Confederate Veteran* XXXII (April 1924):138–140.

28. Davis, *Sherman's March,* 218.

29. Daniel Oakey, "Marching Through Georgia and the Carolinas," in *Battles and Leaders of the Civil War* (New York: Meridian, 1989), 598.

30. Blackburn, 169.

31. Mark L. Bradley, "Bentonville," *Confederate Veteran* IV (1995), 17.

32. James M. McCaffrey, *This Band of Heroes: Granbury's Texas Brigade, C. S. A.* (Austin, TX: Eakin Press, 1985),152.

33. Bradley, 17.

34. Giles, 97.

35. *Ibid.*

36. A. P. Harcourt, "Terry's Texas Rangers," *The Southern Bivouac* (November 1882).

37. Stanley F. Horn, *The Army of Tennessee* (Norman and London: University of Oklahoma Press, 1993), 425.

38. Davis, *Sherman's March,* 239.

39. Blackburn, 171.

40. Harcourt.

41. Bradley, 21.

42. Scott, "Shannon's Scouts," 3:19; obituary of A. M. Shannon, *Confederate Veteran* XV (Feb. 1907):84–85.

43. Scott, *op. cit.,* 3:18.

44. Letter, Tom Burney to Lucy Burney, "The Famous Terry Rangers," undated.

45. Blackburn, 171.

46. *Ibid.,* 171–172.

47. Edward Kennedy, "Last Work of Wheeler's Special Confederate Scouts," *Confederate Veteran* XXXII (January 1924):60.

48. Blackburn, 171–173; Letter, Tom Burney to Lucy Burney, "The Famous Terry Rangers," undated.

49. John G. Walker commanded the "Greyhound Division" at this time. The division consisted of Steele's, Bee's, and Bagby's divisions and the

brigades of Cooper and Slaughter (Roberts). John G. Walker was also a Roman Catholic.

50. Ben Stuart Papers, "The Death of General Wharton," 13–15, Rosenberg Library, Galveston.

51. Tom Cutrer, "Thomas McKinney Jack," *The Handbook of Texas Online*.

Chapter 8

1. Erika Bourguignon, *Psychological Anthropology* (Winston, NY: Holt Rinehart and Winston, 1979), 166.

2. Emanuel F. Hammer, *The Clinical Application of Projective Drawings* (Springfield, IL: Charles C. Thoms, 1980), 6–7.

3. Some of the men in the regiment preferred using the term "banner" rather than "flag."

4. Charlie C. Jeffries, *Terry's Rangers* (New York: Vantage Press, 1961), 62.

5. Barry Shlater, "Terry's Texas Rangers' famed Civil War battle flag returned," *Houston Chronicle*, April 21, 1996, 6E.

6. This flag was lost near Rome, Georgia. After the war, the flag's finder, John J. Weiler, urged the governor of Indiana to return it. In 1899 Governor James A. Mount of Indiana returned the flag to members of the 8th Texas Cavalry Regiment. The veteran's group then turned the flag over to the UDC (United Daughters of the Confederacy), who held it as a public trust. The flag was displayed at the Confederate Museum in Austin, Texas, in a glass case. The flag's condition was poor due to handling and age. On January 30, 1980, the flag was stolen in a nighttime burglary. Its location was a mystery until a military expert overheard a conversation mentioning it. The conversation concerned two Civil War artifact collectors in Florida who had acquired the flag and were offering it for sale. The expert informed the UDC, who in turn alerted the Texas Rangers and the State Capitol Police. After negotiations, the collectors returned the flag. The flag was returned by Paul Fuentez of the Florida Department of Public Safety to the UDC on April 15, 1996. The UDC began work on restoring the flag. Upon restoration, it will be displayed at the Confederate Museum in Hillsboro, Texas. Barry Shlater, "Terry's Texas Rangers' famed Civil War battle flag returned," *Houston Chronicle*, April 21, 1996, 6E; Allan Turner, "Old Flag's New Life," *Houston Chronicle*, September 29, 1996.

7. See *Christ in the Camp* by J. William Jones for documentation on how many of the participants viewed the War for Southern Independence as a "holy war."

8. Giles, 90.

9. The Bonnie Blue also served as the unofficial flag of the Republic of Mississippi during the initial stages of its formation in 1861. The Bonnie Blue design was eventually incorporated into five of the Confederate States flags adopted in early 1861.

10. Two examples of such hats are known to exist. One, Clem Bassett's hat, is located in the Museum of the Confederacy in Richmond, Virginia, and the other in the San Jacinto Monument Museum textile collection.

11. The hat of Ranger Clem Bassett contains this design embedded in the

hat itself. The hat is on display at the Museum of Southern History, Richmond, Texas. A second hat, with similar design is in San Jacinto Monument Museum in Deer Park, Texas.

12. It is now illegal to sell Texas Ranger badges in the state of Texas, since the design has changed little over the years. Original badges were made from Mexican 50 peso pieces.

13. Several autobiographical accounts of the Rangers contain a mixture of reminiscing and folktales. Among these are those written by J.K.P. Blackburn and L. Giles.

14. Bourguignon, 165.

15. A. C. Jones of Company B from Matagorda County was the color sergeant. He was often called "Count." Prior to the war, he owned 6,000 acres.

16. Lois Hill, ed., *Poems and Songs of the Civil War* (New York: Outlet Book Company, Barnes and Noble, Inc., 1990), 214.

Chapter 9

1. Pompeo Coppini also designed the statue for Sam Houston's grave in Huntsville, Texas, and Hood's Texas Brigade on the State Capitol grounds. Other Confederate monuments include locations in Corpus Christi, Victoria, and Paris, Texas. He also designed monuments to Texas Independence such as the Alamo Centopath in San Antonio and "Come and Take It" in Gonzales, Texas. Coppini also designed the Texas Centennial commemorative coin issued by the U.S. mint in 1934.

2. The Wheeler letter follows:

Headquarters
Cavalry Corps
April 24, 1865

Gallant Comrades,

You have fought your fight. Your task is done. During four years of struggle for liberty you have exhibited courage, fortitude and devotion. You are the victors of more than 200 sternly contested fields. You have participated in more than 1000 conflicts of arms. You are heroes, veterans, patriots. The bones of your comrades mark the battlefields of Kentucky, Tennessee, North Carolina, South Carolina, Georgia, Alabama and Mississippi. You have done all that human exertion could accomplish. In bidding you adieu I desire to tender my thanks for your gallantry in battle, your fortitude under suffering, and the devotion at all times to the holy cause you have done so much to maintain. I desire also to express my gratitude for the kind feeling you have seen fit to extend to myself and to invoke upon you the blessings of our Heavenly Father in the cause of freedom.

Joseph Wheeler
Liet. General Commanding
Cavalry Corps
Army of Tennessee

3. Among other notable Houstonians in Glenwood Cemetery is Howard Hughes.

4. The Rangers took sixty servants with them in their campaigning.

5. Michael O. Shannon, "Shannon, Alexander May," *The Handbook of Texas Online.*

6. Randolph Campbell, "Rector, John B.," *The Handbook of Texas Online.*

7. Walter Prescott Webb, ed. *The Handbook of Texas,* 2 volumes (Austin, TX: The Texas State Historical Association, 1952), 447.

8. J.M. Claiborne, "Terry's Texas Rangers," *Confederate Veteran* V (June 1897):252–254.

9. C. E. Avery, and David Williams, "Confederate Images: Brigadier General Thomas Harrison," *Confederate Veteran* II (1999), 11. The cemetery is now known as Oakwood. Tom Harrison's body is in Lot 19, Block 86.

10. Tom Cutrer, "Harrison, Thomas," *The Handbook of Texas Online*; Webb, *The Handbook,* 780.

11. *Ibid.,* 245.

12. *Ibid.*

13. Rose M. Harris, "Love, James," *The Handbook of Texas Online.*

14. Ben C. Stuart, "Ben C. Stuart Papers," Archives, Rosenberg Library, Galveston, Texas. Judge Terry was killed in an angry altercation with a United States Supreme Court justice while traveling by train in 1898.

15. Thomas Cutrer, "Jack, Thomas McKinney," *The Handbook of Texas Online.*

16. Robert Lee Williamson, "Pope, William Henry," *The Handbook of Texas Online.*

17. Cutrer, "Williamson, Robert Lee," *The Handbook of Texas Online.*

18. Diana Kleiner, "Fletcher, William Andrew," *The Handbook of Texas Online.*

19. Barbara Donalson Althaus, "Kyle, Fergus," *The Handbook of Texas Online.*

20. Anne Leslie Fenstermaker, "Maverick, Samuel Jr.," *The Handbook of Texas Online.*

21. Nowlin Randolph, "Combs, David St. Clair," *The Handbook of Texas Online.*

22. Brian Hart, "Cochran, Archalus M.," *The Handbook of Texas Online.*

23. Nowlin Randolph, "Blackburn, James Knox Polk," *The Handbook of Texas Online.*

24. Among the works by the artists are Carl G. Iwonski, "Sam Maverick and the Terry Rangers"; Jack Amirian, "Ranger Willie"; Mort Kunstler, "Battle of Fallen Timbers"; Don Trioni, "8th Texas Cavalry, Terry's Texas Rangers"; Bruce Marshall, "Terry's Texas Rangers," "Charge of the Eighth Texas Cavalry," "Terry's Empty Saddle," "Charge of the Texas Rangers," "Terry's Texas Rangers-Into the Breach" and others; Raymond Desvarreux Larpenteur, "C.S.A. 8th Cavalry Terry's Texas Rangers."

25. Anthony F. C. Wallace, "Revitalization Movements: Some Theoretical Considerations for their Comparative Study" in *American Anthropologist* 5: 264–281.

26. During that time the nations of Latvia, Lithuania, Estonia, Khazakstan, Slovakia, South Africa, Germany, Czech Republic, Serbia, Croatia, and Ukraine achieved their independence after a renewed sense of national identity and breaking free of dominating powers. The national identity movement of Scotland, Catalonia, Tyrol, Quebec, and Chiapas continued struggling for acceptance and independence.

Appendix I

1. Since the delivery of the eulogy, it was discovered that this information is incorrect. The original was included to maintain the integrity of the eulogy.

Colonel Benjamin Franklin Terry. Commander and namesake of Terry's Texas Rangers.

Colonel Gustav Cook. By war's end, he was promoted to regimental commander.

Lt. Colonel S. P. (Pat) Christian. An influential officer in the regiment.

1862
July 26th

Confederate State
To J K White

To Cash paid for Subsistance while
in private Hospital near Camp
Pond Spring ____ from July 15 to July 26
Eleven days at 75 ¢ pr day $8.25

I Certify that the above a/c is
correct the above named J K White
having been sent to private Hospital
by my directions   J H Gulick Acting Surgeon

I certify that the above a/c is
Correct and the money expended is
Charged to the above named J K
White having been sent to
private Hospital with my
prescription   W R Jarmon
                  Capt. comdg 9 o 9 9

The A/c will pay the above a/c
                  J G Walker
                  Lt Col Texas
                  Rangers

A request for reimbursement for James K. White while he was in a private hospital. The request was countersigned by J. W. Gulick, company surgeon, Captain W. R. Jarmon, and Lt. Col. J. G. Walker. Courtesy of James K. White family.

Confederate States

1862   To Lieut J. K. White   Dr

July 21   For Bread Rat for 45 men   3.10
  "   22   "   Dr   "   "   "   "   2.00
  "   23   "   "   "   "   "   "   2.00
  "   24   "   Dr   "   "   "   "   2.00
  "   25   "   "   "   "   "   "   2.00
  "   26   "   Dr   "   "   "   "   2.00
  "   27   "   "   "   "   "   "   2.00
  "   "   "   94½ # Bacon ⊃ 25¢ ——   23.65 ✓
                                            $38.65

I certify on honor that the above bill
is just & correct; that the men were
detached by me, and that it was impracti-
cable to carry rations in kind & the A.C.S.
will pay said acct.   John G Walker
                        Lt Col Commdg 8th Regt Tex. Cav.

Recd Aug 16 1/62 of R. H. Simmons Capt & A C S of 8th Regt Texas
cavalry Thirty Eight dollars & Sixty five cents in full of above
account
                        J. K. White Lt
                        Com Detachment

A request for reimbursement for bread rations for men under Lt. James K. White.
Courtesy of James K. White family.

Blockhouse used to guard the railroads. This is similar to those attacked by the Rangers.

Close-up photo of monument to Terry's Texas Rangers. Note the set of six-shooters on the waist and additional saddle holster.

—From Author's Collection

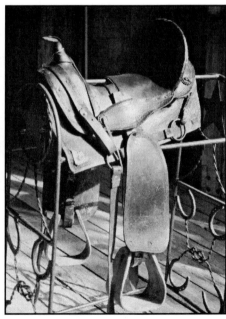

(Left) Confederate cavalry officer's saddle. Note the saddle holster. (Right) Saddle purportedly belonging to a member of Terry's Texas Rangers.

—Courtesy of Donnie Roberts collection

Bibliography

Primary Sources

Manuscripts
Batchelor-Turner Letters. Archives, Rosenberg Library, Galveston, Texas.
Bragg, Braxton. Papers. Archives, Rosenberg Library, Galveston, Texas.
Bunting, Robert Franklin. "True Merit Brings Its Own Reward." John A. Wharton Papers, Rosenberg Library, Galveston, Texas.
Bunting, Robert Franklin. Archives, University of Texas, Austin, Texas.
Hill, James Monroe. Diary of Jim Hill. In possession of Hill family, unpublished manuscripts, 1907.
Love, Cyrus W. Letter to Jas. M. and T.A. Love, 1862.
Wharton, John A. Archives, Rosenberg Library, Galveston, Texas.
Terry, Benjamin Franklin. Archives, Rosenberg Library, Galveston, Texas.
Shannon-Scott Papers. Woodson Research Center, Fondren Library, Rice University, Houston, Texas.
Stuart, Ben C. Papers. Archives, Rosenberg Library, Galveston, Texas.

Books
Diary of E. S. Dodd, Co. D, Terry's Texas Rangers & An Account of His Hanging as a Confederate Spy. Austin: Ranger Press, 1979.
Ford, John S. *Rip Ford's Texas.* Austin, TX: University of Texas Press, 1963.
Gainer, William T., and M. Yeary, eds. *Reminiscences of the Boys in Gray: 1861–1865.* Morningside, 1986.
Giles, L. B. *Terry's Texas Rangers.* Brasada Reprint Series. Austin, TX: The Pemberton Press, 1967.
Jones, J. William, ed. *Christ in the Camp: Religion in the Confederate Army.* Reprint. Harrisonburg, VA: Sprinkle Publications, *1986.*

209

Lubbock, Francis R. *Six Decades in Texas: The Memoirs of Francis R. Lubbock, Confederate Governor of Texas.* Austin and New York: Pemberton Press, 1968.

Miller, Francis Trevelyan, ed. *The Photographic History of the Civil War, vol. 4–The Cavalry.* New York: Castle Books, 1957.

Pollard, E. A. *The Lost Cause.* Reprint. New York: Grammercy Books, 1994.

Roberts, O. M., and Clement A. Evans, eds. *Confederate Military History: Texas and Florida.* Vol. XI. Reprint. The Blue and Grey Press.

Rugley, Helen, ed. *Batchelor—Turner Letters, 1861–1864: Written by Two of Terry's Texas Rangers.* Austin, TX: Steek Co. 1961.

Wright, Marcus J., and Harold B. Simpson, eds. *Texas in the War, 1861–1865.* Waco, TX: Texian Press, 1965.

Yeary, Mamie (comp). *"Reminiscences of Boys in Gray 1861–1865."*

War of the Rebellion: A Compilation of the Official Records of the Union and Confederate Armies. 128 vols. Washington, D.C.: Government Printing Office, 1880–1901.

Articles and Excerpts from Books

Affleck, Dunbar. Letter to Mr. and Mrs. Thomas Affleck, June 29, 1862, in "With Terry's Texas Rangers," *Civil War History:* 308.

Anderson, Mrs. John H. "What Sherman Did to Fayetteville, North Carolina." *Confederate Veteran* XXXII (April 1924).

Battle, Frank. "General Forrest's Order to Colonel Baxter Smith." *Confederate Veteran* VII (February 1899).

Baylor, George Whythe. "With A. S. Johnston at Shiloh." *Confederate Veteran* V (1897):609.

Beauregard, Pierre G. T. "The First Battle of Bull Run." Ned Bradford, ed. *Battles and Leaders of the Civil War.* New York: Meridian Press, 1989, 41–60.

Blackburn, James Knox Polk. "Reminiscences of the Terry Rangers." *Southwestern Historical Quarterly* XXII (July and October 1918):38–77, 143–179.

Claiborne, John M. "Terry's Texas Rangers." *Confederate Veteran* V (June 1897):252–254.

Davis, W. H. "Cavalry Service Under General Wheeler." *Confederate Veteran* XI (1903): 353–354.

Darst, M. "Robert Hodges, Jr.: Confederate Soldier." *East Texas Historical Journal* IX (March 1971):20–47.

Dunman, R. L. "One of Terry's Texas Rangers." *Confederate Veteran* XXXI (March 1923).

"Flag of Terry's Texas Rangers." *Confederate Veteran* VII (December 1899).

Graber, Henry W. *The Life Record of H. W. Grabaer, A Terry Ranger, 1861–1865.* Reprint. Austin: State House Press, 1987.

Grant, Ulysses S. "The Battle of Shiloh" in *Battles and Leaders of the Civil War.* New York: Meridan, 1989, 83–96.

Groce, William Wharton. "Major General John A. Wharton." *Southwestern Historical Quarterly* 19 (January 1916): 271–278.

Harcourt, A. P. "Terry's Texas Rangers." *The Southern Bivouac* I, no. 3 (November 1882).

Hood, John B. "The Defense of Atlanta." in *Battles and Leaders of the Civil War.* New York: Meridian, 1989, 511–526.

Johnson, Robert, and Clarence C. Buel, eds. *Battles and Leaders of the Civil War.* Vol. 4. New York: Thomas Yoseloff, 1956.

Johnston, Joseph E. "Johnston Halts Sherman at New Hope Church," in Henry Steele Commager, ed., *The Blue and The Gray.* The Fairfax Press, 1982: 933–935.

Kennedy, Edward. "Last Work of Wheeler's Special Confederate Scouts." *Confederate Veteran* XXXII (January 1924):60.

———. "The Mills of the Gods." *Confederate Veteran* XXXII (April 1924):126.

King, William H. "Forrest's Attack on Murfreesboro, July 13, 1862, *Confederate Veteran* XXXII (November 1924).

McDonald, Ward. "Sensation in Kentucky Backwoods." *Confederate Veteran* III (May 1895).

Oakey, Daniel. "Marching Through Georgia and the Carolinas" in *Battles and Leaders of the Civil War.* New York: Meridian, 1989, 591–599.

"Obituary of A. M. Shannon." *Confederate Veteran* XV (February 1907): 84–85.

Peake, Michael A. *Indiana's German Sons: A History of the 1st German, 32nd Regiment Indiana Volunteer Infantry,* Deutches Haus-Athenaeum, Indianapolis, Indiana, 1999, foreword.

Prestridge, J. N. *Modern Baptist Heroes and Martyrs.* Louisville, KY: The Word Press, 1911.

Ridley, B. L. "Echoes from the Battle of Murfreesboro." *Confederate Veteran* XI (February 1903).

Scott, H. H. "Fighting Kilpatrick's Escape." *Confederate Veteran* XI (December 1903): 588.

Sherman, William Tecumseh. "General Sherman Thinks His Name May Live," in Henry Steele Commager, *The Blue and The Gray.* The Fairfax Press, 1982, 966–968.

Sherman, William Tecumseh. In Joseph H. Ewing, "The New Sherman Letters." *Civil War Chronicles*, 1994:20–35.

Smith, William Fort. "Presentation of Bonnie Blue Flag." *Confederate Veteran,* volume 3, number 7, July 1895, 216.

Witcher, J. C. "Shannon's Scouts." *Confederate Veteran* XIV (October 1906).

Wyeth, John Allen. "The Destruction of Rosecrans' Great Wagon Train" in Francis Trevelyan Miller, ed., *The Photographic History of the Civil War, vol. 4—The Cavalry.* Reprint. New York: Castle Books, 158–166.

Newspapers

Burney, Tom. "Shannon's Scouts." *Groesbeck Journal,* Thursday, December 9, 1909.

Claiborne, John M. "Terry's Texas Rangers." Paul R. Scott, ed., *New Birmingham Times,* 1891–1892.

Secondary Sources

Books

Armstrong, Robert M. *Sugar Land Texas and the Imperial Sugar Company.* Houston, TX: D. Armstrong, 1991.

Bate, W. N. *General Sidney Sherman: Texas Soldier, Statesman and Builder.* Waco, TX: Texian Press, 1974.

Bedwell, Randall, ed. *May I Quote You General Forrest?* Nashville, TN: Cumberland House Publishing, 1997.

Benson, Al. *A Theological and Political View of the Doctrine of Secession.* Arlington Heights, IL: Al Benson, Jr., 1995.

———. *The Socialist Supporters of Honest Abe.* Arlington Heights, IL: Al Benson, Jr., 1993.

Bowen, J. J. *The History and Battlefields of the Civil War.* Seacaucus, NJ: Wellfort Press, 1991.

———. *The Exodus of Federal Forces From Texas: 1861.* Austin, TX: Eakin Press, 1986.

Bowman, John S., ed. *The Civil War Almanac.* New York: World Almanac Publications, 1983.

Chance, Joseph E. *The Second Texas Infantry: From Shiloh to Vicksburg.* Austin, TX: Eakin Press, 1984.

Davis, Burke. *Sherman's March.* New York: Random House, 1980.

Farber, James. *Texas, C.S.A.* New York and San Antonio: Jackson Co., 1947.

Gallaway, B. P., ed. *The Dark Side of the Confederacy.* Dubuque, IA: William C. Brown Book Company, 1968.

Hair, Denny G. *Terry's Texas Rangers 8th Texas Cavalry, C.S.A.: A History and Chronology 1861–1865.* Part One. Privately published, August 1994.

Hill, Lois, ed. *Poems and Songs of the Civil War.* New York: Outlet Book Co., Inc., Barnes and Noble, Inc., 1990.

Horn, Stanley F. *The Army of Tennessee.* Norman, OK: University of Oklahoma Press, 1993.

Hurst, Jack. *Nathan Bedford Forrest: A Biography.* New York: Vintage Books, First Vintage Civil War Library Edition, 1994.

Jeffries, Charlie C. *Terry's Rangers.* New York: Vantage Press, 1961.

Longacre, Edward G. *Mounted Raids of the Civil War.* Cranbury, NJ: A. S. Barnes and Company, 1975.

Lytle, Andrew Nelson. *Bedford Forrest and the Critter Company.* Nashville, TN: J. S. Sanders and Company, 1984.

McCaffrey, James M. *This Band of Heroes: Granbury's Texas Brigade, C.S.A.* Austin, TX: Eakin Press, 1985.

McWhiney, G., and Perry D. Jamison. *Attack and Die: Civil War Military Tactics and the Southern Heritage.* University of Alabama Press, 1982.

Nevin, David, et al. *Sherman's March: Atlanta to The Sea.* Alexandria, VA: Time-Life Books, 1986.

Oates, Stephen B. *Confederate Cavalry West of the River.* Austin, TX: University of Texas Press, 1992.

Sowell, A. J. *History of Ft. Bend Co.* Houston, TX: W. H. Coyle, 1964.

Sword, Wiley. *Shiloh: Bloody April.* New York: William Morrow and Co., 1974.

————. *The Battle of Shiloh.* Eastern Acorn Press, 1982.

Tucker, Glenn. *The Battle of Chickamauga.* Jamestown, VA: Eastern Acorn Press, 1981.

Wakelyn, Jon L. *Biographical Dictionary of the Confederacy.* Westport, CT: Greenwood Press, 1977.

Webb, Walter Prescott, ed., et al. *The Handbook of Texas.* 2 volumes. Austin, TX: The Texas State Historical Association, 1952.

Wharton, Clarence R. *History of Ft. Bend County.* San Antonio, TX: Naylor Company, 1939.

Young, Kevin R. *To The Tyrants Never Yield: A Texas Civil War Sampler.* Plano, TX: Wordware Publishing, 1992.

Articles, Theses, and Excerpts from Books

Avery, C. E., and David Williams. "Confederate Images: Brigadier General Thomas Harrison." *Confederate Veteran* II (1999):11.

Bradley, Mark L. "Bentonville." *Confederate Veteran* IV (1995): 16–21.

Brazoria County Museum Bulletin."Following the Trail of B.F. Terry," November 1999.

Cutrer, Thomas. "Jack, Thomas McKinney." *The Handbook of Texas Online.*

Dabney, Robert L. "Terry's Texas Rangers, an address given to the Sons of Confederate Veterans," Albert Sidney Johnston Camp, #67, August 16, 2000, Houston, TX.

Fitzhugh, Lester N. "Terry's Texas Rangers," in *Soldiers of Texas.* Waco, TX: Texian Press, 1973.

————. "Terry's Texas Rangers," an address given before the Houston Civil War Round Table, March 21, 1958.

Heidler, Jeanne. "Embarrasing Situation: David E. Twiggs and the Surrender of United States Forces in Texas, 1861. In Ralph E. Wooster, ed., *Lone Star Blue and Gray.* Austin, TX: Texas State Historical Association, 1995.

Jeffries, Charlie C. "The Character of Terry's Texas Rangers." *Southwestern Historical Quarterly* 64 (April 1961): 454–462.

Kellog, Joan, et al. "The Use of the Mandala in Psychological Evaluation and Treatment." *American Journal of Art Therapy* 16 (July 1977):123–134.

Lester, Tom. "Guide to 202nd Battalion, 2nd Military Police Group, Texas State Guard."

Mangum, William Preston. "Kill Cavalry's Nasty Surprise." *America's Civil War* (November 1996).

Mayes, Maxine. "Coppini's Passion." *Texas Highways* 46 (January 1999): 44–51.

Oates, Stephen B. "John S. 'Rip' Ford: Prudent Cavalryman, C.S.A." *Southwestern Historical Quarterly* 64 (January 1961).

————. "Recruiting Confederate Cavalry in Texas." *Southwestern Historical Quarterly* 65 (April 1961): 463–477.

Quigley, Mike. "Heart of a Communist/Mind of a Prussian," Civil War Interactive, 2001 (http://www.civilwarinteractive.com/wc_heart_of _a_Communist.htm.);

Kunze, Peter, August von Willich (1810-1878), Faecher (http://www.kant.step net.de/FAECHER/GE/1848/hp1848/artikel/willich.htm.

Rigelon, John. "Sherman's March Through Georgia." Eastern Digital Resources, *Researchonline.*

Sandbo, Anna Marie. "Beginnings of the Secession Movement in Texas" in *Southwestern Historical Quarterly* 18 (July 1914).

———. "The First Session of the Secession Convention of Texas." *Southwestern Historical Quarterly* 18 (October 1914).

Scott, Paul Robert. "Shannon's Scouts Combat Reconnaissance Detachment of Terry's Texas Rangers." *Military History of Texas and the Southwest* XV:5–23.

Sizemore, Larry W. "The First Confederate Chaplain." *Confederate Veteran* 1 (1998):56–57.

Steele, Edith Lee Lubbock. "The Five Lubbock Brothers." *Heroes in Grey Glory.* Jefferson Davis Chapter #1637, United Daughters of the Confederacy, Houston, Texas, 1983:114–115.

Stockdale, J. "The City of Houston During the War Between the States," a presentation given at the Sons of Confederate Veterans meeting, Houston, Texas, December 21, 1994.

Straw, Russell. "SP's Oldest Line." *S-P Trainline 1996,* no. 48, Southern Pacific Historical and Technical Society.

Terrell, Kate Scurry. "Terry's Texas Rangers," in Dudley Wooten, ed., *A Comprehensive History of Texas.* 2 vols. Dallas: William G. Scharff, 1898.

"Terry's Texas Rangers." *Confederate Veteran* XV (November 1907): 498.

Wallace, Anthony F. C. "Revitalization Movements: Some Theoretical Considerations for their Comparative Study" in *American Anthropologist* 58: 264–281.

Werner, George C. "Houston Tap Railroad." *The Handbook of Texas Online.*

Wooster, Ralph A. "An Analysis of the Membership of the Texas Secessionist Convention" in *Southwestern Historical Quarterly* LXII (January 1959): 322–335.

Zucker, A. E. "The Biographical Dictionary of the Fourty-eighters" in: *The Fourty-Eighters: Political Refugees of the German Revoloution of 1848.* Columbia, NY: Columbia University Press, 1950.

Newspapers
Marshall, Bruce. "Terry's Texas Rangers." *The Texas Star,* August 22, 1971:2–3.
Shlater, Barry. "Terry's Texas Rangers' famed Civil War battle flag returned." *Houston Chronicle,* April 21, 1996:6E.
Turner, Allan. "Old Flag's New Life." *Houston Chronicle,* September 29, 1996.

Theses
Scott, Paul Robert. "Eighth Texas Cavalry Regiment CSA." Master's thesis, University of Texas at Arlington, July 1977.

Index

Brown's Mill, Battle of, 95-96
Buck Head Creek, 100
Buckhead Church, 101
Buckner, Gen. Simon, 55
Buell, Gen. Don Carlos, 53, 55, 56
Bunting, Chaplain R.F., 38, 72, 78,
    121, 137
Burnside, Gen. Ambrose, 81

Camp Cooper, 11
Cape Fear River, 110
Carpenter, Capt. S.D., 11
Cassville, Georgia, 92
Chatham, Ronald, 55
Cheatham, Gen. B. F., 56, 57, 58, 90,
    92
Chicago Historical Society, 117
Chickamauga Creek, 74
China Grove, Brazoria County, 2
Christian, Capt. S. (Pat), 37, 62, 79
Claiborne, George, 95
Cleburne, Gen. Patrick, 28, 29, 90,
    132, 143
Cobb, Gen. Howell, 90, 92
Cochran, Archelus M., 141
Columbia, South Carolina, 105
Combs, David St. Clair, 141
Committee of Public Safety, 10, 12
Confederate Home for Men, 136
Confederate War Department, 17
Connolly, Maj. James, 101
Cooke, Col. Gustave, 6, 18, 73, 79,
    92, 106, 132, 136, 147
Coppini, Pompeo, 128
Corinth, Mississippi, 37-38
Cortina, Juan Nepomuceno, 4, 146
Cortina War, 4, 7, 10, 17, 146
Crittenden, Gen. Thomas, 50-53
Crook, Brig. Gen. George, 79
Crook's Division, 74
Cross, Rev. Dr. Joseph, 64
Cumberland Mountains, 67
Cupp, Lt. Col, 56, 74-75

Dalrymple, William C., 11
Dalton, Georgia, 90 , 96
Daniel Webster, 12

Davis, President Jefferson, 2, 6, 24,
    59, 73, 80, 94, 113, 128
Dean, Mr., 5
Dechard, Lt. George M., 56, 74-76
Democratic convention of 1860, 6
Dennis, Samuel Marion, 18
Department of the Trans Mississippi,
    114
Doctor's Creek, 56
Dover, Tennessee, 68
Downey, Tom, 32, 147
Dred Scott decision, 10
Duck River, 69
Duffield, Col, 52
Dug Gap, Georgia, 89-90

Eagle Island, 5
8th Texas Cavalry, 26, 81-82, 92, 99,
    103, 106
11th Kentucky Cavalry, 83
11th Texas Cavalry, 71, 72, 77, 81-
    82, 83, 87, 99, 103, 106, 111
Elgin, Bob, 56
Elk River, 48
Evans, Mark L., 16, 56

Fairfax County Courthouse, 15
Fallen Timbers, Battle of, 46
Fannin House, 115
Fayetteville, North Carolina, 108
Ferrell, Stephen C., 17, 19, 31-32, 70
5th Kentucky Cavalry, 108
5th Kentucky Regiment, 72
5th Ohio Cavalry, 108
5th Tennessee Cavalry, 88
5th Texas Cavalry, 83
5th Texas Infantry, 23
15th Pennsylvania regiment, 62
51st Alabama Cavalry, 103
51st Mounted Alabama Infantry, 77
1st Alabama Cavalry, 108
1st Georgia Cavalry, 50
1st Kentucky Cavalry, 47, 49, 56
1st Kentucky Regiment, 72
1st Louisiana Cavalry, 49, 50
1st Mississippi Rifles, 136
1st Ohio Cavalry, 74, 76, 79
1st Texas Cavalry, 83